March of America Facsimile Series

Number 93

Travel and Adventure
in the Territory of Alaska

Frederick Whymper

Travel and Adventure
in the Territory of Alaska
by Frederick Whymper

ANN ARBOR
UNIVERSITY MICROFILMS, INC.
A Subsidiary of Xerox Corporation

56691

Foreword

In 1864 the Russian government granted permission to the Western Union Telegraph Company to make a survey for a possible telegraph line extending from British Columbia through what was then called Russian America (Alaska), thence by cable over the Bering Strait to connect with another telegraph line to be strung across Siberia to connect with one already in operation from St. Petersburg to the Amur River. Such a line, when completed, would have connected Europe with the United States by telegraph. The Western Union survey began in 1865. One of the participants was Frederick Whymper, a young English adventurer, writer, and artist, who joined the expedition and wrote *Travel and Adventure in the Territory of Alaska* (London, 1868), one of the earliest and best accounts of Alaska during the transition from a Russian to an American possession.

Whymper's book had a New York edition in 1869 and another American edition in 1871. It was translated into French and published in Paris in 1871. One of the attractions of the book was its sketches by the author, excellent illustrations of Indians, Eskimos, and local scenes.

Whymper left England, bound for Vancouver Island via Cape Horn, in June, 1862. After a hazardous voyage he arrived at Victoria, where he spent three years before joining the Western Union surveying expedition. Among his fellow passengers on the outward voyage from England were sixty well-chaperoned young women being sent out to marry in British Columbia, that colony being then virtually destitute of women suitable for marriage.

Whymper's *Travel and Adventure in...Alaska* is both entertaining and informative. Unlike many travel narratives of the period, it is uncluttered with irrelevancies and is concise and accurate in its descriptions. Whymper, who later contributed geographical and ethnological essays to scientific journals, was a trained observer with an eye for both colorful and significant material. During more than two years, he participated in explorations by sea and land and made an overland trip from the Alaskan coast to the Yukon River at the beginning of the winter of 1866. His narrative of the events provides an invaluable insight into conditions in this wild and then little-known region.

Among the most fascinating portions of the book are Whymper's descriptions of contacts with the Russians, who still maintained trading posts in Alaska when he visited the country. The deal which the United States government made for the purchase of the territory from Russia was consummated on March 30, 1867, while Whymper was still in the Northwest. He mentions the formal transfer on October 18, 1867: "It is said that the Russian flag showed great reluctance to come down, and stuck on the yard-arm of the flag-staff. A man was sent up to detach the halyards, when it fell on the heads of the Russian soldiers appointed its defenders." The Russians, whether on the Siberian coast or in Alaska, were invariably hospitable and friendly, Whymper reports. Indeed, their hospitality was so strenuous that it took a man of strong constitution to survive. The Russian informality with their servants shocked the sensibilities of this Englishman who marveled that servants in this frontier zone "almost invariably addressed their masters and mistresses by their Christian names, and often by abbreviations thereof." Other English travelers were similarly shocked by American informality on the frontier.

The value of Whymper's book lies in its accurate descriptions of life in Alaska at the time of the American take-over. Further information on the expeditions reported by Whymper will be found in W. H. Dall, *Alaska and Its Resources* (Boston, 1870). Dall was one of Whymper's companions on the survey. See also H. W. Clark, *History of Alaska* (New York, 1930).

Travel and Adventure
in the Territory of Alaska

TRAVEL AND ADVENTURE

IN THE

TERRITORY OF ALASKA.

AURORAL LIGHT SEEN FROM NULATO, YUKON RIVER   DEC. 27, 1866.

TRAVEL AND ADVENTURE

IN THE

TERRITORY OF ALASKA,

FORMERLY RUSSIAN AMERICA—NOW CEDED TO THE
UNITED STATES—AND IN VARIOUS OTHER
PARTS OF THE NORTH PACIFIC.

By FREDERICK WHYMPER.

WITH MAP AND ILLUSTRATIONS.

LONDON:

JOHN MURRAY, ALBEMARLE STREET.

1868.

The right of Translation is reserved.

TO

SIR RODERICK I. MURCHISON, BART., K.C.B.,

D.C.L., LL.D., F.R.S., ETC.,

PRESIDENT OF THE ROYAL GEOGRAPHICAL SOCIETY, AND FOREIGN
ASSOCIATE OF THE INSTITUTE OF FRANCE,

This Volume is Dedicated,

IN ADMIRATION OF HIS GREAT SCIENTIFIC ATTAINMENTS,

AND AS A GRATEFUL ACKNOWLEDGMENT OF

MUCH KINDNESS SHOWN TO

THE AUTHOR.

PREFACE.

So little is known of the interior of Russian America, that I trust even this imperfect and meagre narrative may prove not altogether uninteresting. A large portion of these pages refers to a journey made in the Yukon region, which though containing one of the grandest streams on the North American continent, has hitherto remained almost unnoticed. Sir John Richardson, indeed, when on the Mackenzie, collected some information respecting it, but never visited any portion of it, whilst the travels of Zagoskin, of the Russian Imperial Navy, have never been popularly known.

This country has recently acquired some notice from its transfer to the United States Government, and within a few years we shall doubtless hear more of it. The natives have been hitherto so isolated from civilization, that perhaps in no other part of America can the "red-skin" be seen to greater perfection. In a few generations he will be extinct.

"Alaska Territory"—the title by which the whole of Russian America is to be known in future—though as good a name as any other, is founded, apparently, on a misconception. It seems to have been derived from the title of that long peninsula (Aliaska) with which we are all familiar on the map, but the title does not properly belong to the whole territory.

I have before me a 'Report on the Resources of Iceland and Greenland,' issued this year (1868) by the State Department at Washington. It was compiled, at the desire of the Hon. W. H. Seward, by B. M. Peirce, Esq. From that production I glean that the United States Government, so far from regretting the purchase of Alaska, are almost ready to bid for Iceland and Greenland! Mr. Seward's mania for icebergs and snow-fields seems insatiable.

The opening chapters contain some earlier reminiscences of British Columbia and Vancouver Island, whilst in the concluding pages I have attempted to sketch California of our own time. I have also briefly recorded some visits paid by me to the eastern coasts of Siberia and Kamchatka.

Some of the most pleasant days of my life were spent with the two Expeditions with which I have been connected; and of many of my old friends and companions I shall ever think with much kindness. To Colonel Bulkley, Engineer-in Chief of the Russo-American Telegraph Expedition; to Captain Scammon (U. S. Revenue Service); and to my good friends Messrs. Wright, Chappel, and Lewis, all American gentlemen with whom it was a pleasure to be connected, I am indebted for courtesies which it would be difficult for me to sufficiently acknowledge.

To the President and Council of the Royal Geographical Society I am specially obliged for the use of the map, illustrating the course of the Yukon, &c., which is to appear in their 'Journal' in connection with the paper contributed by me. To Mr. Arrowsmith, for the trouble he has taken to work out the crude material laid before him; to Mr. H. W. Bates and Captain George; to Mr. Murray, and to my father and brother, for their constant and kind assistance, I cannot be too grateful.

The illustrations are taken, with but two exceptions, from the original sketches made on the spot; they have gained considerably in the hands of my friends, Messrs. Skelton, Mahoney, and Zwecker. The portrait of an Aht native (Vancouver Island), page 53, has been copied from an excellent photograph by Mr. Gentile, now of San Francisco; and the picture of a Tchuktchi house, page 89, is from a photograph by Mr. Ryder, who was for the season of 1866, attached to the Telegraph Expedition.

CONTENTS.

———•◇•———

CHAPTER I.

THE VOYAGE OUT.

Leaving England — Our passengers — Old Mo' — Freight for the matrimonial market — Storm *on board* — Mutiny — Volunteer coal-heaving — Falkland Islands — Port Stanley — The Horn — Out of coal — San Francisco — The Straits of Fuca — Cook — Vancouver — Juan de Fuca — Victoria — Cariboo mines — The gold — The discoverers of William's Creek — Journalism on the Pacific   Page 1

CHAPTER II.

THE GLACIERS OF BUTE INLET, BRITISH COLUMBIA.

The mountains of British Columbia and adjacent coasts — Bute Inlet — Chilicoten Indians — A "blow up" — Indian packers — Route through the forests — Indian guide — Chinook jargon — Trackless forests — Lost in the woods — The glacier streams — Camp — Great Glacier — Description — Return journey — Second Glacier   .. 18

CHAPTER III.

THE TRAGEDY AMONG THE GLACIERS.

Reported murder — Canoe trip on the sea — Dodd's Narrows — Island on fire — The massacre at Bute Inlet — Reports of survivors — Second massacre — Excitement in the Colony — Expeditions in search of the Indians — Capture of a part of the murderers — The

ideal and real Indian — His ultimate extinction — Reasons for it —
Indian traders — Proposed semi-secular, semi-missionary settlements
— The mission at Metlakahtla   ..   ..   Page 29

CHAPTER IV.

THE INTERIOR OF VANCOUVER ISLAND.

Pleasures of labour — Unknown interior of Vancouver Island —
Expedition organized — Cowichan River — Somenos — Kakalatza
and his hat-box — Travel up the river — Our camps — Camp yarns
— Indian version of the Book of Jonah — Cowichan Lake — Rafting
experiences — The " Rampant Raft " — Brown's camp — Acquisition
of a canoe 41

CHAPTER V.

THE INTERIOR OF VANCOUVER ISLAND.

Nittinaht Inlet — " Whyack " — The Indians — Aht tribes — The
breakers — Port San Juan — Indian yarn — Sooke Basin and
River — Discovery of gold — Gold on Queen Charlotte's Island —
Nanaimo — Coal - seam at Comox — Ascent of Puntledge River —
Wreck of Canoe — Interior lakes — Barclay Sound — Game list —
Camp-mark 52

CHAPTER VI.

ALASKA TERRITORY.

Acquisition of Russian America by the United States — American
criticisms on the purchase — Coal and gold discoveries — Mock
advertisements — America for the Americans — Geographical literature of the Pacific — Of Russian America — The Treaty — W. U.
Telegraph Expedition — Its organization — Preference for young
men   64

CHAPTER VII.

A VISIT TO THE CAPITAL OF ALASKA.

The voyage — Sitka Sound and harbour — Baranoff — Early history — The town — Water supply — Agriculture — Former Russian settlements in California — Russian American Company — The fisheries — Kalosh Indians — Our experiences of Russian hospitality — Sitka in new hands — Two Sundays in a week — Kodiack ice — Formal transfer of Alaska ..   ..   Page 72

CHAPTER VIII.

VOYAGE IN THE NORTH PACIFIC.

1865.

Departure from Sitka — Oukamok — Ounga — Breakers ahead — Volcanoes in Ounimak Pass — St. Michael's, Norton Sound, Alaska — Soundings of Bering Sea — Plover Bay, Eastern Siberia — The Tchuktchis — Tents — Canoes — Tchuktchis' strength — Children — The irrepressible "Naukum" — Native's idea of the telegraph — The 'Shenandoah' pirate — Avatcha Bay   84

CHAPTER IX.

PETROPAULOVSKI AND OUR RETURN VOYAGE TO SAN FRANCISCO.

The Harbour — Town — Monuments — The fur trade — Kamchatka generally — The volcanoes — The attack of the Allies in 1854 — Their return in 1855 — The 'General Teste' — Rejoin the steamer 'Wright' — Gale — Incidents of storm — Covert's "smoke-stack" 94

CHAPTER X.

VOYAGE IN THE NORTH PACIFIC.

1866.

Organization of the expedition — Thirsty medical man — Our fleet — Voyage — Petropaulovski again — The Russian corvette — Russian wedding — Heat — International pic-nic — Voyage north — Bering's voyages — Shipwreck — Death of Bering — Gulf of Anadyr — The " Wandering Tchuktchis " .... Page 105

CHAPTER XI.

THE ANADYR RIVER AND PLOVER BAY, EASTERN SIBERIA.

Tchuktchi with letter of recommendation — Boat expedition to the river — Our explorers — Their experiences — The Anadyr River — Tchuktchi thieves — Plover Bay — Naukum again — Advertising in Bering Straits — Telegraph station erected — Foraging with a vengeance — Whaling — Norton Sound, Alaska — Death of Major Kennicott 117

CHAPTER XII.

RUSSIAN AND INDIAN SETTLEMENTS.—NORTON SOUND.

St. Michael's — The fort and its inhabitants — The ' Provalishik ' — Russian steam-bath — " Total immersion " — The island — Incident of break-up of ice — Arrival of dead Indian sledge-driver — Steamboat trip — Steamer laid up — Russian post at Unalachleet — Malemute and Kaveak Indians — Skin clothing — Intertribal commerce — Trade with the Tchuktchis — Underground houses — Fishing through the ice 127

CONTENTS.

CHAPTER XIII.

UNALACHLEET—NORTON SOUND.

Indian town-hall— Preparations for dance — Smoke-consuming Indians — Feast — Dance — Chorus — The Malemutes and Kaveaks — The chiefs — " Parka-mania " — Erection of quarters — Preparations for sledge journey   ..   ..   **Page 141**

CHAPTER XIV.

SLEDGE JOURNEY TO THE YUKON.

Routes to the Yukon — Sledges and dogs — Our start — Our party — Unalachleet River — Brought to a standstill — Dogs desert — Ingelete Indians — Underground houses, &c. — Beans *versus* rice — Indian cleanliness — Medical aid — Ulukuk — The river — Indian trading..   ..   ..   **148**

CHAPTER XV.

SLEDGE JOURNEY TO THE YUKON.—*Continued.*

Cross the Ulukuk River — Walking on snow shoes — Ulukuk Mountains — Land travelling — Versola Sofka — Patent camp — Our frozen breath — Indian honesty — The use of snow shoes — Warm springs — First glimpse of the Yukon — Coltog — Old " Stareek " — Travel on the Yukon — Alikoff's " barabba " — Meet a Russian sledge-train — Arrival at Nulato **159**

CHAPTER XVI.

LIFE AT NULATO—YUKON RIVER.

First explorers of the Yukon — Nulato — Our quarters — Water sledge — Fish traps — Winter sketching — Frozen provisions —

Coldest day — Departure of a sledge train — Dinner party — Indian
arrivals — Shortest day — Merry Christmas — Bill of fare — Aurora
— Temperatures — Supplies — Principal winter trip of our
explorers .. .. Page 169

CHAPTER XVII.

THE CO-YUKON INDIANS.

Co-Yukon tribe — Fashions — The Nulato massacre — Incidents of
the attack — Indian murders — Mourning observances — " Wake "
— Four-post Coffins — Superstitions — " Corralling " deer — News
travels fast — Furs and trading — Indian women — Indian " goggles "
— Children's dolls 182

CHAPTER XVIII.

CANOE JOURNEY.—ASCENT OF THE YUKON.

Spring — Thaw — Break-up of the Yukon — Preparations for journey
— Our canoes — Start — Dangerous condition of river — Its size —
Current — Perilous navigation — Submerged islands — Co-Yukuk
— Birch - bark fleet — Sachertelontin — Lagoon — Newicargut —
Purchase of supplies — Tooth - brush experiences — Medicine-
making — Indian dissipation — Child's birch-bark chair 192

CHAPTER XIX.

CANOE JOURNEY—(*continued*).—ASCENT OF THE YUKON.

Meet a deserter — Indian taste for " Nigger " minstrelsy — Tracking —
Lagoon — Piles of drift wood — Nuclukayette — Unsophisticated
Indians — Ceremony — Leave the Russians — The Indian's head —
Mountain gorge — Indian dogs — Canoe leak — The rapids — The
" Ramparts " — Moose-hunting — Islands — Overhanging banks —
Shallows — Shortest night — First English Indians — Porcupine
River — Fort Yukon 207

CHAPTER XX.

FORT YUKON.

Return of the Commander and Missionary — Information received from them — Mackenzie and the Yukon — The Indians — Numerous tribes — The furs — Fictitious black fox — Missionary work — Return of our explorers from the Upper Yukon — Fort Yukon, sledges, &c. .. .. Page 219

CHAPTER XXI.

DESCENT OF THE YUKON.

Drifting down the stream — Yukon salmon — Arrival at Nulato —
• Overdose of arsenic and alcohol — Trip resumed — Indian music — Anvic — The mission — Earthquake *on the water* — Andreavski — The mouths of the Yukon — Smith's observations — Pastolik — St. Michael's — Progress of the telegraph — Frozen soil — Scurvy — Arrival of our barque — Plover Bay — Return to San Francisco 231

CHAPTER XXII.

THE VALUE OF ALASKA. — THE ORIGIN OF THE ESQUIMAUX OF NORTHERN ALASKA AND GREENLAND.

The value of Alaska — The furs and fisheries — The purchase, an act of justice to Russia — The Aleutian Islands — Volcanoes — Bogoslov Island — The Asiatic origin of the Esquimaux — The Tchuktchis — Sea-going canoes — The voyages of two Japanese junks — The connecting links between the Tchuktchis and the Esquimaux — Language — Degeneration of the Esquimaux — Community of goods — The " Schaman " and the " Angekok." 244

CHAPTER XXIII.

W. U. TELEGRAPH EXPLORATIONS IN ASIA.

Major Abasa appointed Chief — Arrival in Petropaulovski — Travels
in Kamchatka — Ghijega — The town, &c. — Route betwen Ghijega
and Ochotsk — The explorations of Mahood and Bush — Nicolaiefski,
Mouth of the Amoor — Travel to Ochotsk — Reindeer riding — The
Tunguse — Ayan — Ochotsk — MacCrea and Arnold's wanderings
among the Tchuktchis — Anadyrsk ..   ..   Page 257

CHAPTER XXIV.

CALIFORNIA.

California in 1849 — To-day — Agricultural progress — Wine manufacture — Climate — Lower California — San Francisco — No paper
money — Coinage — Growth — General prosperity — Scarcity of
labour — Hiring a domestic — Luxuries of the land — The "Mission" — Hotel *carte* — Home for the Inebriates — Immigration
desired — Newspapers — Chinese population — "John's" status —
John as a miner — Dead Chinamen — Celestial entertainment —
Merchant's pigtail   269

CHAPTER XXV.

CALIFORNIA.—*Continued.*

San Francisco Society — Phraseology — Ladies of Fr'isco — Sunday
in the city — Free criticism on parsons — Site — Steep streets —
San Francisco calves — Earthquakes — House-moving — Fire companies — "Wells Fargo's Express" — The three-cent stamps — The
men of the Pacific   282

CHAPTER XXVI.

CALIFORNIA AS A FIELD FOR EMIGRATION.

Early American opinions of the country — California steamers — The public lands — Extent — Price — Labour — Wages — The wine interests — Table of temperatures — The vineyards, &c. — Classes suitable for immigrants — Education — Schools — School ma'ams — Investments 292

APPENDIX.

I.—THE PROPOSED OVERLAND ROUTE FROM THE ATLANTIC TO THE PACIFIC, THROUGH BRITISH TERRITORY 309

II.—THE W. U. TELEGRAPH SCHEME 312

III.—NOTES ON SITKA 315

IV.—PORT CLARENCE, NORTHERN ALASKA 316

V.—INDIAN DIALECTS OF NORTHERN ALASKA 318

VI.—NOTES ON THE GEOLOGY OF THE YUKON 329

LIST OF ILLUSTRATIONS.

———◆◇◆———

Auroral Light seen from Nulato, Yukon River, December 27th, 1866 .. .. *Frontispiece.*
Vignette. Loading a sledge in Alaska .. .. *Title-page.*

	PAGE
The Great Glacier, Bute Inlet	to face 25
Island forest conflagration in the Gulf of Georgia	,, 31
The " Raft Rampant "	,, 49
Aht native, west coast of Vancouver Island	,, 53
Example of mask worn by Aht natives of Vancouver Island	54
Camp with " blaze " or camp-mark	63
Sitka, or New Archangel, capital of Alaska	to face 73
Kalosh Indian grave-boxes	78, 79
Indian stone-carving, representing a Russian soldier at Sitka	83
Tchuktchi skin-canoe—Frame-work of Tchuktchi house	to face 89
Tchuktchi pipe	90
Petropaulovski, Kamchatka	to face 94
Monument to Bering, Petropaulovski	95
The volcanoes of Koriatski, Avatcha, and Koseldskai, Kamchatka	to face 97
Fort St. Michael's, or Michaelovski	128
Malemute native	134
Malemute skin-clothing	135
Malemute pipe	142
Diagram of underground-house	152
Snow-shoe	159
Arrival at the Frozen Yukon	to face 164
Fish-traps on the Yukon	172
Co-Yukon four-post coffin	187
A Co-Yukon deer corral	to face 188
Co-Yukon goggles	191
The Yukon River at the break-up of the ice	to face 197
Indian summer encampment, Newicargut, Yukon River	,, 202
Yukon fire-bag, knife, and sheath, &c.	203
Indian child's birch-bark chair	206
Tanana Indian	to face 210
Moose hunting in the Yukon River	,, 215
Yukon Indian's knife	216
Fort Yukon, Hudson's Bay Company's Post	to face 219
Fort Yukon sledge (loaded)	230
Map—the course of the Yukon, &c.	To be placed at the end.

TRAVEL AND ADVENTURE

TERRITORY OF ALASKA.

CHAPTER I.

THE VOYAGE OUT.

Leaving England — Our passengers — Old Mo' — Freight for the matrimonial market — Storm *on board* — Mutiny — Volunteer coal-heaving — Falkland Islands — Port Stanley — The Horn — Out of coal — San Francisco — The Straits of Fuca — Cook — Vancouver — Juan de Fuca — Victoria — Cariboo mines — The gold — The discoverers of William's Creek — Journalism on the Pacific.

IN 1862, the Pacific coast, and especially British Columbia, attracted much attention at home. Having, thank God, like a good proportion of my countrymen, a little superfluous energy—which was then lying fallow—I determined to see something of those coasts, and accordingly commenced getting together my traps for the voyage. I need not say that I laid in a stock of things said to be "portable," essential, or absolutely "indispensable," and that the larger part of them proved to be exactly the reverse. Such, I take it, is the experience of most young travellers. On the 6th June of the above mentioned year—with some slight feelings of regret, it must be admitted—we left the Thames; and on the 9th saw the last of old England's shores, after a brief halt at peaceful, sleepy Dartmouth. A few hours later "the waves," to use an expression of Lamartine's, when starting on a cruise

B

in the Mediterranean, "had our destinies in their power," and
made us aware of the fact.

"Winds *are* rude in Biscay's sleepless bay : "

at least we found them so, for a breeze increased into a gale
before we were clear of its outer waters. Our craft was a
staunch iron screw-steamer, the 'Tynemouth,' which had won
a good reputation during the Crimean war by weathering out
that terrible storm in the Black Sea, in which so many vessels
(including the 'Black Prince') were lost. We were bound
for Vancouver Island, *viâ* the Horn, and expected to call
at one or two ports by the way. On board were some
three hundred passengers, two-thirds of whom shewed a total
loss of dignity and self-respect during these early days, and
made our vessel much resemble a floating hospital. But
there is an end to all things; and by the time we reached
the tropics, our friends had recovered their appetites, and,
clad in light attire, lounged, smoking, chatting, and reading
under the awnings, giving our decks the appearance of a
nautical pic-nic. Our passengers were a study in themselves.
They included a number of young men, much too large a
proportion of whom had apparently no profession, business,
or definite aim in life, to augur well for their future career
in a new country. Still, most branches were represented;
from farmers, tradesmen, and mechanics, to lawyers, artists,
and literary men. The greatest character on board was a
venerable Jew, generally known as "Old Mo'." He was an
Israelite of the conventional stage type, and did not neglect
turning a penny, by selling to the passengers stale lemons
and bad cigars, or by organizing raffles and mock auctions.
Towards the end of the voyage, he purchased all the odds

and ends on which he could lay his hands, offering the
"highestch prishe for old closhe and zhewellry;" and with
these he afterwards stocked a small shop in Victoria. Moses,
like Shylock, had much to stand in gibes and sneers, but
bore it "with a patient shrug."

Our most noticeable living freight was, however, an "invoice" of sixty young ladies destined for the colonial and
matrimonial market. They had been sent out by a home
Society, under the watchful care of a clergyman and
matron; and they must have passed the dreariest three
months of their existence on board, for they were isolated from the rest of the passengers, and could only look
on at the fun and amusements in which every one else could
take a part. Every benevolent effort deserves respect; but,
from personal observation, I cannot honestly recommend
such a mode of supplying the demands of a colony. Half
of them married soon after arrival, or went into service; but
a large proportion quickly went to the bad, and, from appearances, had been there before. The influence of but a few
such on the more respectable girls could not have been
otherwise than detrimental. To speak ungallantly, but truly,
many of these ladies were neither young *nor* beautiful, and
reminded me of the crowd who answered the advertisement
in the farce of 'Wanted 10,000 Milliners!' Of course much
might be said about giving the poor creatures a chance! but
the fact is, that the market would in the course of affairs
more naturally supply itself. The prosperous settler would
send for his sweetheart, or come home in search of one, and
could always get suitable domestics sent out by his friends,
and meet them at the port of arrival. It will be readily
understood too, that in a new country there is a floating

population, among whom some individuals by "chance," or by industry, have acquired a little money, and are ready to plunge into matrimony on the slightest provocation; whilst there is also a large proportion of "black sheep," who are quite ready to amuse themselves at the expense of the poor girls.

We were beginning to find life somewhat tedious, when a storm arose *on board* that altered the aspect of affairs. In common with a large proportion of ships—as far as my experience goes—we were considerably undermanned, and the overworked crew rebelled. They came aft to the captain; and a scene ensued, in which very high words passed, and at length one of the more daring mutineers "planted" (to use the language of the fraternity) a blow between the skipper's "peepers," which brought the "claret" very freely from his nose. In consequence, the fiat went forth—instantly and indignantly—"Put them in irons!" which was, however, a thing easier said than done. At last the officers—with the assistance of some of the passengers—succeeded in handcuffing the rebels, and they were then stowed away in a rather warm compartment near the engine-room, till such time as mutiny should be melted out of them.

Our captain was in a dilemma. We were almost becalmed; our sails flapped idly in the wind, while the arrangements for the coals were such, that with these men off duty, our engine must soon come to a standstill. The coal was chiefly in the fore-hold, and had to be raised, wheeled along deck, and deposited in the "bunkers."

At this juncture a committee of the passengers was convened, and it was agreed that the more active of all classes should be invited to volunteer, and act as crew for the time being. All the younger men came forward readily, were solemnly enrolled, and set to work at once, glad of an interruption to the monotony of the voyage. We scrubbed the decks, hauled at ropes, filled the coal-sacks, and hoisted them on deck, getting a fair taste of a modern sailor's life on board a steam-vessel. It is more than doubtful whether any of us would have echoed the words of England's sea-song writer, who says—

> "Then, Bill, let us thank Providence
> That you and I are sailors!"

but we found it good exercise, and worked with a will. Did we not know that the eyes of sixty maidens were looking on approvingly, as we helped them on to the consummation of their dearest wishes? We did, and even our parson creditably proved his "muscular Christianity," and soiled his irreproachable garments at one and the same time. I tasted the dignity of labour in the *rôle* of an amateur coal-heaver, and in the more sinecure employment of keeping the "lookout." We cooled our fevered frames with libations of beer, and buckets of diluted lime-juice; in this matter having an undoubted advantage over the old crew, who didn't get much of such luxuries. At last the tropical heat, superadded to that of the furnaces, brought the men to their senses, and the larger part of them went back to work; three, however, held out, and were kept in irons.

After some rough weather off the Rio de la Plata (known familiarly by sailors as the River Plate), in which we stove in our bulwarks and lost a boat, we at last made the Falkland Islands, and came to an anchor in Stanley Harbour. This is a land-locked basin some six miles long by half a mile

or so wide, and is on East Falkland. We arrived there early
in August, but it was the end of their winter. The snow had
just disappeared from the low lands, leaving them in places
very swampy. The island was thick with peat-moss, which
affords the inhabitants their only fuel, no timber except a
very limited amount of drift wood being attainable. There
are no trees whatever on the Falklands, and it is said that
attempts to introduce them have been unsuccessful. It was
from these islands that Col. Moody, when Colonial Governor,
brought the " Tussac " grass.

The Falklands had been in the hands of both the Spanish
and French before we obtained possession of them, and they
were not formerly valued as they are now. Port Stanley is
a pretty little town of 700 or 800 inhabitants, with a church,
government buildings, and school-house. Vessels returning
from China, Australia, or California, find these islands directly
in their course, and often put into Port Stanley for repairs,
water, coal, or supplies. Vegetables and fresh meat are
abundant, the latter selling for two-pence or three-pence a
pound. The cattle on the islands are very numerous, and
for the most part wild; they were introduced by the Spaniards. Stanley was a free port at the date of our visit, and
our passengers took advantage of the fact to lay in stocks of
hollands and brandy, much to the disgust of our steward, who
firmly believed in monopoly.

As our ship's cow had given up the ghost—frightened to
death in a storm—and the fowls were things of the past, we
were all glad to get ashore, luxuriate on milk and fresh
provisions, and stretch our legs. An English company had
—and I presume has—a large store there, and exported
hides and furs, employing some 150 persons directly, and

a larger number indirectly, in their collection. Our vessel coaled at this settlement.

We spent several days in excursions from the ship, shooting wild-fowl, and amusing ourselves with watching the penguin, which were very abundant. On the beach, when waddling away from us in a hurry, they suggested the idea of old women tripping over the stones with many a fall! We visited the excellent lighthouse at Cape Pembroke, the easternmost point of East Falkland, about eight miles from the port. Here we found the keeper's wife, with a family of youngsters, some of whom had never seen even the glories of Port Stanley, and yet were happy. The lighthouse, 110 feet in height, stands at the termination of a barren sand waste, and the beach near it is everywhere strewed with kelp and sea-weed of the most enormous growth, resembling in fact *sea trees.* Kelp is so thick in some parts of the harbour that it is next to impossible to row through it.

Our mutineers were tried in due form, and sentenced to a spell of hard labour, which in this case consisted of amateur gardening, and sanding the floors of the government buildings. They were apparently rather glad than otherwise of a brief residence in a place where fresh food was so abundant, and knew moreover that the next vessel touching there short-handed would probably be glad to take them at higher wages than those ruling in the port of London.

We were detained—partly by bad weather—for twelve days, but at last the favourable moment arrived, and we steamed out in good style. In the evening of the same day we passed Staten Land, over the rugged shores of which a canopy of mist hung gracefully. In the valleys a lace-work of snow still remained. Next morning we were in the Pacific in sight of the broken jagged coast of the famed and dreaded " Horn." The weather was superb, the sea almost a lake and the regulation terrors of the passage were nowhere! For the reader's sake, this was a great pity, but our passengers felt a kind of relief from the lingering dread of the more usual bad weather of the Cape. We soon got the " trade winds," set all sail, and knocked off steam.

Before we made the Californian coast, the wind died out, and having again to steam, our coal got reduced to the last gasp. All loose wood on deck, and even some valuable spars, had to be cut up for the furnaces, and the day before our arrival in San Francisco it was seriously contemplated to strip the second and third cabins of their berths and furniture!

But if we had been glad to go ashore at the Falklands, how much more so were we to land in San Francisco, to walk about its handsome streets, and enjoy its good things. Some of our passengers were so well satisfied with it that they abandoned all idea of going any further, and others, who could not imagine that our captain would start from it in such a hurry, were in consequence left behind. Of San Francisco, I shall speak in my concluding chapters. I have watched its growth for five years, and believe its history to be almost unexampled among cities that have arisen in modern times, and that its future teems with the greatest promise.

Resuming our trip, we at length reached Cape Flattery and the Straits of Fuca, and obtained a first glimpse of the interminable forests on Vancouver Island, that were to be the home of some of us for many a day. As late as the days

of Cook, it was believed that Vancouver Island was a part of
the mainland, and it was so laid down in the atlas accompanying his great work.   The Straits of Fuca were in effect
so named in 1792 by Vancouver, after their real discoverer,
Juan de Fuca, an old Greek sailor, whose pretensions, in re
gard to their exploration, were long scoffed at by geographers.
Cook sailing up the coast of *New Albion,* now known as
Oregon and Washington Territory, reached the promontory
which has always since borne the name he gave it—Cape
Flattery.   " It is in this very latitude," says he, " where we
now were, that geographers have placed the pretended Straits
of Juan de Fuca.   But we saw nothing like it ; nor is there
the least probability that ever any such thing existed."
Tolerably positive language!—more especially when we know
the real facts of the voyage, as later given to the world by
Captain James Burney,* who served with Cook on this identical voyage. He says, " After making the coast, unfavourable
winds and weather forced the ships as far south as to 43°,
and when we again made way northward, blowing and thick
unsettled weather prevented our tracing a continuation of the
coast, so that between a cape in lat. 44° 55′ N., named by
Captain Cook *Cape Foulweather,* and a point of land in
48° 15′ N., which he named *Cape Flattery,* because the
prospect of the land near it gave it a doubtful promise of a
harbour, we obtained only now and then a glimpse of the
land.

" We were near the last-mentioned point on the evening of
the 22nd (March, 1778), and a little before seven o'clock ; it

---

* 'A Chronological History of North-Eastern Voyages of Discovery,'
Chap. xix.

growing dark, Captain Cook tacked to wait for daylight, in-
tending to make closer examination; but before morning a
hard gale of wind came on with rainy weather, and we were
obliged to keep off from the land.   At this time a port was
necessary to both ships, to repair the lower rigging, as well
as to recruit their stock of fresh water.   On the 29th, in the
forenoon, we again made the land.   At noon, the latitude was
observed 49° 28′ N."   The reader who has followed me thus
far, will see that Cook missed the entrance to the Straits of
Fuca.   There is nothing surprising in the fact, though there
is in his hasty conclusion with regard to the existence of a
strait.   The last latitude is approximately that of Nootka
Sound, Vancouver Island, of which both Cook and Burney
give us full descriptions.

Between 1787-9, Captains Berkely, Duncan, Meares, and
Kendrick—the three first-named English, the latter American
—all confirmed Fuca's discovery by visits which they paid
to various parts of the Straits; and one of the objects of
Vancouver's great voyage was to determine the truth of their
statements.   He arrived in the Straits—the supposed Straits
of Fuca, as he terms them—on Sunday, the 29th April,
1792, and from that date commenced the survey which has
immortalised his name.   On the day of his arrival he met
Captain Grey, an American, who had made a trip up the
Straits, and had been wintering on the coast.

And now let us speak of Fuca, who seems to have been
in his own day neglected and misunderstood, as he was afterwards doubted and ignored.   His real name was Apostolus
Valerianos; and all that we know of him is recorded in the
celebrated work entitled '*Purchas his Pilgrimes*,'—first published in 1625—under the title of " *A note made by me,*

Michael Lok *the elder, touching the Strait of the Sea, commonly called* Fretum Anian, *in the South Sea,* through the North-west passage of Meta incognita."

In substance the narrative is as follows:—Lok being in Venice in 1596, was introduced to a Greek pilot—an old man of "three-score yeares," commonly known by his companions as *Juan de Fuca*, although his real name was that recorded above. He said that he had been in the Spanish service "*fortie yeares*," and that, on one of his voyages, he had been in the galleon taken off Cape California (? Cape St. Lucas), by "Captaine *Candlish Englishman,* whereby he lost sixtie thousand Duckets, of his owne goods."

In 1592, the Viceroy of Mexico sent him on a voyage of discovery to the Straits which now bear his name. He followed the coast of California and Oregon, &c., "vntill hee came to the latitude of fortie-seuen degrees, and there finding that the land trended North and North-east, with a broad Inlet of Sea, betweene 47 and 48 degrees of Latitude: hee entered there into, sayling therein more then twentie dayes, and found that land trending still, sometime Northwest and North-east, and North, and also East and South-eastward, and very much broader Sea then was at the said entrance, and he passed by diuers islands in that sayling. And at the entrance of the said Strait, there is on the North-west coast thereof, a great Hedland or Island, with an exceeding high Pinacle, or spired Rock, like a pillar thereupon.

"Also he said, that he went on Land in diuers places, and that he saw some people on Land, clad in Beasts skins: and that the Land is very fruitfull, and rich of Gold, Siluer, Pearle, and other things, like *Noua Spania.*

"And also he said, that he being entered thus farre into the said Strait, and being come into the North Sea already (which means that he had rounded Vancouver Island), and finding the Sea wide enough every-where, and to be about thirtie or fortie leagues wide in the mouth of the Straits, where hee entred, hee thought he had now well discharged his office, and done the thing which he was sent to doe ; and that hee not being armed to resist the force of the Saluage people that might happen, hee therefore set sayle and returned homewards againe towards *Noua Spania*, where he arrived at *Acapulco*, *Anno* 1592."

The Viceroy welcomed him with empty compliments, and recommended him to go to Spain, and lay his discoveries before the King, "which voyage hee did performe." The King received him courteously with "wordes after the Spanish manner," but did nothing for him, and giving up all hopes of reward, he went to Italy, where Lok met him.

He there offered to enter the English service, hoping at the same time to be remembered in regard to his great loss to Candlish. Lok wrote immediately to Lord Treasurer Cecil, Sir Walter Raleigh, and Master Richard Hakluit the geographer, asking them to forward 100*l*. to fetch Fuca to England, he not being in a position to afford it. Answer came that the idea was well liked, but the money not being forthcoming, the matter was allowed to drop. Later, Lok—who had been English Consul at Aleppo—corresponded with Fuca, and when himself in the island of Zante, wrote to Cephalonia, offering to take the old pilot at his own expense to England. But poor old Fuca was by this time—Christmas, 1602,—dead, or at the point of death, and we lost the chance of making an early discovery of an important coast.

The Straits of Fuca have been often described, and I will not enlarge upon the subject. Although the scenery is in parts very beautiful, and occasionally grand, there is a monotony about them inseparable from pine-forests, rocks, and islands. We soon arrived off Esquimalt, obtained a pilot, and entered the harbour, now one of our most important naval stations in the Pacific, as it is also one of the healthiest. It is, in effect, the port of Victoria, as only moderate-sized vessels can safely enter the harbour of the latter place, owing to a bar at its entrance.

Of Victoria, in which town I spent three winters, what shall I say? Its career has been a forced and unhealthy one, and it is at the present day suffering from the effects. For a time, indeed, the British Columbian mines gave it an impetus, and had there been a really good agricultural country in the neighbourhood, it would have doubtless become a permanently prosperous settlement. But although Victoria has much in its favour,—a climate almost unsurpassed, provisions abundant and cheap, and fair facilities of communication with neighbouring countries,—it has dwindled down to a very low ebb indeed. I may be excused for alluding to one fact well known in the colony, although most writers on the subject have persistently ignored it. It is this: that men who have made large fortunes in the mines, and other ways,—and there have been many such,— do not, as a rule, become settlers in that country. In Australia and California they *do* become attached to the soil; they find abundance of available and open lands, and end by becoming prosperous and contented residents. This point is of great importance. The discovery of minerals, however profitable to individuals, *will not make a country ;*

but the discovery of minerals *and* rich lands fit for agricultural pursuits may do so.*

I spent many pleasant days in Victoria: it was my resting-place in the intervals between many lengthened journeys. It is a very bright, clean, well-built little town, with all the latest improvements. There are episcopal, dissenting, and Roman Catholic churches, a mechanics' institute, theatre, and gas-works. There are many private and public societies, masonic, national or charitable; and the traveller can always be sure of much hospitality if he comes with good credentials. The naval gentlemen from Esquimalt give life and tone to the society of the place, while the active or retired servants of the Hudson's Bay Company are its principal residents. This Company has in Victoria a very fine warehouse and wharves, and now does a miscellaneous business, in addition to the collection of furs.

Our fellow-passengers, who had come to make a rapid and gigantic fortune in Cariboo, now for the most part awoke to the fact that the mines were yet some five hundred miles away, and out of our list of three hundred persons not more than

---

* The mainland of this now united colony, British Columbia, has a fair amount of good land. The Governor in a recent Blue Book says, " The most important advance made by British Columbia in 1866 was the rapid development of agriculture occasioned by the increasing number of waggon roads and other communications. Home-manufactured flour of superior quality is already taking the place of the imported article. Use is being made of the magnificent timber covering the sides of the harbours and inlets; and spars and lumber of superior quality were exported in 1866 to the value of 10,000*l.* The yield of gold in the year is roughly estimated at 600,000*l.*, and, as there were certainly not more than three thousand miners engaged, the average product reached 200*l.* per man,—far exceeding any average ever reached in California or Australia."

twenty-five ever reached the Northern El Dorado. When, in 1863, I made a sketching and pedestrian tour to that district, I met some of my fellow passengers already on the way down, disgusted and crestfallen. They knew nothing of mining, and their only chance of obtaining an interest in a company was in the same way as in Cornwall or Wales— by buying it. This too was a rather shaky undertaking. If bought on the spot, there was a great probability that the ground was "salted," a technical term for a well known *ruse*, that of scattering a few ounces of gold among the dirt; the seller (true in a double sense) re-discovering it there before the victim's eyes. He did not always get even this satisfaction; fragments of brass candlesticks and dutch metal have sometimes done duty for the precious deposit, and it is said that Chinese miners are excellent at manufacturing fictitious nuggets and quartz specimens.

A friend of mine purchased in Victoria a share in a Cariboo mine, and on arrival there was unable to find or hear of any traces of it. It existed only on paper. On the other hand Cariboo was, and *still is*, a very rich field. A single company once realized 180 lbs. of gold as the result of one day's work.* I have myself seen 200 oz. collected from the "dump-box," as the proceeds of one "shift," or eight hours' work. Much of this kind of thing has been already laid before the public, but the deductions made therefrom have not been by any means correct. The fact is, that in a large

---

* For the week ending July 9th, 1865, the Ericson Company took out 1400 oz. The following week reached still higher,—1926 oz., worth over 6000*l*. I well remember the first gold "struck" in that claim, and the general surprise that anything whatever was to be found in that locality.

number of cases the working expenses were very heavy, and one, two, or even three seasons' work had often to be first expended before there were any returns. The price of provisions, at the date of my visit, averaged all round a dollar (4s. 2d.) a pound, and labour commanded ten dollars a day. Even the hardy pioneers, men who had been " broken in " in California or Australia, were by no means universally lucky. The fate of the discoverers of " William's Creek," the richest valley in Cariboo, is a case in point. One of them, William Dietz, a German, broken down by hardship and exposure, was dependent on charity while I was in Victoria ; and the second, Rose, a Scotchman, died of starvation in the woods, and was afterwards found by horror-stricken friends. On his tin-cup he had attempted to record his sufferings, by scratching thereon a few broken words.

Of my experiences on the grand Cariboo road, a work of great engineering skill, especially in the Cañons of the Fraser, of that great river itself, of lakes, forests and torrents, " ranches " and road-side houses, I could relate enough to fill this volume, but will say nothing ;* for the very good

---

* But I must mention one fact interesting in the history of journalism on the Pacific. In 1865 a small newspaper was started in the mines, and was named 'The Cariboo Sentinel.' It consisted of one (foolscap) sheet of four pages, and with an occasional supplement, sold at one dollar (4s. 2d.) a copy! The editor, Mr. Wallace, whom I knew well, was the all-in-all of the office. He was his own compositor, pressman, advertisement agent, publisher, and collector, and doubtless would have been his own paper maker on the spot if rags had been less valuable! He was very successful in a pecuniary point of view, and afterwards sold the concern to some one else. He then commenced the publication of a paper at the town of Yale,

reason that the country has already been admirably described
in the work of Lord Milton and Dr. Cheadle.† These gentlemen went over exactly the same ground, and have presented
a faithful picture of the whole, as far as the subject can
possibly,interest the public. The succeeding chapters contain
some account of my trips in other and less known parts of
the same country, while the bulk of this volume describes
visits paid to much more northern climes.

---

in the Cañons of the Fraser, and has since returned to England, having
retired with a competency.

† Capt. Mayne's ' Four Years in British Columbia,' a very reliable and
interesting work, touches on the same subject.

CHAPTER II.

THE GLACIERS OF BUTE INLET, BRITISH COLUMBIA.

The Mountains of British Columbia and adjacent coasts — Bute Inlet —
Chilicoten Indians — A "blow up" — Indian packers — Route through
the forests — Indian guide — Chinook jargon — Trackless forests —
Lost in the woods — The glacier streams — Camp — Great glacier —
Description — Return journey — Second glacier.

A GLANCE at the map of British Columbia shows us one of
the most broken jagged coast lines in the world, with arms
of the sea innumerable, into each of which some river, small
or large, finds its way. These streams, fed by numerous
tributaries, born of the snow and ice, pass through the
valleys of the Cascade and coast ranges, bordering on the
Gulf of Georgia, Straits of Fuca, and adjacent coast.
The general character of these mountain ranges is Alpine;
perpetual snow reigns in their upper regions, and glaciers
exist in their valleys. Such are known to exist at the
Stekine River in particular.

A direct route from the coast into the Cariboo mines by
the way of Bute Inlet had been projected and partly carried
out in the year 1864; and in consequence the writer was
induced to visit this otherwise inaccessible country. A
schooner, with men and supplies on board, left Victoria
Vancouver Island, on the 16th March of that year; and he
then took the opportunity, kindly given him by the pro-
jector of the road, Mr. Alfred Waddington, of paying the
glaciers a visit.

Omitting all details of a tedious passage, we arrived at Bute Inlet on the 22nd March, and getting a fair breeze, we made the mouth of the Homathco River the same day. On entering the inlet, the transition from the low rocky islands of the Gulf of Georgia to the precipitous snow-capped mountains of the mainland was very marked. The skipper, who knew the Norway coast, said that it exactly resembled the scenery of the " Fiords." The snow, then fast melting, yielded many a streamlet which glided peacefully through the forest to the sea, and many a thundering cataract which fell over bare and abrupt cliffs. Near the river some Chilicoten Indians paddled out in their canoes, and came on board to get a free ride. They had rings through their noses, were much painted, and wore the inevitable blanket of the coast. For the rest, there was nothing very characteristic in their costume ; some having a shirt without breeches, some breeches without a shirt. Two of them were picturesque with wolf-skin robes, hair turned inwards, and the outer side adorned with fringes of tails derived from marten or squirrel. Among them one old hag attracted some notice, from her repulsive appearance and the short pipe which she seemed to enjoy.

On nearing a small wharf already erected at the mouth of the river, a solitary white man, Mr. C——, made his appearance, and was evidently glad to see us. He had been left in charge of stores, mules, &c., during winter, and the Indians had at times threatened his life.

An amusing incident had occurred during his stay. He had missed many small things from his log house, and could not catch the thief, whoever he might be, but who he had reason to believe must have entered the cabin by the large open chimney. At last he got a friend to go inside with a quarter of a pound of gunpowder, and locking the door, made pretence of leaving, but crept back near the house to watch the result. Soon, an Indian came stealthily along, *sans culottes*, *sans* everything. He climbed on the roof, and got nearly down the chimney, when the man inside threw the powder on the smouldering ashes, and off it went. The Indian went off also! and with a terrific yell; but over his condition a veil must be drawn. He afforded for some time afterwards a very wholesome warning to his tribe, being unable to sit or lie down.

These people appeared to be very bare of provisions, and disputed with their wretched "cayota" dogs anything that we threw out of our camp, in the shape of bones, bacon rind, or tea leaves, and similar luxuries. Many of them were subsequently employed in packing goods on their backs, always carrying their loads fixed to a strap which came round and over their *foreheads*. As they would pack 100 lbs. and upwards this way, their heads must be regarded as tolerably strong and thick! Some of them were also employed in building the road.

After making sundry arrangements, we started up. The route lay through a magnificent forest of cedar,* hemlock, and Douglas pine, individual specimens of which almost

---

* Cedar, as it is popularly known on the coast, is the *Thuja gigantea* of botanists. Douglas Pine, *Abies Douglasii*, and Hemlock (*Abies Bridgei*, 'Proc. California Acad. Natural Sciences,' Vol. 2.). Maple (*Acer macrophyllum*), Alder (*Alnus Oregana*), White Pine (*Pinus strobus ?*) and Spruce (*Abies Menziesii*), are also common trees of the coast. For these scientific names I am indebted to Mr. Brown, with whom I was afterwards associated on the Vancouver Island expedition.

rivalled the "big trees" of California. One of the cedars measured forty-five feet in circumference at the butt (about the height from the ground of a man's chest). Although the snow lay on the ground so thickly, that the heavily-laden pack-train of mules could hardly proceed without a path being cleared for them, the musquitoes were already out in full force. So abundant were they that the writer took nine from the back of his hand at one pinch between finger and thumb. They bit through anything from blankets to cord unmentionables, and against their inflictions there was literally "nothing like leather."

The road followed more or less the river valley, the scenery of which was not seen to advantage till, after crossing the stream by a rope-ferry, we commenced the ascent of a mountain by a zigzag trail, in order to avoid the passage of a rock-girt cañon. From this the views were superb. Purple cliffs rose—pine-clad and abrupt—whilst below the Homathco made its way to the sea, realizing the words of our Laureate,

> " Waters between walls
> Of shadowy granite, in a gleaming pass."

Afar off, snow-crowned peaks and blue valleys completed the picture.

On the 19th April, having arrived at the furthest camp of the constructing party, I engaged an Indian who was supposed to know the country well, and started with him for the Great Glacier. The Chinook jargon, the only medium of converse with these Indians, has no equivalent for " glacier." It could only be expressed by *hyu ice, hyu snow,*—" plenty of ice and snow;" and I was very much in the fix of a dignitary of the Church on that coast, who began an address to the Indians with " Children of the forest," but was rather disgusted to find his interpreter could only render it, *Hyu tenass man copa stick*—"Many little men among the sticks (or stumps)!" I could not make the man thoroughly understand, and after two days' wandering it became obvious that it would be better to return and seek another guide. We accordingly returned, and, having secured the services of an Indian of some intelligence—Tellot by name—an old chief, I again started; this time, as it proved, with more success.

Few can have any conception of the old forests through which our course lay, who have not themselves seen such. Thick with living vegetation, they were equally so with decay and death. Now an immense fallen trunk, over which we had to climb, blocked the path; now one under which we were obliged to creep; and now and again, an accumulation of the same, the effect of some wintry storm or natural death. Here, as the tree falls so it lies, and has lain undisturbed for ages. Hence, a log, green with moss, suddenly collapsed as we trod on it, and we were half-buried in tinder. Prickly thickets were common.

Men have frequently been lost in the woods of this country for long periods; and some, unable to discover a way out from them, have suffered protracted and painful deaths.

In 1865, a merchant of Victoria went out on an excursion trip on the occasion of the Queen's birthday, and landed with others at Sooke Harbour—a place sixteen miles from the town, and where, as is common on Vancouver Island, the forest is extremely dense. Being rather short-sighted, he wandered off a trail, and was six days in the woods without food.

A party of sixty men, among whom was the writer, volunteered to go in search of him, and made a detailed examina-

tion of the locality, proceeding in the manner of riflemen
when "extended," with as much regularity as was possible in
that broken country, thick with timber and underbrush, and
where you often could not see the next man ten feet off.
But these efforts were entirely unsuccessful, although continued for several days; and eventually this gentleman
wandered out again on the ill-defined trail, and was found
there—in total ignorance of the fact—by some hunters passing by. It need not be said that he was in a very exhausted
state. He had heard the bugle-calls and shouts of the
searching party, but was at the time in too feeble a condition
to make himself heard. On the fourth day he had made his
will, and having no paper, had written it in pencil on his white
handkerchief!

Later the same year Mr. Butler, an explorer, in a different
branch of the same service as the writer—the Russo-American Telegraph Expedition—was lost for nearly two weeks in
Northern British Columbia, near the Upper Fraser. He had,
when in pursuit of a Cariboeuf deer, wandered far from the
camp of his companions, and attempting to retrace his steps,
found that he had lost his reckoning entirely. In order to
try and discover a way out of the forest he climbed a tree;
but a branch gave way, and he was unfortunate enough to
fall from it, remaining at its base stunned and half-uncon-
scious for two days. At last, partially recovering his strength,
he managed to reach Fraser River, and to construct a raft of
small logs; but from his weakness, and from the rapidity
of the current, he was unable to manage it, and it left him at
last stuck on a bar of the river, with the pleasure of seeing
it float away in the distance. He, however, reached the bank,
and took to the slower but surer mode of following the course

of the river by land through the woods and thickets. He at length reached a small " clearing " owned by Chinamen, who treated him kindly and took him to the " city " (a board and shingle one) at the Mouth of Quesnelle. He had subsisted for twelve days on fern and " gamass," or lily roots, and a few berries.

To return to our narrative :—we found that rotten snow covered the ground, logs, and underbrush, to a depth of several feet, and travelling with the loads we carried was hardly pleasurable. We, however, pushed on, and, after following the Homathco River more or less closely for the greater part of a day, we reached the first glacier stream, and soon obtained a distant view of the great " frozen torrent " itself, with the grand snow-peaks behind it.

This stream, with several others derived from the same source, ran with great violence, and had to be waded; it was as much as I could possibly do to cross them, and I thought that but for the additional fifty pounds on my back I should have been taken off my legs.

To this point several Indians had accompanied us, and I was not over-grieved to see them continue following the main river; they were bound for Tatla Lake. They begged for a " potlatch " or gift, and, glad to get rid of them, I acceded to their request for a little flour, tobacco, &c. To one of the children I gave a sixpence, explaining in doubtful Chinook that her Majesty, as thereon portrayed, was *Victoria, Klootch- man tyhee copa King George illi-he,*—or " Woman-chief of the King George Land " or England,[*] and he immediately sug-

---

[*] " King George man," in the Chinook jargon (a mixture of English, French, and Indian, used as a means of converse among most of the white

GREAT GLACIER, BUTE INLET.

gested by motions that he intended to hang the coin from his nose!

We pitched our camp in an open space from which the snow had melted, on the flat of land extending for several miles below the glacier. On the next morning (24th April) after our simple repast, and one pipe, I left Tellot in camp to look after the traps, as he was unwilling to take any more trouble, and struggled up by myself to the base of the glacier, a distance of about two and a half miles, through very deep, but rotten and thawing snow. The flat was strewed with boulders and drift-wood, with here and there a sand-bar, and covered with snow so soft, that I frequently slipped in between masses of rock up to my chest, or higher, and occasionally jerked down, without any warning, into a streamlet that had undermined it. The streams were large and swift; one of them in fact was a small river, too deep and strong to be waded. Pine and alder woods enclosed this open space on either side.

On reaching the glacier, its presence was rendered very obvious, by the cracking of the ice, and the careering of the stones from its surface. This was incessant; now a shower of pebbles, now a few hundredweight of boulders, and now a thimbleful of sand, but always something coming over. The ice—very evidently such, at the cracks where you saw its true colour, and its dripping lower edges of stalactite form— yet appeared for the most part like wet smooth rock, from

---

men and natives of the coast) simply means an Englishman, and was originated by the fact that our first acquaintance with them was made in the Georgian era. "Boston man," or "Boston" simply, stands for an American; the first vessels bearing the stars and stripes, hailed from that port.

the quantity of dirt on its surface. At its termination the glacier must have been three-quarters of a mile in width; it was considerably wider higher up. Whilst sketching it, all around was so supremely tranquil, that its action was very noticeable. Rocks and boulders fell from it sufficient to crush any too eager observer. A great quantity of snow was on its surface, but fast melting and forming streamlets that glistened in the sun, whilst from innermost icy caverns, torrents of discoloured water poured. The day was extremely warm, and the glacier in full activity. It ran east and west, the sun setting behind the grand peaks, from whose snows it derived its existence.

The terminal moraines were very distinctly marked by pyramids, islands (between the streams), and heaps of boulders, some of them a quarter of a mile in advance, on the flat. That these pointed to a former period when the glacial mass extended thus far cannot be doubted. The green pine woods came almost to the glacier in places. Its surface was strewed with boulders, and both the lateral and medial moraines were strongly marked. Here and there a sapling, either detached from the side precipices, or possibly sprung from a wafted seed, was peacefully moving on to its destruction. The crevasses were large and yawning. Square hummocks of ice, forced up by the closing of crevasses, existed in many places on its surface, whilst at the western or upper end, pinnacles, peaks, and pyramids of ice were seen in the distance. I have little doubt that nearly all the features usually observable in connection with glaciers were to be found there.

The mountains behind were lofty, and one peak was slightly horned; whilst one immense black mass of rock, with precipitous sides, reared itself from the surrounding purity. After spending the day in such crude examination as my time would permit, I returned late in the evening to the camp, where Tellot had remained all day. From his manner, I should suppose that he thought me a fool for my pains, although he showed some little interest in my sketches.

After joining once more the camp of the road party, and resting there a day or two, I turned my face coastwards—proceeding leisurely to the Ferry station, and sketching in the neighbourhood. There I stopped two days with S——, the man in charge, and later with the Superintendent, and some of the workmen who came down for supplies; I then started down for the coast with a pack-train then returning· When within eleven miles from the sea, I left them; and this time proceeded entirely alone to visit a second glacier, which could be seen from the trail, and very much resembled in general appearance the Mer de Glace. This was less troublesome to reach, but the streams had to be waded constantly. Often an accumulation of drift-wood on a bar or " riffle," as it is termed on that coast, would assist me in crossing; but the principal stream from the glacier could not be crossed at all, and so turbulent was it that it had swept away a substantial bridge, formerly built over it (at the crossing of the road).

The ice of this glacier, and the water from it, were comparatively pure, and it was really a very beautiful sight. The mountains behind it seemed of less height, and more rounded in form, than in the case of the other glacier. One immense slope of dazzling purity was very striking. The cliffs and hills, by which it was shut in, were more precipitous. The woods almost extended to its base. The flat in front was strewed with trees swept from the river's banks at times when its waters were unusually swollen, or in some instances doubtless brought down on the glacier itself. The boulders here were neither so large nor so abundant, but there was more sand.

As a canoe was to leave Bute Inlet* the following day, and it was getting late, after sketching the glacier, I reluctantly made my way back to the trail, and followed it through the woods to the station at the mouth of the river.

---

* In a paper read before the Royal Geographical Society last session (1868), Bute Inlet was mentioned as the terminal point on the Pacific of a proposed railway and steam-boat route from the Atlantic sea-board. See Appendix (I.). The same scheme has been more recently laid before the British Association.

CHAPTER III.

THE TRAGEDY AMONG THE GLACIERS.

Reported murder — Canoe trip on the sea — Dodd's Narrows — Island on
fire — The massacre at Bute Inlet — Reports of survivors — Second
massacre — Excitement in the Colony — Expeditions in search of the
Indians — Capture of a part of the murderers — The ideal and real
Indian — His ultimate extinction — Reasons for it — Indian traders —
Proposed semi-secular, semi-missionary settlements — The mission at
Metlakahtla.

I REACHED the station late in the evening, and, after a little
refreshment, turned into my blankets immediately, and was
soon fast asleep. Early next morning, whilst I was yet
sleeping soundly in company with the packers and two of
the workmen who were about to leave the party, some
friendly Indians broke into the room without warning, and
awoke us, saying, in an excited and disjointed manner, that
the man in charge of the ferry (thirty miles higher up the
river) had been murdered by the Chilicotens for refusing to
give away the provisions and other property in his care.
We simply laughed at the idea, knowing that although
S——, the man in question, was sometimes living alone,
the working-party was near him, engaged in blasting rock,
bridging, and otherwise building the road. Moreover, constant communication was necessarily held between them,—
his station being a temporary depôt for provisions, tools,
and blasting-powder. The pack-train from the mouth of
the river made a regular trip to him about every six days,

and we believed that he and the party generally were well armed.

The superintendent had gladly entrusted letters of import-ance to me, and had in fact rather hurried my departure in order that they should reach Victoria by an early date. I therefore, on the noon of the same day, the 30th April, left the river by canoe, in company with two of the work-men, and one Clayoosh Indian. The latter being the owner of the canoe, proved an inexorable tyrant, and kept us paddling for three days, from early dawn to dewy eve. Although these "light kanims," built of cedar, appear too frail for the sea, we came down the inlet, and crossed the Gulf of Georgia to Nanaimo Point, Vancouver Island, in perfect safety, getting then a fair breeze till the end of our trip.

I have many times seen the Indians of that coast, when migrating from one village to another, employ *two canoes*, set a little apart, but parallel to each other, and covered with planks. Their household gods, their strings of clams, and dried fish, are piled on the top of this arrangement, and a man seated in *one* of the canoes can steer it. It is a capital contrivance for use on the sea: a small sail is often hoisted on the top of the planks.

As long as the weather is moderate there is nothing more pleasurable than lying at the bottom of a canoe, smoking or dozing, whilst it cleaves through the water, but in a rough or chopping sea one's time is occupied in keeping it baled out, and the Indian's in steering,—a careful and difficult opera-tion. We camped on some of the numerous islands of the Gulf, and had capital weather. Whilst passing through "Dodd's Narrows" we had a near tussle with fate. The

ISLAND FOREST CONFLAGRATION; GULF OF GEORGIA.

water there at ebb or flow comes with the whole force of
the tide through a small rocky passage in eddies and currents,
and our Indian, usually so impassible, was evidently scared,
as we passed between two opening whirlpools, and within a
few feet of them. We paddled for life, and got through
safely. He afterwards told us, pointing back to the place
with a shudder, "*Hyu si-wash hyack clattawa keekwully
ya-wa!*"—"Many savages (Indians) had quickly gone to
the bottom there," or had found a watery grave.

At one of our mid-day halts for tea, &c., we set a whole
island on fire. Our camp-fire being built at the basé of a
shelving cliff, set light to some dry grass, which in its turn
communicated the flame to the underbrush at a short distance,
and in a little while the forest itself, covering the whole
island, formed one immense conflagration. The last we
saw of it was a cloud of smoke on the horizon some hours
afterwards as we skimmed away from it with a favouring
breeze. These forest fires are often very grand sights, and
burn for weeks. New Westminster, on the Fraser, has had
some very narrow escapes from total destruction from them.

We arrived safely in Victoria without meeting with any
further incidents of special interest, and were generally con-
gratulated by persons of experience on having made a very
quick trip. The distance, 185 miles, had occupied us five
days, camping every night.

But a week after our arrival—on the morning of the 12th
May—the writer, in common with all Victoria, was startled
and horrified by news just arrived from Bute Inlet viâ
Nanaimo. Fourteen out of seventeen men of the working

party had been massacred by the Chilicotens under circumstances of peculiar atrocity, *on the very morning* (the 30th
April) that the Indians had awoke us at the station (forty-
three miles distant), with the reported death of the ferry-
keeper.   He, poor fellow, *had* indeed been killed the day
before, but they had not been satisfied with his blood.   On
the early morning of the day following his murder, whilst the
workmen were yet soundly sleeping, the Indians had surrounded the camp, cut the tent-poles, and dropped the tents
on their victims, firing into them with their muskets, and
running knives into their bodies till all but three were
despatched.

One of the survivors, Petersen, a Dane, told the writer that
hearing the shots, he jumped out of his blankets, and was
immediately struck at by an Indian with an axe; he stepped
aside just to see it fall heavily on the ground, and a few
seconds after this was shot in the arm.   Faint, and bleeding
copiously, he plunged into the river hard by, and its swift
waters carried him down half a mile over the stones and
"snags," bruising him much.   He managed to reach the bank,
and was soon after rejoined by Mosley, a man who had
escaped almost unhurt, although he had, whilst struggling to
release himself from the fallen tent, seen long knives,
on either side of him pierce the prostrate bodies of his companions.   The third man, Buckley, an Irishman, who
afterwards joined them, had been stabbed repeatedly by the
Chilicotens, and fell, faint from the loss of blood, remaining
unconscious for hours, and they left him, imagining he was
dead.   These men, sick and down-hearted, on arrival at the
rope-ferry found that the boat or "scow" had been cut
adrift, and the swift current had carried it away.   In their

weak condition, they had no means of crossing till Buckley, who had been a sailor, managed to rig up a "travelling loop," as he termed it, and succeeded in hauling himself over on the cable stretched across the river, which was 200 yards wide at that spot.   He then sent over the "travelling block" (formerly attached to ropes fixed to the boat), and Petersen and Mosley were at length brought over safely.   They eventually reached the coast, and leaving the river's mouth by canoe, travelled slowly to Nanaimo, Vancouver Island, where they got the mail steamer for Victoria.   The superintendent, and two others who on the morning of the attack were camped a little way a-head of the main party, had risen early, and were at work "blazing," i. e. marking the trees with an axe to show where the trail should go.   They were attacked and shot before they could offer any resistance.   It is said that the Indians, glutted with blood, tore the heart out of one of them and ate it!   With these poor fellows I had just been stopping; with three of them, indeed, I had camped as late as the 28th of April, or but two days before this brutal transaction.   I had reason indeed to be grateful for my escape.   The Chilicotens were well provided with fire-arms. As it afterwards appeared, a number of guns, sent for the protection of the workmen, had been paid away to these natives for various services, and it was therefore true that the party was killed by its own weapons.   On the other hand, the men were virtually unarmed, having, as it was afterwards shown, but one gun and one revolver among them.   These, from the sudden and treacherous nature of the attack, do not appear to have been of the slightest assistance.   From the apparent friendliness of the natives, a fatal security had reigned among the party, nor could any of us detect the

slightest ground for alarm. I was myself, also, totally
unarmed, but got at that time a lesson which I have taken
to heart. I have always since carried a trusty revolver, and
have found that except in those rare cases where pistols
have been traded to natives, they have a wholesome dread
of it.

Alas! the story is but half told. Three weeks later a
large party of packers, with a train of well-laden mules, were
attacked by the same tribe on the Bentinck Arm trail,* and

---

* Bentinck Arm is on the northern coast of British Columbia. A second
route by a trail exists from the head of this arm of the sea to the Cariboo
road. The particulars of the second massacre were as follows:—"On the
17th of May M'Donald and his party started from New Aberdeen, at the
head of Bentinck Arm, for Fort Alexandria on the Fraser. They had forty-
two pack animals, twenty-eight of which were loaded with goods for the
mines, valued at between four thousand and five thousand dollars. On
arriving at Nancootioon Lake, about seventy-five miles from the Arm, they
met with a party of Indians, composed of the Chilicoten, Tatla, and Sitleece
tribes, among the number being two of the murderers of Mr. Waddington's
party at Bute. M'Dougall's squaw, who was a daughter of one of the
Chilicoten chiefs, here learnt from one of her old *tillicums* (friends) that
the Indians intended to rob and murder the whole party, and at once
informed the packers, who, becoming alarmed, began to retrace their steps,
when they were attacked by the savages. Two of the number, M'Dougall
and Higgins, fell from their horses at the first fire, the latter shot through
the breast; M'Donald's horse was shot under him, on which he at once
mounted another, which was also shot down; he then took to the bush,
and when last seen was standing behind a tree, shooting at the Indians with
his revolver. Barney Johnson was badly wounded in the face and breast
by heavy shot, and a ball passed through his horse's head, killing the
animal and tearing open the rider's cheek. Malcolm M'Leod was wounded
with shot, and his hand badly torn by a ball. Grant got a ball through
his arm, and his side filled with shot. Frederick Harrison was also considerably cut up. Farquharson was the only one who escaped unhurt,
although his horse was shot under him. He escaped into the bush, where
he was four days wandering about without food, except berries, not daring

most of these men were also murdered. It need hardly be said that intense excitement prevailed in the colony; many settlers having relatives and friends in isolated spots of this thinly settled country, and being apprehensive of further danger from the natives. Great sympathy was naturally expressed for Mr. Waddington, who had, in an almost unparalleled manner, undertaken a grand work at his own expense,—one which, if completed, would have been of great value to the country. The Colonial Government acted with great promptness. A force of marines, an additional selected and paid body of men, and the New Westminster Volunteers, with the assistance of friendly Indians, endeavoured to catch the murderers. Parties proceeding from the coast at Bentinck Arm and Bute Inlet, and from the interior, attempted to hem them in from all sides, and Governor Seymour himself took a prominent part in these undertakings; but, from the inaccessible nature of the country, a part only of the Indians concerned were ever captured, and that with the loss of an excellent and well-known Hudson Bay Company's man, —Captain MacLean. He was shot by the Chilicotens whilst

---

to return to the trail for fear of being seen by the Indians. He at last made his way back to the head of the Arm. M'Dougall's squaw was also shot by the Indians, and all the horses and property carried off. Grant found his way to Mr. Hamilton's ranch, about twenty-five miles above the settlement, at the head of the Arm, and burst in upon the family, his face and body streaming with blood, telling them of the massacre. They at once packed up a few valuables, and, taking their arms and ammunition, hastened down to the river and embarked in a canoe. They had hardly got afloat when the bloodthirsty villains appeared on the high bank above them. They did not fire, however, being intent on plundering the house, and the little party fortunately made their escape unhurt."—' British Colonist,' June 28th, 1864.

incautiously riding in advance of his party. The Indians taken were afterwards tried in due form, and hanged, and among them was old Tellot, my companion to the glacier.

It may very naturally be asked, What motives led the natives to perpetrate this crime?

I believe the answer is a simple one: a strong desire for plunder, accompanied by the knowledge of the improbability in that country of ever being taken and brought to justice. That any provocation had been given them I do not believe; Mr. Waddington was well known to have been specially indulgent to them.

The Indian is to this day but little understood. By some he is looked on as an animal, by others as almost a hero of romance. The ideal Red-skin, the painted and much adorned native with lofty sentiments, is certainly, as far as my experience goes, a very rare being at the present day, if indeed his existence at any time is not to be considered mythical. A creature, half child—half animal, a mixture of simplicity and ferocity, certainly exists; but though a partial civilization may have varnished his exterior, beneath the thin crust the savage nature lurks, ever ready to break forth, like those volcanic mountains' whose pure snows only hide the molten lava within.

It is easy enough to find natives who have abandoned that simple costume—a blanket, for more decorous clothing, who can swear in broken English, sing " Sally come up !" and drink all the camphine* whiskey they can obtain, but it is very rare

---

* In Victoria, V. I., a comparatively small town, there were between 1858–64, inclusive, no less than 336 "whiskey cases," *i. e.*, men taken up on suspicion of having sold ardent spirits to natives, and 240 of the number resulted in convictions.

to find those who are the better for intercourse with the "pale faces." My experience is decidedly this, that the least degraded Indians were those who had least to do with the white man.

But the importation of "fire-water" is not the only evil: diseases unknown, or little known before, are introduced, and the mere fact of the white man's presence among the Indians seems to foreshadow their ultimate extinction. This very curious point is carefully discussed by a recent writer, Mr. Sproat, in his 'Scenes and Studies of Savage Life.' He had excellent opportunities for a detailed examination of the subject, at his saw-mill settlement of Alberni, Barclay Sound, V. I. He was a large employer of native as well as of white labour, and from personal observation I can confirm his statements with regard to it. The place was conducted on temperance principles, while no violence was used or permitted towards the natives. They were perhaps better fed, better clothed, and better taught than they had ever been before. "It was only," says Mr. Sproat, "after a considerable time, that symptoms of a change, amongst the Indians living nearest the white settlement, could be noticed. Not having observed the gradual process, my mind being occupied with other matters, I seemed all at once to perceive that a few sharp-witted young natives had become what I can only call offensively European, and that the mass of the Indians no longer visited the settlement in their former free independent way, but lived listlessly in the villages, brooding seemingly over heavy thoughts." Their curiosity had been satisfied, they had been surprised and bewildered by the presence of "machinery, steam vessels, and the active labour of civilized men," and they seemed to have acquired a

distrust, nay almost a disgust for themselves. They began
to abandon their old habits, tribal practices, and ceremonies.
" By and bye," continues Mr. Sproat, " it was noticed that
more than the usual amount of sickness existed among the
Indians " and " a high death-rate continued during the five
years I was there." " Nobody molested them, they had
ample sustenance and shelter for the support of life, yet
the people decayed. The steady brightness of civilized life
seemed to dim and extinguish the flickering light of savageism
as the rays of the sun put out a common fire."

Now supposing these views to be correct, and the Indian
to be aware of all this—as he must be if there is truth in it
at all—can we wonder if he takes any chance, fair or foul, to
expel those whom, at the best, he looks upon as intruders
on his native soil ?

There are few places more favourably situated than
Alberni, placed as it is on a secluded canal or arm of the sea,
and it was really a model settlement. Yet—if the above
statements represent the actual facts of the case, and it is
my belief they do—how infinitely worse is it for the Indian
in places open to every trader, and where there is no check
on him but a half-sustained law. Great corporations like
the Hudson's Bay and the Russian American Companies did
not usually sell spirits to natives at all; but private traders,
from the large profits attached to their sale, did, and do it
without hesitation, and the mixtures sold would infallibly
kill any ordinary person,—in fact frequently do kill them.
For the Indian who has acquired a love of liquor there is
little hope, for with him there is no middle course. Catlin
concisely summed up our relations with the red men when
he said, " White men — whiskey — tomahawks—scalping-

knives—guns, powder, and ball—small-pox—debauchery—extermination."

The subject is a sad and wearying one, for the Missionary can hope to do but little, in counteracting such influences. Mr. Sproat suggests the formation of half-secular, half-missionary establishments in native villages at a distance from white settlements. He considers that five white men—men of courage, energy, and proved morality, and willing to forego the use of alcoholic drinks—might form such an establishment, and that at least two of them should know a trade. The leader might act as a magistrate; and, from the writer's observation, he would have enough to do in keeping white traders from the neighbourhood, and in preventing such men from overturning the very objects of the settlement.

Success would depend purely on the earnest, unselfish, and, in a word, Christian efforts of those employed in the work. In the United States, the "Indian Agencies," something very similar in theory, have not been satisfactory in practice, solely owing to the greediness of those engaged, who used them as a means of personal aggrandizement, and left the Indians for whose benefit they were intended "out in the cold."

The Missionary Duncan, at the Metlakahtla village on the coast of British Columbia, has inaugurated such an experiment. Among the natives there are now to be found expert carpenters, builders, gardeners, and road makers. A part of them own a small vessel which takes their produce—oil, furs, and manufactured articles—to Victoria. On her periodical return to the settlement, dividends are declared: on one such occasion, they termed her *Ahah*, "the slave," signi-

fying that she did the work, and they reaped the benefit.
The success of this station is, doubtless, due in part to its
isolation from any large white settlement, but Mr. Duncan
must have laboured earnestly and incessantly in his noble
work.

I think it is fair to allude to one objection I have heard
used—both in and out of the colony—to Mr. Duncan's work.
It is this, that—for a missionary—he is "too much of a
trader." I cannot say to what extent, or in what sense, this
may be true; I do not myself believe it in any offensive sense.
If, however, Mr. Duncan, from a little pecuniary advantage
accruing to him, should be induced to prolong his stay
among the Indians, and follow out the work of civilization he
is engaged in, no one can rightly complain. The majority
of missionaries do not stop long enough in any one locality
to acquire a thorough knowledge of the native dialects, and
this of itself must be a fatal hindrance to their efforts.

If this gentleman, by giving up a large part of his life for
the benefit of these savages, can at the same time make a
fortune, may success attend him!

CHAPTER IV.

THE INTERIOR OF VANCOUVER ISLAND.

Pleasures of labour — Unknown interior of Vancouver Island — Expedition organised — Cowichan River — Somenos — Kakalatza and his hat-box — Travel up the river — Our camps — Camp yarns — Indian version of the Book of Jonah — Cowichan Lake — Rafting experiences — The "Rampant Raft"— Brown's Camp —Acquisition of a canoe.

TRAVELLING in the interior of Vancouver Island exhibits little beyond an alternation of various shades of monotony, so that the narrative of one month's experiences is as good, or a good deal better, than the details of five. Notwithstanding the truth of this statement, I count some of the happiest hours of my life in the time spent there. Although no believer in the "dignity" of labour, I can well believe in its pleasures. When a man can enjoy any diet, even one of beans—of a kind at home only given to horses—when he considers tea the best and most refreshing of drinks, it is a pretty good sign that he is in vigorous health, that he sleeps well, and that life is no burden to him. Such was our experience at times when we carried on our backs loads from 50 to 120 lbs. in weight, through a rugged country where rivers were mountain torrents, the woods almost a jungle, and where we rarely turned into our blankets at night, except in a wet condition.

In 1864, but few of the settlers in this colony had penetrated ten miles back from the towns and settlements of the East coast ; for although Captain Richards (now Hydrogra-

pher to the Navy), Captain Mayne, and Messrs. Pemberton
and Pearce had already made very interesting journeys into
the interior, yet the results of their explorations were little
known. Victoria had been built and sustained by the
British Columbian mines, and fluctuated with them. In the
spring of the above-mentioned year her citizens woke up to
this fact, and an expedition organized by a popular committee, and endorsed by the Colonial Government, was
immediately started. A naturalist—Mr. Robert Brown, of
Edinburgh—was unanimously chosen leader. For astronomer
we had Mr. P. Leech, formerly of the Royal Engineers; and
the writer accompanied the expedition as artist. Our party
numbered nine persons exclusive of Indians, and was at
a later period slightly increased. The men were selected
for special qualifications; many of them were miners by profession, and the V. I. E. E. had no cause to be ashamed of its
members.*

On the 7th June, 1864, after an address from Governor
Kennedy,† himself in truth the originator of the expedition,
we left the Hudson's Bay Company's wharf in Victoria on
board H.M. Gun-boat 'Grappler,' bound for Cowichan, a
settlement thirty-five miles north of Victoria, on the east
coast of the island. Her commander, Captain Verney, was

---

* Our party comprised the following men, in addition to those named
above:—Mr. John Buttle, assistant naturalist; Messrs. Barnston, Macdonald, Lewis, Meade, and Foley, pioneers and miners; and Thomas
Antoine, and Lazare de Buscay, half-breed hunters. At a later period
Mr. Foley left our party, and Messrs. Drew and Hooper were added
to it.

† Now Sir Arthur Edward Kennedy, C.B., Governor of the West Africa
Settlements.

also an ardent promoter of the proposed explorations, and to him the writer is indebted for much kindly courtesy.

On arrival at Cowichan Bay we landed at the pretty little settlement of Comiaken, a place which boasts a Roman Catholic mission and several farms and settlers' houses. In one of the latter we enjoyed so much hospitality that it was a serious question whether some of us would not stop there, and let our travels end where they had begun!

On the 9th June, after a "hyas wa-wa" (big talk) with the Indians, Brown at length succeeded in hiring a canoe, and, putting the larger part of the stuff therein, sent it up the Cowichan River in charge of one white man of our party and several Indians. The larger part of us proceeded by land direct to the village of Somenos, where we found several large lodges, or "rancheries," as they are termed in the colony. The natives were drying fish and clams on strings hanging from the rafters of their dwellings, and were by no means anxious to engage in our service. There were two reasons for this reluctance, which was one of the main drawbacks of our journey. The first was simply that they lived so easily, getting salmon, deer, and beaver meat in abundance, and consequently were indifferent to anything but extremely high pay. The second and main reason was fear of surrounding tribes, especially those of the west coast, who were accustomed occasionally to kidnap "unprotected males," and carry them off as slaves. At length "Kakalatza," an old "tyhee" or chief, of grave but dignified appearance, and who persisted in wearing a battered chimney-pot hat, given to him by some settler, was engaged to act as our guide to the Cowichan Lake, but this was on the understanding that we allowed him to take his hat-box with him; and every night afterwards he carefully deposited his beaver in it, before retiring into his blankets. Kakalatza and his hat were inseparable. Here, too, a half-breed, Thomas Antoine by name, but known elsewhere as "Tomo," joined us, and proved a great acquisition. He could speak any number of Indian dialects, was a good shot, though he had but one arm, could travel or "pack" with the best, and was reliable except when he got hold of some whiskey, when he was a perfect devil. Spirits seem to have even more attraction for the half-breed than for the full Indian, and more influence upon him.

The succeeding days much resembled each other, most of us proceeding through the forests with packs of no light weight, whilst the canoe was poled up the strong current of the river,—paddles being useless, and oars impracticable. The river was a succession of "riffles," or rapids,—small and large—alternating with comparatively quiet water. Sometimes the canoe had to be towed, and sometimes carried bodily; in several places all hands had to make a "portage," or carry the goods over the rocks, to a higher and better part of the stream. We found the banks thickly timbered, and where the Douglas pine, spruce, and hemlock had grown under favourable circumstances, the place resembled a beautiful park; but for the most part it was a tangle of underbrush, mingled with fallen logs in all stages of decay, and woods in all degrees of luxuriance. But if our travelling was troublesome, the evening camp more than made up for all, when a good log-fire, a bed of fir-brush, and a pipe made us happy, and where we could comfortably sleep—for the most part, with no canopy but that of heaven. There is no climate in the world, California not excepted, more delicious than that

of Vancouver Island. We were generally fortunate, too, at
this time in getting grouse or deer meat; and our party
thought nothing of polishing off a whole deer at a couple of
meals. We had to abandon and leave behind many a rib,
and even haunch of venison, it being impossible to carry
any more than we already had on our backs in the shape
of beans and flour, blankets, frying-pans, pots, and instruments.

And then the yarns of those evening camps! Mac
Donald's story—often begun and never ended—the narrative
of his eventful life. Born on Fraser River, the son of a
Hudson's Bay chief trader, the tedious barter with Indians
for their peltries had proved distasteful to him, and he ran
away, when quite young, to sea, got shipwrecked and detained a prisoner in Japan. Here he was closely confined,
but on the whole well treated, till he was rescued from the
Japanese by Commodore Perry, U. S. Navy, when he called
there on his well-known expedition. After many wanderings
Mac brought up in Australia, mined, made money, and
spent it; had once kept a gambling-house and dancing-
booth at the "diggings." Later the British Columbian
mines had attracted him back to his earliest home; he had
"run" a ferry on Fraser River, kept a grog-shop at Lillooet,
and played the "honest miner" in Cariboo, and now, hale
and hearty as ever, was a member of the V. I. E. E. Or
else the Indian yarns of Tomo—many of them childish,
some incomprehensible, but sometimes showing that the
natives have inventive power and a sense of humour. Here
is one of them, apparently a native version of the book of
Jonah! "An Indian, paddling in his 'frail kanim' on the
great 'salt chuck' or sea, was swallowed—canoe and all—

by a great fish, and lay down at the bottom of its belly, sad at heart, thinking it was all up with him, and that never more would he see his people. But in the midst of his affliction comfort came to him; a brilliant idea flashed through his brain,—sweet revenge was at least possible! and he proceeded to execute a hastily conceived project. He cut his paddles into shavings—'wittled' them, as a Yankee would say—broke his canoe into fragments, and lighted a great fire on the floor of the creature's stomach. It was not long before the fish showed, by a tortuous uncomfortable wriggling of his body, that this operation did not agree with him, and he consequently attempted, by swallowing wave after wave, to cool his fevered body, but did not succeed in putting out the fire, though our hero was nearly drowned in the operation. Our Indian, averse to water at all times, appeared at this juncture to get in a very bad temper, and drawing his long knife, stabbed the lining of the creature's inside, till the coats of its stomach were in a very dilapidated state. It was evidently expiring fast, and swam ashore on the beach. Here, while it lay in the agonies of death, our friend cautiously crept up its throat, and through its gasping mouth, just in time to avoid the collision of its jaws, which came together with a terrific crash, and the great fish was dead!" This formed part only of a long story,—many such we had, and varied them by making the woods echo with the latest gems of "nigger" minstrelsy, or even more classical productions.

The Cowichan River is about forty miles in length; but a much shorter route to the great lake, its source, is possible by land. In several places it passes through cañons,—small rocky gorges, in which the water boils and frets in eddies and rapids over sunken rocks. It was but a type of three parts of the streams on the island. Every locality on its banks had appropriate native names. One fresh verdant spot near a deserted Indian lodge was *Saatlam*, "the place of green leaves;" another, an open prairie in the woods, was *Qualis*, "the warm place."

On the 15th June we found the forest getting thicker, the trees larger, and the soil evidently richer, a sign that we were nearing the lake; and later the same day we camped by its placid waters. One cedar near this spot measured thirty-five feet in circumference, at a height of five feet from the ground. In this country very valuable timber is necessarily useless at the present time, from the fact that there are in most cases no available means of transport to the coast,—the rivers usually being tortuous, and blocked at intervals by accumulations of drift-wood. One occupation is alone possible—so far as the interior forests are concerned —and that has hitherto attracted little attention on Vancouver Island: I allude to the manufacture of rosin and turpentine. In forests in Oregon, of almost exactly the same character, it has become a profitable employment, and the products are items of export from that country.

The Indian name for Cowichan Lake, a very calm, beautiful sheet of water, is "Kaatza," and a long peninsula stretching into it, and widening at its termination into a thickly-wooded knoll, is "Kanatze," "the island in tow." One considerable stream and several minor ones enter it.

After making sundry surveys and explorations, we divided our forces: one party, under Leech, proceeded in as direct a course as might be to Port San Juan; while Brown, myself, and four of the men, started for the Nittinaht River,

in the direction (as we had learnt on Indian authority) of its
upper waters.

Bidding then adieu to "Kakalatza" and his hat, we
shouldered our packs, and, travelling through the forests,
at length reached a stream flowing in a westerly direction,
which we concluded was the one in question. Our supplies
were down to starvation point; and we lost no time in
commencing the construction of a raft. On the 26th June,
this being finished, we started down, going smoothly enough,
except when our bark was brought to a standstill on the
shallow "riffles." Then all hands lightened her by getting
into the water, lifted her over the boulders, and then all
aboard! and away we went, shooting some of the deeper
rapids very successfully. But at length the distant, though
unmistakable roar of a fall, warned us that we must resume
our travel by land. It was fortunate that we did so in time,
for on examination of the rapid we found it to be one of a
serious nature, and, had we proceeded, it is questionable
whether there would have been one left to tell the tale.
We resumed our packs, and followed an Indian trail, which
brought us at night to a deserted lodge, and there we
camped. Near it on the bank lay an old cedar canoe, and
we at once set to work to caulk it, and make it as water-
tight as possible. Mr. Brown, who had planned the routes
with care, knew that an inlet existed at the termination of
the Nittinaht River; but it was a matter of uncertainty
whether we had reached that stream, and it behoved us all
to bestir ourselves on account of the state of our supplies.

On the morning of the 27th, Brown and Barnston started
down in this shaky old canoe, which leaked like a sieve; and
an hour or so afterwards MacDonald and myself got on

THE RAMPANT RAFT.

board a raft of very limited dimensions, to follow them. It was composed of boards and logs, mostly taken from the Indian lodge, and was held together by the ropes of our blanket packs, the necessary holes pierced in some cases by pistol bullets. We left our companions, Buttle and Lewis, to follow through the bush, and to attempt, as they fondly hoped it might prove, a "short cut." We tied our bundles to two upright posts fixed on the raft, poled into the stream, and off we shot.

We found the river a series of rapids alternating with silent and deep pools. These last gave us really harder work than any other part of our journey. We could not usually touch bottom with our poles, whilst it was very difficult to keep the raft in shore. On the "riffles" it was pure fun mixed with a dash of danger. The current acting on the stern of our craft with 300 lb.—MacDonald's weight, as steersman—took it under water several feet, while the bows were elevated in the air. Several times a curious sight might have been witnessed, that of a raft shooting past at the rate of six or eight miles an hour, and, *standing nearly upright in the water*, a "raft rampant," as it were, with a couple of half-drowned explorers hanging on with comical desperation. It need not be stated, that on such a river our bark whirled round in the eddies every few minutes, and the stern became the bows and *vice versâ*. Twice we were directly spilt in the water, and once sucked in beneath a number of huge logs, under which the current swept violently, but we escaped with a few bruises. Accumulations of drift-wood occurred constantly on the river, and made navigation an affair of constant watchfulness.

We often as before brought up against boulders in the

E

river, and had to lighten her, the water meantime rushing past with fury, and then had to scramble on again, or we should have been left behind. A few moments after this the cry, a very constant one, was " Duck your head ! " as we shot under overhanging banks, branches, and half fallen trees. I was reminded ever and anon of early experiences in donkey-riding, when that patient but vicious animal *would* bruise my legs against every wall, and *would* run under trees that just allowed him to pass completely, but that nearly swept me from the saddle. Our raft seemed to be " possessed " in like manner. Mac was as usual thoroughly good-tempered, and the events of that day made us faster friends than ever. We went ashore two or three times, and had several luscious though unsatisfying meals of " salmon " and " salall " berries. In other respects our provisions were so low that we were well inclined to make a quick trip.

We despaired of reaching Brown's camp that evening, when smoke wafting up the river—the grateful smell of a camp fire reached our nostrils, and a few minutes afterwards, turning a bend of the stream, we discovered our friends camped on a flat bar at what was virtually its termination. After their experiences in the canoe they were surprised to see us, and as it proved we were more fortunate than the men who followed us. The next afternoon they arrived fatigued and hungry, and perfectly satisfied that " short cuts " in that country were a delusion and a snare. They had like us essayed a raft, but had not been able to manage it.

Before they arrived our companions had found, at a little distance below the mouth of the river, an uninhabited lodge, and near it a canoe, which was immediately " pressed," says

Brown, in his Report to the Colonial Government, "into the service of the Expedition, in the name of her most gracious Majesty, Queen Victoria, and her faithful Deputy, his Excellency Arthur Edward Kennedy." We set to work to caulk it with flour-bags and pine-gum, preparatory to an early start on the morrow.

CHAPTER V.

THE INTERIOR OF VANCOUVER ISLAND.

Nittinaht Inlet — " Whyack " — The Indians — Aht tribes — The breakers — Port San Juan — Indian yarn — Sooke — Basin and river — Discovery of gold — Gold on Queen Charlotte's Island — Nanaimo — Coal-seam at Comox — Ascent of Puntledge River — Wreck of canoe — Interior lakes — Barclay Sound — Game list — Camp-marks.

VERY early the next morning we made a start, a light favourable breeze had risen, and, hoisting a blanket sail, we skimmed away gaily before it. Even now we were not absolutely certain that we had reached the wished-for Nittinaht Inlet, but appearances were in favour of that view. We passed several Indian villages with, however, no signs of life about them, and towards evening found the Inlet narrowing. The tide swept through it in many an eddy and whirlpool, and we could hear the noise of breakers outside, a convincing proof that we had almost reached the coast. A few minutes of specially hard paddling took us out of the current into a quiet bay behind the Nittinaht village of "Whyack," where a troop of wild-looking savages watched our approach with evident surprise.

"Mokoola," the chief, was absent, and a part of his tribe with him; but those remaining in the village treated us well, and pointed out a flat place behind it for our camp. We were soon engaged in bartering for halibut, &c., and they crowded round to see how we cooked it, and perhaps to watch an opportunity for pilfering. Their blankets give

AHT NATIVE, WEST COAST OF VANCOUVER ISLAND.

an excellent chance for obtaining and concealing anything lying round a camp: we lost two axes and an auger at this place.

It was on this coast and neighbourhood that Mr. Sproat made the careful studies and observations on Indian habits and character, which he has recently laid before the public. The annexed portrait of an *Aht* * native is no imaginative production, but is taken from a photograph made on the spot, and gives a fair idea of the type of native we met at this village. The unkempt hair, the wreath of leaves put on much for the same purpose as they are often put on the heads of cart-horses—to keep off flies and musquitoes, and also for ornament—and the limited amount of costume, are all characteristics of the west coast natives. The pin stuck in one side of his nostril is simply put there for convenience, when not required for fastening the blanket across his manly bosom! A large number of these people have small holes drilled through the cartilage between the nostrils, in which they not unfrequently wear rings; it is no uncommon thing for them to insert their blanket-pins in them temporarily, for want of a better place.

But on festive occasions and dances these "nasty Injiens" do not deem themselves sufficiently ugly, and therefore put on masks carved from wood, and often very grotesque and curious. The original of our illustration is nearly two feet in height, but much larger ones are worn, and some of the chiefs have a complete series of "properties" of this kind.

---

* *Aht* is the generic name given by Mr. Sproat to the tribes of the west and south coast of Vancouver Island, or rather is the generic termination of most of the native names; thus Nittinaht, Klaho-quaht, &c.

Some of them are ingeniously constructed, and have strings

arranged to move the eyes, open the beak, &c. They are common to all the tribes of Vancouver Island.

The Nittinahts bear a bad reputation, and owing to the inaccessible coast round "Whyack," the heavy surf and breakers off the entrance to the Inlet, and the fact that they have stockaded their village,

Example of Mask worn by natives of Vancouver Island.

they consider themselves almost impregnable, and safe from attack. They have in days gone by often waged war on surrounding tribes, and even on those of the opposite coast of Washington Territory. The terrible Bute Inlet massacre was so fresh in our memories that we kept a careful "watch" by turns all night. "Whyack" is famous for the manufacture of cedar canoes, and we saw many there in course of construction *from single logs*. The models of these craft were extremely good; I have not seen better in any other part of the island.

Next morning, after a couple of hours' haggling, we hired a large canoe and three Indians to manage it. Our goods being put on board, it was hauled to the water's edge, where we all stood more or less in the surf. The right moment at length arrived, the retreating wave lifted our bark, we scrambled on board, and paddled with all our might till clear of the breakers. We then hoisted a mat sail, and, leaving the Indians to manage it, lay down at the bottom of the canoe, and smoked our pipes in comfort.

We rounded the southernmost end of Vancouver Island, and arrived at Port San Juan, or Pachenah, without accident, finding there Mr. Lawton, a well-known trader, who welcomed us kindly, and immediately spread a meal that seemed a princely banquet after our week of semi-starvation. A few days after our arrival, Leech and his party came in, worn out with fatigue and hunger, and their clothes in tatters. A distance of twenty miles—*on the map*—had occupied ten days to travel, and they used very strong and emphatic language in regard to an old Admiralty chart on which their route was marked as "level plains"! Their journey had been of the most difficult nature, over a constant succession of mountains, and through the usual thick forests. To proceed one mile they had to travel five, and when they at length reached the San Juan River, it was found to pass through gorges specially inaccessible, and to be in fact, for the larger part of its course, a brawling torrent. Among other specimens brought in by Leech was a fragment of undoubted plumbago. Coal was also observed by us in the neighbourhood, but in thin seams only.

Mr. Lawton, then living by himself, and with no white neighbours within thirty or forty miles, was very glad to see us, and had an unlimited budget of yarns. Once during his stay at Pachenah, the Nittinahts had made a warlike excursion to the Cape Flattery Indians of the opposite coast (Washington Territory), and had brought home twenty-six human heads as their spoil, which they brought up to his log house with savage glee. They then left for their own village, and Lawton knew well that a return visit would be made by the outraged tribe, and that they would not be particular whom they attacked, even though they were white settlers. He accordingly, with one white man then with him, barricaded the doors and windows of his house, and kept a constant watch. They had a large quantity of trading guns lying there, and they determined to load every one of them, and give the attacking party a thorough good peppering. They had not long to wait; but one night elapsed before the plash of paddles was heard approaching in the bay. They stopped opposite the Pachenah Indian lodges; all was silent as the tomb, the inhabitants had fled. Enraged, they made for Lawton's house, their hearts full of vengeance, and ready to wreak it on the first man they met. Their canoes were just touching the beach, when the two men inside let fly at them, and took up musket after musket so rapidly, that the Indians thought there must be a large party inside, and, howling with disappointment, made off in the greatest confusion, paddling for dear life. They never gave any further trouble.

After the arrival of a sloop from Victoria with provisions for the ensuing month, we left for Sooke Basin or Harbour in two canoes, and in the lovely Straits of Fuca soon got a favourable breeze. This increased so suddenly, that we lost one of our sails by a squall of wind, and we had to make a tent do duty for it. On this trip we noticed fair outcroppings of coal on a low cliff on the coast near Sooke. This may well be considered a continuation of the coal measures already worked on the opposite coast, at Clallam Bay, Washington Territory.

On the 13th July we commenced the ascent of the Sooke River ("Soak" more nearly expresses the Indian pronunciation), a stream much resembling the Cowichan River before mentioned, but even less navigable. It was there that we made the first important discovery of our expedition,—one that for a time revolutionised Victoria. In brief, gold was found in paying quantities; a "rush" took place when the news reached Victoria, and before the end of the season, 100,000 dollars' worth of the precious metal had been taken out. It is admitted that few persons made extremely large "piles" or stakes, but many made for the time very high wages. Board and "shingle" stores, grog-shops, and hotels, were run up in numbers out of all proportion to the wants of the locality, and, as in other places, it was a question whether for every dollar obtained, *two* had not been spent in the operation!

Large numbers of Chinamen eventually worked this ground, and as provisions were tolerably cheap on the spot, especially after trails were made from the nearest road, the discovery was deemed one of value, and a reward in hard cash was voted and paid to us by the Colonial Government. The principal stream was, by the general wish of the members of the expedition, named after Leech, our astronomer.

As yet nothing equal to these diggings has been found on the island, but from the indications observed by us in innumerable other places,* and from the well-known yield of the mainland, it cannot be doubted that Vancouver Island has

---

* On a stream entering Cowichan Lake, on rivers falling into Barclay Sound on the southern side, and on streams falling into the Puntledge Lake, near Comox, very good "colours" of gold were obtained.

other fields of the same character, as yet undeveloped. On
Queen Charlotte's Island also, the precious metal is known
to exist, although the precise locality of the deposit has
never been satisfactorily ascertained. It is stated that a
gentleman in the Hudson's Bay service found the Haidah
Indians of that island using golden bullets in place of leaden
ones !

For very interesting reports of the explorations once
made on Queen Charlotte's Island by Captain Torrens, and
also by Major Downie, both gentlemen well known to me,
I must refer the reader to Captain Mayne's work on that
coast.

The gold on Vancouver Island was usually found in small
specks and scales (dust), but nuggets up to six and a half
ounces have been obtained. The great drawback was the
scarcity of the "pay-dirt," that is to say, that there were
more rocks and boulders, than earth impregnated with gold
resting on them ; sometimes in cracks and corners, however,
of the former, very nice little "pockets" or accumulations of
nuggets were struck. I cannot leave this subject without
alluding to the great assistance afforded us in the first
discovery by Mr. Foley, then a member of the expedition, a practical miner of considerable experience, who knew
more of gold and its whereabouts than any five of the other
men.

On the Sooke River deer were especially abundant, and
when once we had arrived at the lake of the same name, one
of its sources, we lived for a time in clover, catching some
salmon trout in its limpid waters. Owing to the dryness of
the weather at this period, our camp fires were on several
occasions the means of setting the forest on fire ; and at the

lake we were burnt out of our camp, and had to retreat to an island, from which we could watch the conflagration in safety. Here we should have been happy, but for the musquitoes. It has been distinctly stated that they do not exist on Vancouver Island, but the writer knows, from this and subsequent trips, that they are abundant in the interior, though not perhaps as bad as those in British Columbia. We always kept a pan of smouldering ashes at our tent door, when camped for any length of time in one spot, yet we passed many a restless night from their inflictions.

From Sooke Lake we proceeded by Shawnigan Lake and Cowichan to Nanaimo, where a delay occurred owing to the difficulty of obtaining Indians. Nanaimo, seventy miles north of Victoria, is the second town in point of size on the island : in fact the list ends here ; there is no third as yet. It owes its existence mainly to the valuable coal deposits which are successfully worked by an English company, and it has had a steadier and more healthy career than Victoria. It lies in a pleasant bay sheltered by islands, and there is depth of water sufficient for large vessels close in shore. A quantity of the coal is shipped to San Francisco, Victoria, and Fraser River, while there is an expectation that the recent annexation of " Alaska " will create a further demand for steam-ship purposes. The main deposit is situated at about a quarter of a mile from the town, and the coal reaches the wharf by means of a railway and locomotive. The principal shaft is a hundred feet in depth, and a "drift" runs in an inclined plane for 1200 feet, sinking in that distance 170 feet, so that the perpendicular depth from which the coal is now taken is 270 feet. The bed has naturally varied considerably in thickness ; in 1867 it was about five

feet through.   150 to 300 tons are taken out daily; the coal
brings an average of six dollars a ton on delivery at the ship.
In San Francisco it is retailed at an average price of twelve
dollars (or about £2 10s. gold: there are no "greenbacks"
accepted in California except at the regular discount).   The
Hudson's Bay Company, which had formerly a fort at
Nanaimo, were the first to work this seam, hiring Indians
to dig it from the outcroppings, and paying them at the rate
of one blanket for eight barrels.   It is an undoubted fact
that the coal of Vancouver Island is its most valuable production, and that it is abundant.   After leaving Nanaimo,
we discovered, on a stream entering the Puntledge River near
the small settlement of Comox, a very important deposit.
A seam from two to eight feet in thickness, disappearing and
again reappearing on the rocky walls of a small cañon,
extended for a mile of its course.   This occurred five miles
from navigable water, and would require the construction of
a tramway through the woods for its successful development.
We camped by the principal seam, and made a gigantic fire
of the coal, which really appeared to be of excellent quality.
The stream on which we observed it was named in honour of
our leader, Mr. Brown.

Our journey from this place up the Puntledge River to the
lake of the same name was one of difficulty.   We had determined to take a canoe there, and it had to be carried or
towed nearly the whole distance.   Piles of drift-wood blocked
the river, while its bed consisted of boulders of all sizes.   We
all spent more of our time in the water than out of it; and
often, when dragging the canoe by main force through the
shallow but swift current, got into holes out of our depth,
and clung to it with great pertinacity, till once more we

could get a foothold. There were two falls of importance on this river, one of them bearing the poetical name of *Ski-ep*, " the whirl of waters." At last we reached the lake, one of the most picturesque on the island, and our canoe was of much service to us. Alas! it was near here that our craft, that had gone through so much, at length came to grief. Descending a tributary of the lake which we had previously examined, owing to the bad steering of one of our party it came broadside on a log, and in a second was cracked up like a nut-shell into a hundred pieces, and we were all spilt in the swift current. We hung on to the larger part of the fragments, and succeeded in getting ashore. After several hours' patching, sewing, and caulking, we managed to rig her up again, but had subsequently to treat her as a very cripple of a canoe, and to get out at all the rapids and shallows and carry her tenderly over. With great care we at length reached our camp by the lake, where doubtless she still lies, the wreck we left her.

Between the east coast at Comox and the west coast at Barclay Sound, we found a series of seven lakes, extending almost across the island. One of these, the Central Lake, is about eighteen miles long by one to one and a half in width, and our travelling was spasmodic, constantly making halts to construct rafts. On this rather tedious trip our supplies again got down to a very limited ration of flour, and that " strait," that is to say, unaccompanied by tea, beans, or bacon. We varied a diet of soggy bread with a kind of thin paste or soup of flour and water; not very good " working " grub. It was a sad but true fact, that, when our commissariat department was exhausted, nothing was to be obtained in the way of game or outside supplies; and we were not sorry when on the 23rd September we reached a " logging camp " near the Opichesaht village on the Somass River, where the workmen, who had been expecting us for some time, spread a repast to which we well knew how to do justice. The same day, descending the river, we reached the large saw-mill and lumber establishment of Alberni, Barclay Sound, where Messrs. Johnston and Raymur, the gentlemen then in charge, received us with great kindness. Two hundred workmen—representing a dozen nationalities, and, including among the number, Kanakas from the Sandwich Islands, and the Indians and half-breeds of many tribes—were busily engaged in the mill and neighbourhood. Seven vessels were, at the date of our visit, loading with lumber for England, California, Chili, China, and Australia, and the settlement presented a lively aspect.

Our subsequent canoe-trips down Barclay Sound — on streams entering which, we again found the " colour " of gold,—our journey once more across the island to Qualicum, and thence by canoe to Nanaimo, would, if narrated be little more than a repetition of what has been said above, and I will not enlarge upon them. Our party in detachments had crossed the island in seven directions.

In the interior game is fairly abundant, and our list included three elk, twenty-five deer, and two beaver, shot mainly at the commencement of our journeys. Owing to the noise made in travelling through the thickets and woods, and the density of the forest itself, we saw but few wild animals, and of those generally only their *hind-quarters* retreating in the distance. The animals above named, with a few bears, panthers, martens, and coons, are about all that the traveller will see at any time on that island.

The future explorer will have no trouble in finding our tracks, for at each camp the trees were " blazed," *i. e.*, marked with an axe, and an inscription affixed as represented below —the artistic part of the work being usually performed by the writer—painter, but not glazier, to the expedition.

Camp with " blaze," or Camp-mark.

CHAPTER VI.

ALASKA TERRITORY.

Acquisition of Russian America by the United States — American criticisms on the purchase — Coal and gold discoveries — Mock advertisements — America for the Americans — Geographical literature of the Pacific — Of Russian America — The Treaty — W. U. Telegraph Expedition — Its organization — Preference for young men.

THE recent acquisition of Russian America by the United States Government is one of the events of our day. 400,000 square miles of territory have been, under the name of "Alaska,"* added to the already vast domain of Uncle Sam, and Russia has rid herself of an isolated possession of dubious value.

The purchase was not allowed to be completed quietly. On its announcement the people of the United States were, in fact, taken by surprise; there was much hostile criticism, and strong political opposition. That has now for the most part passed away, and American enterprise has begun to develop the resources of the country.† For some time,

---

* By this purchase the U. S. Government has acquired also one of the largest mountains of the continent, Mount St. Elias.

† Coal has been discovered at Cook's Inlet, and a recent newspaper paragraph (July 30th, 1868) tells us that "A party of explorers started some time back from the State of Oregon for the Skena River, in Alaska, and were subsequently reported to have been lost in a schooner in Queen Charlotte's Sound. The American consul at Victoria, Vancouver Island, now announces their safety, and adds that they state themselves to have discovered a rich gold-field in the Taquo River, where they are picking up

indeed, Mr. Seward's position in regard to it—he being always considered the originator of the project—was anything but a desirable one. It was regarded as a bad business and as an unfortunate speculation, and was ridiculed as " our new possession of ' Walrus-sia.' " Mock advertisements—purporting to come from the Secretary of State—appeared in the daily papers of New York and the large cities generally, offering the highest price for " waste lands and worn-out colonies," " submerged and undiscovered islands," icebergs, polar bears, volcanoes, and earthquakes, " provided they should not shake the confidence of the State Department." In the House of Congress it was made a party question, and therefore the colony was on the one hand described as the tag end of creation, and on the other as an Elysian field. Virtually there was, and is, little known about it; and the following pages must be regarded simply as an early and superficial contribution to our better knowledge of it.

There are, however, many, both in England and America, who look on this purchase as the first move towards an American occupation of the whole continent, and who foresee that Canada and British America generally, will sooner

---

the precious metal in lumps. This news is credited in Sitka, and every available craft is being brought into requisition to convey adventurers to the spot." Gold has been frequently obtained in the Stekine River, a large stream near the boundary line, running partly through British and partly through Russian America.

It has also been recently stated that a company was prepared to "take " Alaska, pay 10,000,000 dollars in gold to the United States Government (nearly 3,000,000 dollars over the sum to be paid to Russia), and leave the supreme authority to Congress. Their object was of course to trade for furs, mine, and otherwise develop the country.

or later become part of the United States. Looking at the matter without prejudice, I believe that it will be better for those countries and ourselves when such shall be the case. *We* shall be released from an encumbrance, a source of expense and possible weakness; *they*, freed from the trammels of periodical alarms of invasion, and, feeling the strength of independence, will develop and grow; and—speaking very plainly and to the point—our commercial relations with them will double and quadruple themselves in value. No one now supposes, that, had the United States remained nought but "our American colonies," they would have progressed as they *have* done; and it is equally obvious that our commerce with them must have been restricted in equal ratio. That it is the destiny of the United States to possess the whole northern continent I fully believe.

The geographical literature of the Pacific is abundant; but that part of it which has reference to Russian America is comparatively restricted. Müller's* narrative of the voyages of Bering and his companions deservedly heads the list. Bering and Tschirikoff may be fairly regarded as the discoverers of the country, and their names will ever be associated with the North Pacific. Immediately following their adventurous voyages, a number of Russian merchants of Eastern Siberia sent vessels from Ochotsk and neighbouring ports on trading excursions, mainly to the Aleutian Islands. "Within a period of ten years," says Coxe,† their historian, "more important discoveries were made by these individuals at their own private cost, than had been hitherto

---

* Müller's 'Voyages from Asia to America,' &c.
† Coxe's 'Russian Discoveries.'

effected by all the expensive efforts of the Crown." Byron, Carteret, Wallis, and Cook follow next in chronological order; the latter especially helped to clear up the fogs that encompassed the coast. Cook's Inlet, Ounalaska, Norton Sound, and Bering Straits were all examined by the great circumnavigator.

Passing over the illustrious La Perouse, who explored portions of the N.W. coast, adjacent to Mount St. Elias, and several Spanish commanders who did next to nothing for Russian America, we come to our countryman Vancouver, whose laborious surveys have left their mark on the whole of the coast from San Francisco to Cook's Inlet, and whose great work deserves a fuller recognition from the public than it has ever yet received.

Russia has naturally done much towards the exploration of her colony; and some of her naval officers hold a deservedly high rank as geographers. Lisiansky, Kotsebue, and Lütke are names as familiar to men of science as to navigators. Among our own countrymen, Moore, Kellet, Collinson, and McClure, when engaged in the search for Sir John Franklin, also examined some portions of the coasts,* while Captain Bedford Pim, who made some extensive land-trips, is well remembered at some of the (late) Russian posts. But, with the exception of the one visit paid by a Russian, Zagoskin, until our expedition commenced its work, the interior of the country had been little visited,

---

* Findlay's ' Directory for the Navigation of the Pacific Ocean ' gives—up to the date of its publication—an exhaustive *resumé* of this subject. Although a little out of date, from the rapid development of the north-west coasts of America, it was used constantly on our vessels, and looked upon as an invaluable work on the subject.

except by the traders of the Russian American Fur Company; and much valuable information has been hitherto locked up in their archives. By the recent treaty all the documents relating to the territory were to be handed over to the United States Government. Let us hope that they may, in the interests of geography, receive a thorough investigation.

The treaty between Russia and the United States establishes the eastern and southern boundary lines as arranged by Russia and Great Britain in 1825. The western line includes the whole of the Aleutian Islands; Attou is distinctly named as the most westerly island ceded. The northern boundary is only limited by the ice and snow of the Arctic.

In 1865, the Western Union Telegraph Company of America, the largest corporation of its kind in existence, commenced the explorations for a proposed overland telegraph, which, by means of a cable, *viâ* Bering Straits, was to unite the old and new world. The project—of itself not entirely new—was virtually started by Mr. P. D. Collins, an enterprising American, who had, after several years' perseverance, obtained the necessary charters and right of way from the British and Russian Governments. The scheme, after an expenditure of three million dollars, was abandoned in 1867, owing to the success of the Atlantic cable, and not from any overwhelming difficulties in the way of the undertaking itself. There was, at the date at which our explorations commenced, no faith in the great submarine cable, at least among telegraphic engineers.*

---

* It is by no means improbable that this enterprise may be again

It is needless to state that an expedition employing several hundred explorers, who examined six thousand miles of country on both sides of the Pacific—from Fraser River to Bering Straits, and thence southward to the Amoor—has added something to our knowledge of those countries. In point of fact, five volumes like the present would hardly give a fair idea of the amount of travel undertaken. Much of the information acquired is in the hands of the Telegraph Company, and much more in the possession of individuals, and is virtually lost to the world. I have confined myself almost exclusively to the narration of my own experiences, ranging over nearly two and a half years.

Colonel Bulkley, engineer-in-chief of the projected line, in the spring of the above-mentioned year, left San Francisco (where the head-quarters of the expedition were established), and paid a preliminary visit to Sitka. He there left Dr. Fisher, the surgeon-in-chief, to collect information while he himself returned to California to organise the expedition. I first had the pleasure of meeting Colonel Bulkley in Victoria, V. I., and immediately volunteered to serve on the expedition. He expressed himself gratified at the idea of an artist accompanying him, and we commenced a friendship that has but increased with better acquaintance. Colonel Bulkley inspired affection and esteem in all who knew him.

---

revived, if the Atlantic cable or cables should "give out" or work with uncertainty, although it would be an expensive line to construct and to keep in good order. That the scheme is practicable there can be no doubt. Portions of the line which *were* completed between New Westminster and the Mouth of Quesnelle—both on Fraser River—are now used for the transmission of messages. See Appendix (II.).

Our expedition had a military organization, and to each man was assigned a special duty. The principal officers for the first season (1865) were as follow:—

Col. Bulkley, Engineer-in-Chief (on leave of absence U.S. regular army.)
Capt. Scammon, Chief of Marine (U.S. Revenue Service).
Major Wright, Adjutant.
Major Chappel, Chief Quartermaster.
Mr. Lewis, Assistant Engineer.
Dr. Fisher, Surgeon-in-Chief.
Major Kennicott (in charge of Yukon party).
Lieut. MacCrea (in charge of Anadyr party).
Major Abasa (in charge of Siberian party).
Major Pope (in charge of British Columbian party).
Capt. Conway (in charge of building party).
E. K. Laborne, Interpreter.
Fredk. Whymper, Artist.

It would occupy an unnecessary amount of space to give the details and numbers of each party, more especially as reference will be made to them subsequently; but I may add that several collectors for the Smithsonian Institution at Washington accompanied us, among the principal of whom were Messrs. Dall, Rothrock, Bannister, and Elliot. Major Kennicott, besides being selected on account of his previously acquired knowledge of the country, was the appointed director of the scientific corps.

The men selected by Colonel Bulkley were nearly all young, and hardly one beyond the prime of life. He more than once said that no old man (or old woman either) should serve on his expedition, and he could have hardly found a better place than San Francisco for the selection of active and "live" men. There, nearly every one has been more or less a traveller, and knows something of the many acquirements valuable in a new country.

Doubtless Colonel Bulkley's preference for youth, activity, and "go" is that of Americans generally. Here, in England, I have sometimes thought that youth was considered more of a crime than a recommendation, and that you were nowhere until you had—like old port—acquired "body" and "age"!

CHAPTER VII.

A VISIT TO THE CAPITAL OF ALASKA.

The voyage — Sitka Sound and Harbour — Baranoff — Early history — The town — Water supply — Agriculture — Former Russian settlements in California — Russian American Company — The fisheries — Kalosh Indians — Our experiences of Russian hospitality — Sitka in new hands — Two Sundays in a week — Kodiak ice — Formal transfer of Alaska.

On the 30th July, 1865, I bade a final adieu to Victoria, joined the W. U. Telegraph Company's steamer 'Wright,' and the following day we were *en route* for Sitka, the then capital of Russian America.

Our voyage, made in calm summer weather, was not specially eventful. Early in our trip we were unfortunate enough to lose one of the fans of our screw, which of course somewhat diminished the speed of our vessel. At Port McNeil, near Fort Rupert, V. I., we stopped to take on board a small quantity of native coal to test its value for steaming purposes.

After threading Johnstone Straits we passed to the north of Vancouver Island, and outside Queen Charlotte's Island. I mention this fact because there is well known to be an "inside passage" threading the archipelago of islands north of Vancouver Island. In winter it may possibly be the better route, but it is of a difficult and tortuous nature.

On the 8th August we reached the intricate and rock-girt shores of Sitka Sound, and soon came to an anchor imme-

SITKA OR NEW ARCHANGEL; CAPITAL OF ALASKA.

diately abreast of the town of Sitka. The harbour, though small, is commodious, and the water is usually as smooth as a mill-pond. It is in lat. 57° 2′ 45″ N., long. 135° 17′ 10″ W.

Sitka, or New Archangel, is as yet the only " city " in the country, and therefore deserves some little notice. Formerly it was exclusively the headquarters of the Russian American Fur Company; but has now become a town of some life, and will probably much increase in size.

The island on which Sitka is built is one of a group or archipelago, discovered in 1741 by Tschirikoff, the companion of Bering, who, unlike that brave commander, lived to return from his adventurous voyage, the third and last of an important series. The island is named in honour of Baranoff, the real founder of the settlement of New Archangel, who for a long period managed the affairs of the Russian American Company in the days of its early history,—a troubled and eventful time. Baranoff had been a merchant in Siberia, and was a man of education and superior attainments, with a large amount of courage and perseverance. After the establishment of this post the Kalosh Indians, a neighbouring tribe, gave the Russians much trouble; and in 1804, while the commander was absent, they attacked and murdered the larger part of the garrison, one or two Aleuts alone escaping to the island of Kodiak. Baranoff returned shortly afterwards, and with the assistance of a part of Admiral Krusenstern's fleet, then on a voyage in the North Pacific, attacked and besieged the Kaloshes till they acknowledged themselves beaten; not, however, until they had murdered all the old and helpless of their number who could not go off with them. They have threatened and attacked the town subsequently, and the Russians feared them a good deal. At the date of our visit, a palisade or stockade divided the Russian and Indian habitations, and no native, unless working in some private house, was allowed in the town after dark.

Sitka was not overlooked during our war with Russia, and after the second visit to Petropaulovski, recorded later in these pages, the English and French admirals, with a portion of the combined fleet, visited the coast. No vessel, however, of the squadron entered the port except Her Majesty's steamer 'Brisk,' and the object of their visit was merely to ascertain whether any naval force belonging to the Czar was to be found there. A compact had been entered into by the British and Russian Governments, that the property of the Hudson's Bay Company, and of the Russian American Company, should be respected. The right of blockade was, however, reserved, although not exercised in this case. The admirals, satisfied that no government vessels or supplies were there, left Sitka undisturbed. No special defences had been prepared.*

The town is situated on a low strip of land, the Governor's house rising on a rocky height a hundred feet or so above the general level. Snow-capped and peaked mountains, and thickly-wooded hills surround it, and Mount Edgcumbe on Crooze Island immediately opposite the town, an extinct volcano of eight thousand feet in height, is the great landmark of this port—the most northern harbour on the Pacific shores of America. The colouring of the town is gay, and the surroundings picturesque. The houses yellow, with sheet-iron roofs painted red; the bright green spire and dome of the Greek Church, and the old battered hulks, roofed in and

---

* See 'Nautical Magazine,' October, 1855.

used as magazines, lying propped up on the rocks at the
water's edge, with the antiquated buildings of the Russian
Fur Company, gave Sitka an original, foreign, and fossilized
kind of appearance.

Landing at the wharf, and passing a battery of ancient
and dilapidated guns, we first saw the stores and warehouses
of the Company, where furs of the value of £200,000 were
sometimes accumulated. Sitka in itself had but a moderate
Indian trade, but was the head-quarters of the Company,
whence the peltries of twenty-one different stations were
annually brought. After passing the Governor's house,
which is perched on a rock, and only reached by a steep
flight of stairs, we found the *bureau* and workshops of the
Company, and a number of the better class of houses of
employés. On the left of the street a shrubbery, the " Club
Gardens," with summer-houses, card and supper rooms, and
swings for the children, and a little further the Greek Church
with its dome and spire of oriental style overshadowing a
plainer Lutheran structure within a few steps of it, attracted
our attention. Then came the " Club-house " occupied by
unmarried servants of the Company—the school-house, from
which scholars of promise were sent to St. Petersburg—and
the hospital, a very neat and clean building. Beyond these
were a few dozen cottages and shanties, and then—the
woods! with the one promenade of the place running through
them.

Sitka enjoys the unenviable position of being about the
most rainy place in the world. Rain ceases only when
there is a good prospect of snow. Warm sunny weather
is invariably accompanied by the prevalence of fever and
pulmonary complaints, and rheumatism is looked upon as

an inevitable concomitant to a residence in the settlement. Doubtless the miasma arising from damp and decaying vegetable matter is one reason why Sitka is more unhealthy in fine weather than in wet: a fact which was constantly stated to us by the inhabitants. The winter is by no means severe: the thermometer rarely standing below 20° Fahr.

A vast deal of nonsense has been published and republished in the newspapers of the United States relative to the agricultural resources of their new acquisition. The reader may take my word for it that the culture of a few potatoes and other vegetables is all that has been done in this way, and that the acres of barley mentioned in some of these high-flown paragraphs are purely mythical. There is not an acre of grain in the whole country.

For a long period, from 1812 to 1841, the Russian Company had settlements in California, at Ross, and Bodega, and they have left their name attached to the principal stream in that part of the country—Russian River. In 1841 Captain Sutter, a well-known Californian of the early days, purchased the Company's settlements, stock, &c., for 30,000 dollars. These establishments were kept up expressly for the supply of Sitka and the other posts, and were given up when they found it more convenient to purchase from the Hudson's Bay Company on Vancouver Island. For a full account of this the reader is referred to the fifth volume of Wilkes' 'Narrative of the U. S. Exploring Expedition.'

The white and half-breed population of Sitka was about eight hundred, but has risen since the American occupation to about two thousand persons. A company of Russian infantry formed the garrison, and the soldiers were allowed to work for the Company, receiving extra pay.

The Russian American Company, formed on the model of our Hudson's Bay Company, commenced its existence as a chartered corporation in 1799, but had existed as a body of traders and merchants long before that date.   Between the two Fur Companies there have been disputes.   Latterly the coast, as far as the Chilcat River, had been leased by the former to the latter Company for trading purposes.   The most valuable station of the Russians, without exception, was the Island of St. Paul (Pribylov Group in Bering Sea), which yielded the larger part of the sea-otter obtained by them.

In the neighbourhood of Sitka extensive fisheries existed, and from 100,000 to 150,000 salmon were annually exported to the Sandwich Islands and elsewhere.   Immediately on the arrival of a boat-load of fish at the wharf, a number of the poorer women, some of them Indians, arranged themselves in two long lines, and very rapidly cleaned and gutted the salmon.   A few buckets of water were then thrown over the heap, and they were carried to the vats, and put in brine at once.   Each woman took as her share a large fish weighing 20 or 30 lbs., and worth —just nothing!   It is said that the salmon is so abundant in the streams in the spring time that they impede the passage of boats, and that when a strong south-east wind comes, it drives them ashore, where they lie in piles putrifying.

The Kalosh Indians seen at Sitka inhabit the coast between the Stekine and Chilcat rivers.   At the date of our visit large numbers were absent, but in winter they are said to congregate to the number of 2500.   The Chilcat Indians also come to Sitka.

These people dwell in a long line of rude houses outside the settlement. Their dwellings are shanties on a large scale, with a small entrance, often circular in shape, and a hole in the roof to let the smoke out. The idea of these constructions must have been derived from the Russians; in some cases the very unusual circumstance of the sleeping rooms being apart from the main chamber was to be observed.

The Kaloshes are by no means a prepossessing people, and have a bad reputation. Their dress is commonly a blanket, at least in summer time; they frequently black their faces all over, and sometimes paint themselves in red, black and blue stripes and patches. They wear a pin of bone or metal stuck in their lower lip; this is said to denote maturity; it is at least never worn by the young. They appear to be more than usually lazy natives, probably from the fact that Nature

Kalosh Indian Grave-box.

has been so kind to them; salmon is abundant, deer and bear meat are to be had for the hunting, and the berries are innumerable. Their canoes are much inferior to those of the lower coast, whilst their skin " baidarkes " (kyacks) are not equal to those of Norton Sound and the northern coast. Their grave boxes or tombs are interesting; they contain only the ashes of the dead. These people invariably burn the deceased. On one of the boxes I

Kalosh Indian Grave-box.

saw a number of faces painted, long tresses of human hair depending therefrom. Each head represented a victim of the (happily) deceased one's ferocity. In his day he was doubtless more esteemed than if he had never harmed a fly. All their graves are much ornamented with carved and painted faces and other devices.

We shall not readily forget the reception given us by the residents of Sitka, who seemed bent on making up for the absence of the Governor, Prince Maksutoff. Russian hospitality is proverbial, and we all somewhat suffered therefrom. The first phrase of their language acquired by us, was "Petnatchit copla" (fifteen drops). Now this quantity—in words so modest—usually meant a good half tumbler of some unmitigated spirit, ranging from Cognac to raw *vodka* of a class which can only be described by a Californian term as "chain lightning," and which was pressed upon us on every available occasion. To refuse was simply to insult your host. Then memory refuses to retain the number of times we had to drink tea, which was served sometimes in tumblers, sometimes in cups. I need not say the oft described *samovar* was in every household. Several entertainments—balls, suppers, and a fête in the club gardens—were organised for our benefit, and a number of visitors came off daily to our fleet of four vessels,—strangely enough the only ones in harbour, though the Company owned many sailing-vessels and steamers. We found the Russians there living on terms of great intimacy with their domestics. The latter almost invariably addressed their masters and mistresses by their Christian names, and often by abbreviations thereof. Thus a gentleman by name " Ivan " (John) would be so called by his servants, and his wife whose name was Maria, but by her husband known as Molly, would be so addressed by the servants, to the great scandal of propriety.

But Sitka in the hands of the Russian Company, and Sitka in those of its new owners, are already very different things. An Anglo-Russian newspaper, to be printed in double columns, is projected, and is to appear this spring (1868). Town "lots" are held at fabulous prices; for a small log house 10,000 dollars (£2000) is asked, and I should not be surprised to learn that salmon was half a dollar a pound, that a dozen "saloons," hotels, barbers' shops, and "lager bier" cellars had been started, or especially that the Sitka water-works were a great success! Every "correspondent's" letter from thence, and I have read a score, agrees in one fact, "that our aqueous supply evinces no sign of failure!"

In the " good old Russian times " there were, it is said, about 180 church holidays to the year, now they will be confined to Christmas and New Year's days, Washington's birthday and the 4th of July (Independence day). But if the enlightened citizens of the country choose to avail themselves of the privilege, they can enjoy two Sundays each week. Owing to the fact that the Russians came eastward and we came westward, there is of course a day's difference where the two meet, and their Sunday in Sitka falls on our Saturday. "The San Franciscan," says a Californian newspaper, "who arrives at Archangel on Friday night, according to his reckoning, will find the stores closed and business suspended on the following morning, and so will lose not only that day, but the next, too, if his conscientious convictions and the force of habit are only strong enough. On the other hand, the pious Alaskan merchant, who belongs to the Greek Church, will look with horror on the impious stranger who offers to trade or swap jack-knives on Sunday, but who on Monday morning suddenly assumes a clean shirt, black broadcloth, a nasal twang, and that demurely self-satisfied air which is our national idea of a religious demeanour."

As before stated, Sitka itself yielded but a limited quantity of furs; hence the mistake made last year (1867) by numerous Jews and other traders, who thought they could buy to advantage there. By latest accounts you could almost as cheaply obtain furs in San Francisco! not one of the places in the world *most* celebrated for moderate charges, and in consequence the steamers were well filled by disgusted Israelitish traders on their return trips to California. Yet in the north of Russian America—a country that few perhaps will venture into—there is undoubtedly a large trade yet to be developed, and the energy of the American people will hardly let the opportunity pass unimproved, if the difficulties in the way of the transportation of large quantities of trading goods and provisions do not prove of too serious a nature. I shall have to allude to this subject again, in the chapters on the Yukon River.

A San Francisco company leased from the Russians the privilege of obtaining ice from St. Paul's, Kodiak Island. The Americans, as it is unnecessary perhaps to remark, use ice at table to a far greater extent than we do, and in the Atlantic States it is sold at an almost nominal price. California, about the warmest State in the Union, naturally consumes a large quantity of ice. It is cut from an artificial lake, which has an area of forty acres. The labourers are all Aleuts (Aleutian islanders), and are principally engaged for three or four months of winter, while the ice is firm, in cutting it up and storing it for summer consumption. The larger part of this luxury is consumed in San Francisco, but it finds its way to Mexican, Central, and even South American ports. Kodiak,* which is included in the purchase, is therefore by no means an unimportant acquisition.

The formal transfer of Russian America to the United States authorities took place on October 18th, 1867. It is said that the Russian flag showed great reluctance to come down, and stuck on the yard-arm of the flag-staff. A man was sent up to detach the halyards, when it fell on the heads of the Russian soldiers, its appointed defenders!

---

* On September 5th, 1866, at 4 A.M., there was a very violent earthquake on Kodiak Island. A correspondent of 'The Alta California,' writing thence, said :—" The sensation on shipboard was very terrifying, seeming as though the ship was going at railway speed over the rocks, while many articles came tumbling down which the most violent gale at sea had not disturbed. Other slight shocks were felt at intervals for four hours in some of the southern portions of the island. Huge rocks were torn from their places, and came tumbling down the mountains ; but no lives were lost."

I present the reader with a representation of one of the Sitka "army," copied from an Indian stone carving in my possession. Although it may seem a caricature, it is really an accurate likeness of the stolid features and antiquated cut of the late defenders of Russian America.*

* For some additional notes on Sitka, see Appendix (III.).

Indian stone carving, representing a Russian Soldier at Sitka.

CHAPTER VIII.

VOYAGE IN THE NORTH PACIFIC.

1865.

Departure from Sitka — Oukamok — Ounga — Breakers ahead! — Volcanoes in Ounimak Pass — St. Michael's, Norton Sound, Alaska — Soundings of Bering Sea — Plover Bay, Eastern Siberia — The Tchuktchis — Tents — Canoes — Tchuktchi strength — Children — The irrepressible "Naukum" — Native's idea of the telegraph — The 'Shenandoah' pirate — Avatcha Bay.

DURING our stay at Sitka, Colonel Bulkley, besides collecting much valuable information from the Russian Company, was engaged in organising the parties for the Anadyr and Yukon rivers. Lieut. MacCrea, in charge of the former division, was with his party transferred to the schooner 'Milton Badger,' and despatched to his destination. The Yukon party were mostly on board the barque 'Golden Gate,' then considered the "flag-ship" of our expedition, and to this vessel I was myself transferred. I was the guest of Captain Scammon, to whose kindness I owe much.

We left the harbour of Sitka on the 22nd August, and the entire population turned out to see us depart. They gave us a full though rather irregular salute, which nearly brought down the old wharf, and we returned it in better style. For several days after leaving we kept company with the steamer, being in fact towed by her. On the 28th we again saw land, the grassy slopes and abrupt cliffs of Oukamok Island. There were no trees apparent. On the 29th we sighted the peninsula of Aliaska, a jagged rock-bound coast with many snow peaks, and the next day we got a glimpse of Cape Ivanoff,—a promontory that appeared at a distance to be detached from the mainland. Later in the day we came to an anchor in Zakharovskaia Bay, in the Island of Ounga. Our object in calling there was to examine some coal seams known to exist on the coast. They proved to be lignite of poor quality, and apparently not abundant. The seams have been worked, and the products used on board the Russian American Fur Company's steamers, but not to any great extent. On the 31st August we again started in company with the steamer, but the following night our hawser broke, and we parted company in a fog. The next morning, while I was quietly drawing in the cabin, the steward's boy, a wild Irish juvenile, known as " Brick-top," from the red colour of his moppy head, rushed in with the pleasing announcement of " Breakers ahead!" and that we were all coming to grief. I went on deck, and found some very ugly looking rocks on the starboard side, within a few hundred yards, and the white surf and foam breaking round them. The weather was extremely foggy and thick, and the danger while it lasted was unmistakable. Captain Scammon, seconded by his officers, soon, however, brought the vessel round, and we passed within a hundred yards of them, our craft rolling and pitching a good deal. It proved to be a reef outside Sanak or Halibut Island, —a known yet dangerous coast.

On the 3rd September, when tacking and trying to make Ounimak Pass or passage, between Ounimak and Ougamok, two of the Aleutian Islands, we caught a glimpse through the opening mists of the volcano of Chichaldinskoi. This mountain is, on the authority of Lütke, 8935 feet in height, and is situated on Ounimak Island. It has a very graceful form. Near it is a second mountain of less elevation, with a jagged double summit, of very odd and irregular appearance. On the evening of the 4th Chichaldinskoi loomed out very distinctly, and when the clouds cleared from it we could see smoke issuing from a large cleft near the summit. In Ounimak Passage a second volcano over 5000 feet in height was seen, and Captain Scammon observed during the night the fire of one on Akoutan Island. The whole chain of the Aleutian Islands is volcanic. They deserve an expedition to themselves.

We arrived in Norton Sound on the 12th September, having experienced very rough weather in Bering Sea; in fact, during part of the time we had to "lay to." Approaching for the first time these northern coasts of Russian America, we observed with surprise the dried up and sunburnt appearance of everything on shore. The hills varied much in colour, from shades of crimson and red, to tints of brown and yellow. The summer in this country, though short, is intensely warm while it lasts; late in the season hot days alternate with frosty nights, and the vegetation is much affected thereby. We went into the Sound carefully taking soundings, and indeed it was very necessary, as our later experience will show. We arrived off the Island of St. Michael's at 10 A.M. on the 13th, and found that our steamer had already called there, and had again started for Bering Straits.

On the Island of St. Michael's, or Michaelovski, is a Russian trading-post of some importance, which will be hereafter described. Major Kennicott began at once to land his party with their supplies and personal effects, and also to fit up the 'Lizzie Horner,' a small steamer which had been brought up on the deck of our ship. She was intended for the navigation of the Yukon, but alas! proved worthless, and in fact never left Norton Sound.

Major Kennicott found at St. Michael's an Indian who stated that he had been up the Yukon to its junction with the Porcupine. Colonel Bulkley, before leaving in the steamer 'Wright,' had taken on board a little half-breed boy to give him the advantage of a good education in San Francisco. This was, of course, done with his friends' perfect consent. On leaving, his Indian mother said to the Colonel, "Teach him, sir, nothing but good." Could any mother have said more? *

On the 17th we parted from our exploring friends and turned our ship's bows towards the Asiatic coast. Captain Scammon made a series of very interesting soundings on this trip. Bering Sea is well known to be extremely shallow, but few would suppose that the whalers can and *do* anchor in nearly every part of it on occasions, weather permitting. Between latitudes 64° and 66° N. the average depth is slightly under nineteen and a half fathoms. We passed to the south of the large island of St. Lawrence, and found the bottom very even. At the starting-point of this voyage —St. Michael's—the soundings gave five fathoms, deepening

---

* This boy, with a second taken from Petropaulovski, made good progress in San Francisco. Col. Bulkley's object was, of course, eventually to make these youths of service to the Telegraph Company. They were, at the abandonment of the scheme, returned to their friends. Col. Bulkley also took down a Tchuktchi boy from Plover Bay, who was educated in the same manner, and we had, at different periods, several Aleutian Islanders (Aleuts) as sailors on our vessels.

gradually to twenty-five fathoms off the S.E. end of St.
Lawrence Island. From thence to Plover Bay it averaged
thirty-five fathoms, and shoaled to nineteen fathoms immediately off the bay itself. The bottom was found to
consist mainly of a soft mud and sand: one cast off the
eastern end of St. Lawrence Island, near a rocky islet,
brought up gravel.

On the 22nd we made the land off Port Providence, or
" Plover " Bay, as it has always been called by the whalers who
frequent it, since the winter of 1848-9, when H.M.S. ' Plover '
laid up there, when on the search for Sir John Franklin.*
It does *not* derive its name from whaling pursuits, although
an ingenious Dutchman of our number persisted in calling it
" Blubber " Bay. But we were doomed to disappointment,
for when in sight of the Bay a gale of wind rose, and we were
driven several hundred miles to the southward, not regaining
our position till the 26th, when we went in successfully, to
find the ' Wright ' awaiting us.

Plover Bay, when once you are in it, is a very secure
haven. It is sheltered at its southern end by a long spit of
land, and it is no uncommon thing to find several whaling
vessels lying inside in the summer. It includes two smaller
basins; one known as Emma Harbour, the second to be hereafter mentioned. Bare cliffs and rugged mountains hem it
in on three sides, the mountains composed of an infinite
number of fragments split up by the action of frost. Innumerable and many - coloured lichens and mosses are
the only vegetation to be seen, except on a patch of open

---

* See Lieut. Hooper's ' Tents of the Tuski ' for a full account of the
' Plover's ' stay.

TCHUKTCHI SKIN CANOE.

FRAME WORK OF TCHUKTCHI HOUSE.

country near Emma Harbour, where domesticated reindeer graze.

On the spit before mentioned is a village of Tchuktchi natives; their tents are composed of skin. *The remains of underground houses are seen, but the people who used them have passed away.* The present race makes no use of such houses.

Although their skin dwellings appear outwardly rough, and are patched with every variety of hide,—walrus, seal, and reindeer,—with here and there a fragment of a sail obtained from the whalers; they are in reality constructed over frames, built of the large bones of whales and walrus, and very admirably put together. In this most exposed of villages the wintry blasts must be fearful, yet these people are to be found there at all seasons. Wood they have none, and blubber lamps are the only means they have for warming their tents. The frames of some of their skin canoes are also of bone. On either side of these craft, which are the counterpart of the Greenland "Oomiak," it is usual to find a sealskin blown out tight and the ends secured. These serve as floats when the canoe heels over. They have very strong fishing-nets, made of thin strips of walrus hide.

The Tchuktchis appear to be a strongly-built race, although the inhabitants of this particular village, from intercourse with whaling vessels, have been much demoralized. I have seen one of these natives carry the awkward burden of a carpenter's chest weighing two hundred pounds, without apparently considering it any great exertion. They are a good-humoured people, and not greedier than the average of natives, so far as our experience goes. They were of some service to a party of our men who wintered there in 1866-7.

The children are so tightly sewn up in reindeer-skin clothing that they look like walking bags, and tumble about with the greatest impunity. All of these people wear skin coats, pantaloons, and boots, excepting only on high days in summer, when you may see a few old garments of more civilized appearance that have seen better days, and have been traded off by the sailors of vessels calling there.

The true Tchuktchi method of smoking is to swallow all the fumes of the tobacco, and I have seen them after six or eight pulls at a pipe fall back completely intoxicated for the time being. Their pipes are infinitely larger in the stem than in the bowl; the latter, indeed, holds an infinitesimally small amount of tobacco.

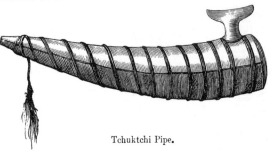

Tchuktchi Pipe.

It is said that the Tchuktchis murder the old and feeble, but only with the victims' consent! They do not appear to indulge in any unnecessary cruelty, but endeavour to stupify the aged sacrifice before letting a vein. This is said to be done by putting some substance up the nostrils; but the whole statement must be received with caution, although we derived it from a shrewd native who had been much em-

ployed by the captains of vessels in the capacity of interpreter, and who could speak in broken English.

This man, by name "Nau-kum," was of service on various
occasions, and was accordingly much petted by us. Some of
his remarks are worthy of record. On being taken down into
the engine-room of the 'Wright' he examined it carefully,
and then shaking his head, said solemnly, " *Too* muchee
wheel, makee man too muchee think!" His curiosity when
on board was unappeasable. "What's that fellow?" was
his constant query with regard to anything from the
"donkey engine" to the mainmast. On one occasion he
heard two men discussing rather warmly, and could not
at all understand such unnecessary excitement, "That fellow
crazy?" said he.

Colonel Bulkley gave him a suit of clothes, with gorgeous
brass buttons, and many other presents. One of our men
remarked to him, " Why, Naukum, you'll be a king soon!"
" King be d——d," was his extremely radical answer! It is
of course obvious where he had got his schooling. The
whalers use such men on occasions as pilots, traders, and
interpreters, and to Naukum in particular I know as much as
five barrels of villanous whiskey have been intrusted, for
which he accounted satisfactorily.

The truth-loving Chippewa, when asked, "Are you a
Christian Indian?" promptly replied, "No, I whishkey Injen!"
and the truthful Tchuktchi would say the same. They all
appear to be intensely fond of spirits. The traders sell them
liquor of the most horrible kind, not much superior to the
" coal oil " or " kerosene " used for lamps.

They appeared to understand the telegraph scheme in
a general way, and had probably been enlightened by the

whaling captains before our arrival. "Enoch," a very intelligent and quiet native, gave us an outline of the project somewhat as follows:—"S'pose lope fixy, well—one Melican man Plower Bay, make talky all the same San Flancisco Melican." Perhaps quite as lucid an explanation as you could get from an agricultural labourer, or a "city Arab," at home.

We had been expecting to meet at some part of our northern voyage, the famed and dreaded 'Shenandoah.' It is an old story to return to now, but I was an eye-witness of the havoc wrought by her. The whole of the coast was strewed with fragments of the vessels burnt by her, and the natives had several boats and other remains of her wanton doings. She had left the Arctic and Bering Sea at the end of June of the same year (1865), but not till thirty American whaling vessels had been burnt by her. The captains and crews had been for the most part sent down to San Francisco, and I have since met a gentleman who was one of the victims. He did not complain of ill-usage from the pirate captain, but spoke much of the wholesale destruction of private property. The captain of an English whaler, the 'Robert Tawns,' of Sydney, had warned and saved some of the American vessels, and he was in consequence threatened by the 'Shenandoah.'

26th—29th September.—The weather was now getting cold and brisk, a skin of ice forming on the bay, and icicles hanging from the shrouds and ship's boats. We learnt on good authority, that the whole of Plover Bay was frozen up by the 5th October, in 1864. The smaller bay (Emma Harbour), leading out of the main one, was frozen up at the above dates.

On the 29th we got a favourable breeze, and set sail for Petropaulovski. The following days were only remarkable for light breezes, or baffling head winds, and we did not make the entrance to Avatcha Bay till the 14th October, on which day we got our first glimpse of the grand volcanoes, which are so important a feature of the scenery in the Peninsula of Kamchatka.* On the morning of the 15th we passed through the entrance to the Bay of Avatcha, and soon dropped anchor outside the harbour of Petropaulovski, not, however, before several of the foreign residents had boarded us.

---

* The above mode of spelling the word represents the sound in a phonetic sense better than the common version. I had opportunities of becoming familiar with the Russian pronunciation of the word on many occasions, and not merely at this visit.

CHAPTER IX.

PETROPAULOVSKI AND OUR RETURN VOYAGE TO SAN FRANCISCO.

The Harbour — Town — Monuments — The fur trade — Kamchatka generally — The volcanoes — The attack of the Allies in 1854 — Their return in 1855 — The 'General Teste' — Rejoin the steamer 'Wright' — Gale — Incidents of storm — Covert's "smoke stack."

THE Harbour of Petropaulovski is protected by a long spit, an apparently common feature of the coast. Inside it there is a good depth of water, and a vessel, once in, can ride in safety though storms rage outside. The town encircles the haven on the north and east sides, and it is shut in by a hilly promontory on the west. Behind the town is some steep hilly ground, through a gap in which the volcano of Koriatski towers grandly. It is over thirty miles distant, and yet, in clear weather, it does not appear five.

With the exception of a few decent houses, the residences of the Russian officials and foreign merchants, the town makes no great show. The poorer dwellings are very rough indeed, and are almost exclusively rude log cabins. The only noticeable building is the old Greek church, which has painted red and green roofs, and a belfry entirely detached from the building. It is to be remarked that the town, as it existed in Captain Clerke's time, was built on the sand spit, but no remains or indications of it were discovered by us. Petropaulovski was once a military post, and had a rather

PETROPAULOVSKI: KAMCHATKA.

larger population than at present. The Cossack soldiers have
now been removed to the Amoor.

There are two monuments of interest in the town: the first
in honour of Bering, the other to the memory of La Perouse.

Monument to Bering, Petropaulovski.

The former is a cast-iron column of no great pretensions; the
latter, a nondescript erection of octagonal form, constructed
of sheet iron. Neither of these navigators is buried in Petropaulovski. Bering's remains lie on the island where he died,
and which bears his name; while La Perouse, and his unfortunate companions, suffered shipwreck, and but little traces
were ever found of their expedition. We looked in vain for
the monument to Captain Clerke (Captain Cook's successor),
which existed as late as the date of Beechey's visit. The
spot (in an inclosure belonging to the captain of the port)
where once it stood was pointed out to us, much overgrown
with nettles and weeds.

The Russian American Company had at one period stations in Petropaulovski, and other parts of Kamchatka, but abandoned them, owing doubtless to the competition of private traders. To such a pitch has competition brought the fur trade of that country, that it is now only a very moderately profitable pursuit. As much as thirty dollars—sometimes in hard cash—is paid for one Siberian sable of good quality; and the merchants have frequently to advance goods to the native traders and hunters a long time before they get any returns. Petropaulovski is one of the centres of this trade, but Nijne (New) Kamchatka is the present capital. Bolcheretsk was considered the principal town formerly, but it has dwindled down to an inconsiderable village, and indeed the population, and with it the products of Kamchatka, are on the decline. Yet the climate is by no means so bad as commonly believed. Colonel Bulkley considered it better than that of some of the New England States and Canada, and it is quite certain that agriculture is possible. The grass round Petropaulovski ripens into hay during the brief summer, and garden stuff is raised in small quantities in the outskirts of the town.

I am convinced that Kamchatka would repay a detailed examination. It is a partially settled country; the Kamchatdales are a good-humoured, harmless, semi-civilized race; and the few Russian officials and settlers would gladly welcome the traveller. The attractions of the country for the Alpine climber cannot be overstated. The peninsula contains a chain of volcanic peaks of the grandest character, attaining, it is said, in the Klutchevskoi Mountain, a height of 16,000 feet. In the country immediately behind Petropaulovski, are the three mountains, Koriatski, Avatcha, and

THE VOLCANOES OF KORIATSKI, AVATCHA, AND KOSELDSKAI, KAMCHATKA.

Koseldskai ; the first of these is between eleven and twelve thousand feet in height, and is an unfailing land-mark for the port.

From the summit of the steep hills which so nearly enclose Petropaulovski, a grand view of these mountains is obtained; a comparatively level country stretches to their base. It is, however, covered with rank grass and underbrush, and intersected by numerous streams: a journey to them would be more easily made in winter time than in summer. To the S.S.W. of the town a fourth peak—that of Vilutchinski—towers above the coast-line, and is a very beautiful feature in the landscape. Petropaulovski has been frequently visited by earthquake, accompanied sometimes by showers of ashes from these volcanoes. The smoke from Koriatski was several times observed by us ; its pure snows only hid the boiling, bubbling lava beneath.

The object of our visit was to communicate, by special courier, with Major Abasa, a Russian gentleman in our Telegraph service who had formed a station at Ghijega at the head of the Ochotsk Sea.* The facilities of travel on the peninsula are superior to those on the coast of the above-mentioned sea. In winter small Siberian horses, reindeer, and dogs are all employed for sledging purposes. The feeding of the dogs of Petropaulovski took place every evening, and their yelps and howlings made night hideous. One dried salmon *per diem* was each dog's allowance, and they were much better off than their Russian-American cousins, who in summer have to forage for themselves.

---

* See the 'Proceedings' of the Royal Geographical Society for Feb. 11th, 1867.

The hospitality extended to us was almost unlimited. Dinners, balls, suppers followed each other in rapid succession; we had a steam-boat excursion in Avatcha Bay. One of the dishes common in Petropaulovski was salmon pie, constructed apparently of eggs and salmon, covered with a crust. Salmon is very abundant in the harbour and neighbouring streams, and some has been put up in salt for export.

We also got a little sledging, when the snow fell just before our departure. The ice was fast forming in the harbour, and it was often a serious undertaking to row ashore.

It is well known that in 1855—during the Crimean war— Petropaulovski was visited by the Allied fleet. The record of *that* visit has been duly laid before the public, commented on, and forgotten; but it is not so generally known that our first attack, the previous year, was by no means a subject of congratulation for us, and (although well understood by naval officers, and especially by those who have served on the Pacific station) it has been kept uncommonly quiet. The fact is, that at the first visit, the wretched little town made —greatly to its own surprise—a successful resistance, and is very proud of the fact. The inhabitants look upon the combat at Petropaulovski as one of the decisive battles of the world !

The narrative I am about to lay before the reader was obtained on the spot, but not merely from the Russians. An Englishman—Mr. Fletcher—who had resided there for thirty years, and several of the foreign merchants who were in the town at the date of the attack, confirmed the Muscovite versions of the story.

In the autumn of 1854 (28th August) six vessels of war—

French and English—comprising the 'President,' 'Virago,' 'Pique' 'La Fort,' 'L'Eurydice,' and 'Obligado'—arrived off Avatcha Bay; a gun, placed near the lighthouse at the entrance, was fired by the Russians, and gave the inhabitants of Petropaulovski notice to be on the alert. Admiral Price immediately reconnoitred the harbour and town, and placed the 'Virago' in position at a range of 2000 yards.

The Russians were by no means unprepared. Two of their vessels, the 'Aurora' and 'Dwina,' defended the harbour, and a chain crossing the narrow entrance shut it in. There were seven batteries and earthworks, mounting about fifty guns of fair calibre.

The 'Virago' commenced the action with a well-directed fire, and several of the batteries were either temporarily or entirely disabled. The one furthest from the town, on the western side, was taken by a body of marines landed for the purpose. The guns were spiked. Four of the Allied fleet were specially engaged, and the Russians returned their fire with spirit. There were three batteries outside and on the spit, two at the termination of the promontory on the western side of the harbour, and one in a gorge of the same, which opens on Avatcha Bay. It is in this little valley that the monument to La Perouse stands.

The town was well defended both by nature and by art. The hills shut it in so completely, that it was apparently only vulnerable at the rear. There, a small valley opened out into a flat strip of land immediately bordering the bay, and, although there was a battery on it, it seemed an excellent spot to land troops.

Our vessels having taken up a new position, and silenced the batteries commanding it, 700 marines and sailors were put ashore. Half of them were English, half French; a large number of officers accompanied them, while they had for guides two Americans, said to know the ground. They appear to have expected a very easy victory, and hurried in a detached and straggling style in the direction of the town, instead of proceeding in compact form, in military order. A number of bushes and small trees existed and still exist on the hill-sides surrounding this spot, and behind them were posted Cossack sharp-shooters, who fired into our men, and either from skill or accident picked off nearly every officer. The men not seeing their enemy, and having lost their leaders, became panic-struck, and fell back in disorder. A retreat was sounded, but the men struggling in the bushes and underbrush (and, in truth, most of them being sailors, were out of their element on land) became much scattered, and it was generally believed that many were killed by the random shots of their companions. A number fled up a hill at the rear of the town. Their foes pursued and pressed upon them, and many were killed by falling over the steep cliff in which the hill terminates.

The inhabitants—astonished at their own prowess, and knowing that they could not hold the town against a more vigorous attack, were preparing to vacate it—when the fleet weighed anchor and set sail, and no more was seen of them that year! The sudden death of our admiral is always attributed to the events of that attack, as he was known not to have been killed by a ball from the enemy.*

Before the second visit in May and June, 1855, every-

---

* See 'Nautical Magazine,' October, 1855. It is there stated that 107 English were killed or wounded in the engagement.

body—except the foreign residents—had vacated the town.
Early in the spring of the same year the Russian squadron
had received orders to leave it to its fate at the break-up of
the ice. The Russian Government had indeed given up all
idea of defending so worthless a town, and, for two reasons,
we also should have left it alone. First, it was an insignificant place, and victory could never be glorious; whilst,
secondly, it has been—from the time of Cook to our own
days—famous for the hospitality and assistance extended to
our explorers and voyagers.*   All is *not* fair in war.

When therefore the Allies landed at their second visit they
found an empty town.†   They, however, captured a Russian
whaler, and burnt some of the government buildings. The
latter it is said was done unintentionally, or more probably
was the work of some wanton jack-tar. The batteries and
earthworks were of course razed to the ground.

We all visited the battle-field, and found it still strewed
with the remains of shells, &c. In getting out ballast from
a bank near the town, several cannon-balls were unearthed.
The monument to La Perouse was peppered all over with
bullet marks.

It was at that period, that an old French captain, commanding a whaler named the 'General Teste,' was saved
from the Russian hands by a rather ingenious *ruse*. He
was in a terrible state of mind, when cruising in Bering
Sea, expecting hourly to lose his vessel, and the American
captains of the whaling fleet, pitying him, came to his aid.

---

* See Cook, Cochrane, Beechey and others.

† For an account of the *second* visit in 1855, see Tronson's 'Voyage to
Japan, Kamschatka,' &c.

They induced him first to substitute 'Washington' for
'Teste.' His vessel then became the 'General Washington.'
Next they got him to hoist the "stars and stripes" in place
of the "tri-colour." Lastly, they made him, much against
his will, keep a bottle of "cocktails" ready mixed for
all-comers; and by these three devices his vessel escaped
detection!

On the 31st October I again joined my old friends on the
'Wright,' and on the 1st November we steamed out of
Avatcha Bay. By-the-bye, why will geographers persist in
spelling the distinctly pronounced *Avatcha* as though it were
a difficult and excruciating word? We have it in all shapes
—*Awatska, Awatscha, Awatcha,* and *Avatska.* From long
intercourse with educated Russians I know that Avatcha
represents the word phonetically (and it is useless to attempt
to render Russian in any other way).

During the next fortnight we experienced very bad
weather, which culminated on the 14th in a gale from the
S.E., in which a series of disasters made us fear for our
vessel's safety. The first was a novelty in its way. A rope
snapped, our "main boom" swung round and knocked the
funnel overboard! and, as the weather was so tempestuous,
we had simply to cut the chains or "guys," which held it,
and let it drop to the ocean's bed. A little later, our steering
apparatus got out of order, and our little steamer lay in
the trough of the sea as helpless as a log, steaming being
rendered impossible by these two accidents. The waves
washed over her every few minutes, and her bulwarks (or
"guards") were so low, that we expected every moment
to see the "house on deck" carried overboard. It was stove
in in a score of places, and the cabins presented a pitiable

spectacle,—a wreck of trunks, furniture, and crockery. Sail after sail was carried away by the sudden squalls, and we were at length left with nothing to lie under. A few long streamers of canvas, hanging from the yards, alone showed where they had been. On the 17th we shipped a sea, which threatened to engulf us. A torrent rushed into the aft cabin, down the stairs, and through the skylight, extinguished the lamps and fire, and left us tumbling about in two or three feet of water. This night our vessel seemed to be constantly driving under water, and our sailors were often thrown down and much bruised, although no one happily was lost. Captain Marston behaved with great coolness, lashed himself on deck, and remained there all night, half-frozen, and with seas washing over him every few minutes. We landsmen did not expect to see *our* native element again, and although I had been in many gales, it was, without exception, the very worst I had experienced. Fortunately, the hull of our vessel was staunch and sound, and our pumps in perfect order.

The storm lasted for nearly a week, and was not devoid of incident. For part of one day, the sea *driving faster than our vessel*, acted in such a manner on the screw, that in its turn, it worked the engine at a greater rate than we had ever attained by steam! In the end the coupling was disconnected, fearing injury to the machine.

In the "state room" of the house on deck, occupied by Mr. Laborne our interpreter, and myself, some boxes of soap were stowed away. This being constantly worked about the floor under water, raised one of the most magnificent lathers ever witnessed, which ran through the series of rooms, and did not improve our possessions. After the storm had subsided, we opened the boxes, to find bars of soap, of about eighteen inches in length, reduced to the dimensions of sticks of sealing-wax.

It became absolutely necessary to rig up something in place of our lost funnel, or "smoke stack," as it is invariably called by Americans. At length Mr. Covert, our chief engineer, hit upon a device. He caused his men to knock out one end of a square water-tank, and, with some extra sheet iron, made a chimney about ten feet high, which gave sufficient draught to the furnaces. Covert's "patent" was a great success, and created some little notice on our arrival in San Francisco, which took place on the 30th November.

Thus ended the not uneventful voyage of 1865, in which we had gone over 10,000 miles of ocean travel, and we were not sorry to reach our head-quarters in the "Bay City," and have once more a spell of civilized life.

CHAPTER X.

VOYAGE IN THE NORTH PACIFIC.

1866.

Organization of the expedition — Thirsty medical man — Our fleet —
Voyage — Petropaulovski again — The Russian corvette — Russian
wedding — Heat — International pic-nic — Voyage north — Bering's
voyages — Shipwreck — Death of Bering — Gulf of Anadyr — The
" wandering Tchuktchis."

THE winter of 1865-6 was spent by Colonel Bulkley and his
staff in San Francisco, and their time was fully occupied
in organizing the parties for the following season. A large
number of labourers were engaged, and these, with assistant-
surgeons,* quartermasters, and foremen, brought our expedi-

---

* One of these individuals soon after his engagement showed a decided
leaning towards stimulating fluids, and, having drunk up his salary, was at
his wit's end to know how to keep up the supply. In each of our company's medicine chests there were a few bottles of wine and brandy,
intended exclusively for medicinal purposes. These our doctor, in the
discharge of his arduous duties, soon discovered and finished, but—like
Oliver—wanted more. Our hero of the bottle next ferreted out a small can
of alcohol, which slightly—very slightly—diluted with water, made a
drinkable mixture, and enabled him to hold out a day or two longer. The
reader may suppose that when this was finished he was nipped in his
career. Not a bit of it! Were there not the ethers, tinctures, and spirits
contained in every well regulated chest? Bottle after bottle, phial after
phial, of spirits of lavender, peppermint, and sweet nitre followed each
other to the same goal. There was still the camphor and tincture of
myrrh, rhubarb, and aloes left, but not for long ; and when there was
nothing remaining but the laudanum, that also went the same way.
About this period his weaknesses were discovered, and he was discharged
from the service.

tion up to a formidable size ; not less than 500 " white men,"
besides bands of Cossacks in Eastern Siberia, Chinamen in
British Columbia, and Indians everywhere, were employed
in building telegraph, exploring the route, or transporting goods, during the season of 1866 and following
winter.

Our fleet alone made a perceptible difference at the
wharves of San Francisco. We had seven sea-going vessels,
besides smaller craft; the steamer ' Wright ' was refitted, a
clipper, the ' Nightingale ' * purchased, and one large and two
small river steamers built specially for our service. We had
five barques—several of them excellent vessels.

During the winter, a commissioner from the Russian
Imperial Government, M. Paul Anasoff, and Mr. Knox,
a well-known " correspondent " of the leading New York
papers, arrived in San Francisco. Both of these gentlemen
accompanied us on our second voyage.

On the 23rd June, 1866, we left California, and after an uneventful trip, made Petropaulovski once more. Our voyage
occupied us thirty-one days, the weather being perfect for
the whole time, and the ocean unmistakably " Pacific." Our
little steamer, now fitted up in the best style, and carrying
heavier spars and more sail, was almost equal in accommodation and appearance to a steam yacht, and our trip, taking
into consideration the pleasant company on board, was simply

---

* The ' Nightingale's ' history had been an eventful one. Built at first as
a model clipper, intended for exhibition in London in 1851, she had been
for a long period used as a slaver, then captured by the U. S. Government,
and employed as a blockading vessel during the war, and was now the
" flag-ship " of our expedition.

a holiday excursion—the very antithesis of the return voyage in 1865. On the 25th July we arrived in Petropaulovski Harbour, and found a Russian corvette, the 'Variag,' awaiting our arrival. She was a fine steam vessel of 2156 tons, and her commander Captain Lund immediately reported, in accordance with his instructions, to Colonel Bulkley, our engineer-in-chief.

The day of our arrival had been fixed for the celebration of two Russian weddings, and a general invitation was at once sent on board. The ceremony commenced at 5 P.M. in the old Greek church, and was rather long and fatiguing. The congregation stood: in fact there were no seats in the church. It is the custom for the bride and bridegroom to be crowned. In this case the brides wore elaborate head-dresses, and considerate male friends—the " best men " of the occasion —held the crowns for three-quarters of an hour a few inches above the ladies' heads. I imagine they were rejoiced when the pairs were satisfactorily spliced; I know that *we* were, for we were in tight uniforms, extremely gorgeous, and equally uncomfortable.

It is the fashion apparently—when the persons, as in this case, are in the lower walks of life—to ask some more wealthy individual to be master of the ceremonies, and it is understood that he stands all the expenses! On this occasion the victim was M. Phillipeus, a merchant, who brings his vessels annually from Hong Kong to Kamchatka, and the neighbouring coasts.* He accepted the burden willingly,

---

* M. Phillipeus took his more valuable furs, &c., annually to St. Petersburgh, *via* the Amoor and Siberia, returning thence to Hong Kong *via* Suez. He had made this lengthened journey five times at the date of our visit.

and gave a very liberal entertainment to the whole town, the officers of the ' Variag,' ourselves, and the captains of several small vessels lying there.   So many were invited that no one house was large enough for the purpose.   The party was therefore divided, and the guests occupied two buildings, one on either side of the main street.   The band of the ' Variag' played outside, and a messenger was kept constantly running between the two houses to keep the merry party in either informed of the nature of the toasts.   Such rousing cheers and "tigers" had never been heard before in that usually sleepy, half-dead town.

After the feast, we adjourned by invitation, to the house of the Captain of the Port, where dancing was kept up with great vigour till the small hours next morning.   The brides had to dance with everyone present, and it was amusing to see them change from one gentleman to another: during the time occupied by one waltz they had ten or a dozen partners.   Petropaulovski had not nearly ladies enough for the invited males, and, in consequence, a number of very clean and sedate Kamchatdale peasant women were asked for the occasion.   Our efforts at conversation with the latter were ludicrous and extremely unsatisfactory; but with our Russian friends of the ' Variag' we got along capitally, and found them splendid fellows.*   The following

---

* These gentlemen all spoke, more or less fluently, French and English, or rather *American*. The reader is doubtless aware that at the termination of the Crimean war, French—once the court language in Russia—got out of favour there; but he may not know that the *American* tongue was ordered to be taught *in place of English* at the universities and schools—a distinction without a difference. So, at least, I was informed by an intelligent Russian officer.

day the brides and their relations paid return complimentary visits.

We found Petropaulovski in its brief summer garb; wild flowers, coarse grass, and musquitoes all abundant. The thermometer stood at 80° in the shade, and the writer found himself nodding over his out-door sketching, which was perhaps partly due to the constant round of festivities. Three months of Russian hospitality would kill most men; and the fortnight spent on this visit was the hardest work I have ever done in my life!—done, too, at a time when the summer heat was intense, and when every one who could, got into silk, duck, or alpaca clothing—like that worn in tropical countries. Our pre-conceived ideas of Kamchatka were entirely upset.

I shall never forget an " international " pic-nic held during our stay, in which the representatives of six or eight countries took part. There were European and Asiatic Russians,— from the Finlander to the Kamchatdale; Americans, North- erners and Southerners; Englishmen, Frenchmen, Germans, and an Italian.

Chatting in a babel of tongues, we walked leisurely by an upland path, skirting beautiful Avatcha Bay, till we found a grassy opening, pleasantly shaded, where the servants and sailors were beginning to unpack the hampers. The weather was perfect, there was scarcely a ripple on the blue water below us, flowers made the air fragrant, and, but for an occa- sional musquito, we should have forgotten we were on earth at all! And then—bliss of blisses!—we not merely raised a cloud of balmy smoke, but were encouraged therein by the sanction of our lady friends, some of whom joined us. At all their entertainments, or at quieter family parties, cigars and cigarettos were always served with the tea and coffee, and the ladies retained their seats with us. Would it were so in our own otherwise—more or less—happy land! When we were tired of games—one of them a Russian version of "hunt the slipper"—and toasts and songs, an *al fresco* repast was served; and we did not leave the place till long after twinkling stars studded the heavens.

It would be a serious undertaking to acknowledge duly all the kindness lavished upon us by the Russians and foreign residents. Messrs. Pflueger, Peirce, and Hunter, of the German and American houses, did everything to make our stay agreeable.

Messrs. Anasoff and Knox now left us, and were conveyed to various points on the Ochotsk Sea on board the 'Variag,' and eventually went to Nicolaiefski at the mouth of the Amoor. From thence Mr. Knox made the trip *viâ* Siberia to St. Petersburgh.

We left Petropaulovski on the 6th of August, and then steamed up the coast, keeping in sight of land for several days. Not merely is it a grand and rugged coast-line, but the ever-recurring volcanic peaks are a great source of beauty and interest.

Many of these mountains appeared at this season to be very bare of snow. The volcano of Koriatski—which as we had seen it, in the late autumn time of the previous year, was one vast sheet of snow—now showed immense sterile rocky sides.

On the 8th August we passed the promontory which terminates in the two capes Kamchatka and Stolbovoy. It had the appearance of two islands detached from the mainland, the intervening country being low. This—a circumstance to be constantly observed on all coasts—was perhaps specially noticeable on this. The island of St. Lawrence in Bering Sea, which I have passed twice, was a very prominent example. It has always appeared to me that the apparent gradual rise of a coast, seen from the sea as you approach it, affords a far better proof of the rotundity of the earth, than the illustration usually employed, that of a ship, which you are supposed to see by instalments, from the main-royal sail (if not from the " sky-scraper " or " moon-raker "), to the hull. The fact is that the royal and top-gallant sails of a vessel on the utmost verge of the horizon may be, in certain lights, barely distinguishable, while the dark outline of an irregular and rock-bound coast can be seen by any one. First, may be, appears a mountain-peak towering in solitary grandeur above the coast-line, and often far behind it, then the high lands and hills, then the cliffs and lowlands, and lastly the flats and beaches.

Immediately by Cape Kamchatka the river of the same name empties into Bering Sea.

It was from this river that Bering sailed on his first voyages, and his name will ever be associated with the coast. He deserves to rank among the great adventurers of the last century; yet his voyages are little known. He was a Dane drawn into the Russian service by the fame of Peter the Great, and his expeditions had been directly organized by that sagacious monarch. Peter did not, however, live to carry them out. Their principal object was to find out whether Asia and America were one, or whether any part of their coasts were contiguous. Müller, the historian of Bering's life, who accompanied him *on land*, but does not appear to have made any sea voyages with him whatever, says, " The

Empress Catherine, as she endeavoured in all points to
execute most precisely the plans of her deceased husband, in
a manner began her reign with an order for the expedition to
Kamtschatka." Vitus Bering was to be commander, and
to be assisted by two lieutenants, Martin Spanberg, and
Alexei Tschirikoff. They left St. Petersburgh on the 5th of
February, 1725, and proceeded to the Ochotsk Sea *viâ* Siberia.
It gives some idea of the difficult nature of the overland route
in those days, to find that it occupied them over two years to
transport their outfit to Ochotsk. From thence, after a vessel
had been specially built for them, they crossed to Bolcheretsk
in Kamchatka, and the following winter transported their provisions and naval stores to the town of Nishni (New),
Kamchatka. "On the 4th of April, 1728" says Müller, "a
boat was put upon the stocks, like the packet-boats used in
the Baltick; and on the 10th of July was launched, and named
the boat *Gabriel.*" On the 20th of the same month they
went to sea. Bering followed the E. coast of Kamchatka and
Siberia, and discovered the island of St. Lawrence. He
reached as far north as lat. 67° 18', and then found the coast
trend to the west, whereon he seems to have come to the
conclusion that he had reached the extremity of Asia, and
that there was no connection between the continents. In the
main point, of course, he was right; but he was totally wrong
in his conclusion as to the Asiatic coast commencing its
westward course from the point reached by him. He returned to the Kamchatka River without serious injury to his
vessel. The second voyage of his first expedition calls for little
remark, as he was unable, from contrary winds, to carry out
his plans, which were virtually to attempt the discovery of
the Pacific shores of America. He eventually sailed round

the south promontory of Kamchatka and returned by Ochotsk to St. Petersburgh.

But it is to the second expedition of Bering that we must look for adventure and interest. He with his two faithful lieutenants proposed it; and they were all promoted, a number of naval lieutenants and midshipmen being ordered to join them. Müller says, " The design of the first voyage was not brought on the carpet again upon this occasion, since it was looked upon as completed ; but instead of that, orders were given to make voyages, as well eastward to the continent of America as southward to Japan, and to discover if possible, at the same time, through the frozen sea the north passage, which had been so frequently attempted by the English and Dutch. The Senate, the Admiralty Office, and the Academy of Sciences all took their parts to complete this important undertaking." Several scientific professors volunteered to accompany Bering (John George Gmelin, Lewis de Lisle de la Croyère, S. Muller, and Steller, a student), and were nominated for the purpose. Two of these individuals never went to sea, but confined themselves to various researches in Siberia. One of Bering's subordinates—Spanberg—made at this time a voyage from Ochotsk to Japan ; but it is aside from the narrative of Bering's life.

After much trouble in transporting their goods and building ships, they at last, on the 4th of July, 1741, went to sea ; their port of departure being this time, Petropaulovski. On the 20th of the same month the vessels of their little fleet got separated during a storm, and each had to prosecute the voyage alone. They discovered many of the Aleutian and other islands nearer the American coast, and had many adventures with the natives. At length the scurvy made its

I

appearance among them, and Bering turned back to try and make the coast of Kamchatka. The sickness increased, and so weakened the crew that "two sailors who used to be at the rudder were obliged to be led in by two others who could hardly walk. And when one could sit and steer no longer, another in little better condition supplied his place. Many sails they durst not hoist, because there was nobody to lower them in case of need." At last land appeared, and a council was held; they determined to sail towards it, and getting near it they dropped anchor. A violent storm rose, and the ship was driven on the rocks, which she touched; they cast their second anchor; its cable was torn in pieces before the anchor took ground. A great sea pitched them clean over the rocks; behind which, however, they found quieter water, and the crew having rested, at last put their boat overboard, and some of them went ashore. There was but little drift-wood, and no trees on the island; hence they came to the determination to roof over some small ravines they found near the beach. On the "8th of November a beginning was made to land the sick, but some died as soon as they were brought from between decks in the open air, others during the time they were on the deck, some in the boat, and many more as soon as they were brought on shore."

On the 9th of November the Commander Bering—himself prostrated by scurvy—was brought ashore on a hand-barrow, and a month later died on this island, which now, in consequence, bears his name. "He may have been said to be buried half alive, for the sand rolling down continually from the side of the ditch in which he lay, and covering his feet, he at last would not suffer it to be removed, and said that he felt some warmth from it, which otherwise he should want in

the remaining parts of his body ; and thus the sand increased
to his belly, so that after his decease they were obliged to
scrape him out of the ground in order to inter him in a
proper manner."

Their vessel, lying unguarded, was wrecked in a storm, and
the larger part of their provisions lost. They subsisted for a
long time on dead whales • that had been driven ashore. At
last, in the spring, they came to the conclusion to try and
break up the wreck and construct a smaller vessel from its
remains, which was done, and they left the island. At last, to
their great joy, they reached the coast of Kamchatka. The
previous autumn Tschirikoff, the companion of Bering, had
arrived at Petropaulovski, with the loss of twenty-one men
by scurvy, and the Professor de la Croyère, who had lingered
to the end of the voyage, died before they could get him
ashore.*

Late in the evening of the 13th Aug. we reached the Gulf
of Anadyr (pronounced *Anärder*, and not "Annie, dear," as
some of our men persisted in calling it), and anchored till daylight next morning. The land round it was low, and, in spite of
the heat of the weather, a good deal of ice and snow remained
packed on the beach. We steamed slowly up the gulf, and
very soon some Tchuktchi natives came off, and convinced
us that they were men and brethren by asking for "lum "
(rum) and "tabak." On approaching the entrance to Anadyr
Bay there is a very curious island, to which we gave the name

---

* In the above narrative I have followed Müller exclusively. A second,
and not very different account was given to the world in the journal of
Heller, which is to be found, translated in an abbreviated form, in the
fourth edition of Coxe's ' Russian Discoveries.'

of "Sarcophagus," from a supposed resemblance. The entrance to the bay is about a mile and a half wide at the narrowest point.

We came to anchor off a Tchuktchi village similar to that in Plover Bay before described. On shore large herds of domesticated reindeer were peacefully grazing. It need not be stated that we immediately bargained for some. These constitute the wealth of the "wandering Tchuktchis;" some of them own many thousands, and employ their poorer countrymen in herding them. They wander from place to place with their deer, and may be regarded as Arctic patriarchs.

CHAPTER XI.

THE ANADYR RIVER AND PLOVER BAY, EASTERN SIBERIA.

Tchuktchi with letter of recommendation — Boat expedition to the river — Our explorers — Their experiences — The Anadyr River — Tchuktchi thieves — Plover Bay — Naukum again — Advertising in Bering Straits — Telegraph station erected — Foraging with a vengeance — Whaling — Norton Sound — Alaska — Death of Major Kennicott.

One of the Tchuktchis, immediately on our arrival, hastened on board with a letter. It was from Mr. MacCrea, the officer in charge of the explorations at the Anadyr, and stated that " a bigger liar never walked the earth " than the· gentleman who delivered the epistle, and cautioned us against him. He bore the euphonious title of " O-cock-cray."

On the 15th a boat expedition to the mouth of the Anadyr River was organised, and I obtained permission to accompany it. The second mate of the steamer, Mr. Laborne, and myself, with three sailors, formed the party. We had nothing to guide us but a sketch chart, constructed the preceding year by two of our captains, and there is little reliable information on any part of the country. On the eastern side of the bay, Mount Dionysius, a mountain of no great height, is the only landmark of the district. We steered due west from it. The weather was foggy and showery, but a favouring breeze helped us on, and we proceeded steadily for several hours, when we noticed an opening in the land, a little to the south of west, and immediately put our boat's head for it.

Soon we found the bay getting very shoal, so much so that in sailing we left a "tail" of discoloured water behind us, from constantly touching bottom on sand-bars. Sometimes we stuck, and had to lower the sail, and get out in the water to help our boat off. We then had to tack and keep off, and by this we lost much time. In the evening we had to give up for the time being, and ran in to a spit of land to the south of the opening. It was raining hard, and we found it rather difficult to raise a fire from the scanty underbrush and drift-wood. We at length succeeded, and the sailors rigged up a shelter tent from the oars, mast, and sail. But for the rain the musquitoes would have been out in full force, for even as it was they gave us very decided intimations of their existence.

Inside the spit there appeared to be a second bay, and from the number of "snags" and small trees stuck on the sand-bars, it was evident that a river entered there. Early the next morning we again started. Laborne's recollections of a trip the preceding year made him decide, as it proved rightly, that the Anadyr must be farther to the west. About 9 A.M. we found the right opening, and a little later reached "Camp MacCrea," at the mouth of the river.

The journey had been undertaken in order to leave a notice for the explorers there, but we did not expect to meet any of them, so that on entering their log house we were much surprised to find four of our old friends. They had been subsisting for about two months on an exclusive diet of salmon, which fish is abundant in the river. They had almost given up expecting to see any of the expedition; we, on the other hand, believed them to be at the Ochotsk Sea. Three of these gentlemen, MacCrea, Harder, and Smith, belonged to this section, but my astonishment was great to find with them Mr. Bush, who had made the entire journey from the Amoor River to the mouth of the Anadyr the preceding winter. His trip of at least 2500 miles, deserves to rank as the most remarkable of the many undertaken by members of our expedition. Nearly the first thing our friends asked was, " Have you brought any grub ? " and we soon satisfied them on the point by fetching up a supply of bread, tea, and salt meat from the boat, and spreading an extempore lunch. They had got heartily sick of " *toujours* " salmon, and infinitely preferred salt pork !

As we all very naturally wished to reach the steamer before night, we stopped but an hour or so and then started back, leaving Harder, by his own agreement to keep camp. We rowed the entire distance, thirty miles, while it rained incessantly; but we made the time pass very quickly in a most animated and disjointed conversation. Our friends had been absent a year from civilization, and we were curious in regard to their travels, and, as each asked for what came uppermost, our spasmodic discussion would have puzzled a stranger. Now it was dog-sleighing, or reindeer riding; now the policy of the President, or the last opera ; now the latest events in California, or those of the Anadyr. Tchuktchi, Lamutki, or Koriak lore was mixed with inquiries for absent friends, and nitro-glycerine explosions with Anadyr scandal.

The Anadyr River, as we learnt from these gentlemen, is subject to violent freshets in the spring ; it then rises fifteen to twenty feet above its usual level, flooding the country in all directions. It is navigable for 300 miles, and has no rapids of importance in that distance. A considerable amount of light timber was found on its banks. Our explorers had constructed eight log-houses, at intervals of twelve miles apart, and we found them in a very tolerable building at the mouth of the river. The logs for the latter had been rafted down forty miles. Mr. Bush told me that the natives catch and dry a quantity of salmon, and that deer are abundant. The latter, crossing the streams in herds, are speared in the water. The Tchuktchis have small canoes constructed of three planks, called "vetkas," which are used mainly for this purpose. Geese are plentiful, and when moulting are driven ashore by the natives, and knocked on the head by others remaining there. Musquitoes are a great pest in the short summer season. The lowest cold experienced by our friends during the preceding winter of 1865-6 was −52° Fahr., or 84° below freezing.

We were also informed that the opening in the land mistaken by us for the Anadyr River *was* the mouth of a large river called by the natives the "Arnoura." A third stream enters Anadyr Bay from the north, and the effect of so much river water falling into what would otherwise be an arm of the sea is to render it entirely fresh. Our steamer watered from the bay itself, the hose being simply put overboard, and the pumps set to work at filling the tanks.

During Mr. MacCrea's absence on lengthened explorations, the natives had broken into his hut, and had stolen a quantity of powdered arsenic intended for the preservation of specimens. They probably mistook it for sugar. The result was never known. They also carried off a bottle of liniment, supposing it to be whisky. It was composed of turpentine, sugar of lead, &c.; the native who drank it will never steal again! One man was known to have been killed by it.

On the 16th we left the Anadyr direct for Plover Bay, and here we met several of our vessels. My good friend, Major Wright, though but just risen from a bed of sickness, had made a very successful exploration through the barren country towards Pentigu Gulf. The irrepressible "Naukum," the native spoken of at our first visit, had accompanied him. "Nothing," said Wright, speaking of this trip, "that the 'white man' did could astonish him or make him for an instant lose his gravity, except the introduction of pepper-sauce into his food. The taste of this was a novelty, and after an experiment nothing could induce him to repeat it. He says: 'Me sabe good deal, but me no sabe white man eat fire on meat.' Having been presented with a complete suit of woollen clothing, he sported it with much dignity, varying his costume now and then by wearing his drawers about his neck. His tent may easily be found by any enter-prising traveller, as over the door is one of Heuston and Hastings' signs, while the door-post is ornamented with a poster directing everybody to go to Lamott's for hats, caps, &c."

This was a fact. The signs of several San Francisco houses were taken up—as a joke,—and left in various parts of the coast, where some future traveller may perhaps see them. In this instance it attracted a good deal of notice from the whalers who frequent the bay, itself within sight of Bering Straits. After this the enterprising advertisers who plastered the Pyramids and Palmyra with their posters must hide their diminished heads.

Colonel Bulkley caused a small house of planks to be con-structed for "Naukum," and made him many presents. My friend Grob—a mechanical draughtsman attached to us, and a genius in every form of sketching—made a drawing, "a dream of the future." It represented the interior of Naukum's dwelling. Madame, seated on a whiskey barrel, was playing the piano, Mr. Naukum engaged in a game of billiards in a further apartment, and a small boy, of blubbery aspect, handing him the "cock-tails" on a salver. The room was picturesque with paddles, skins, preserved-meat cans, dogs, and children; but civilization was triumphant! I am sorry that I cannot include this sketch among my illustrations.

My kind friend, Mrs. Scammon, had accompanied her husband on this voyage, and she invited "Naukum" into the cabin to look at some pet canaries. Although he had never seen such birds, he preserved a gentlemanly apathy, and would show no surprise whatever. Some one, a little piqued perhaps that he would not be astonished, said, "Why, Naukum, they are worth ten dollars each in San Francisco!"—"Ah," replied he, shrugging his shoulders, "too muchee!"

We stopped the larger part of a month in Plover Bay, our carpenters and labourers being engaged in the construction of a station. When the flooring and foundations were ready, the National and Company's flags were raised on a tall telegraph pole, a salute fired, and the health of Kelsey, the captain in charge, drunk enthusiastically. Fourteen men were left with him for the winter of 1866-7, and immediately commenced the erection of the line through a most rugged and difficult country.

In spite of the proximity of Plover Bay to the Arctic, very little snow remained on the barren country round it, except on the distant mountains, or in deep "gulches" or gullies, where it has lain for centuries. "That there snow," said one of our sailors to me, pointing to such a spot, "is three hundred years old if it's a day. Why, don't you see the wrinkles all over the face of it?" Every one has noticed the wrinkles and ridges in snow; but the idea of associating age with them was rather original.

Of course, when our men were landed at their destinations it was frequently found that some trifles, necessary to their comfort, had been omitted in the hurry of preparation. One of the leaders of an exploring party said to his men at the last moment, "I haven't time to tell you all you want, but look round, and take all you can get." Now, although there was much *bonhommie* generally, and every one, at some time or another, helped his acquaintances, not knowing how soon his turn might come, it was not pleasant to miss one's favourite coat or boots, knife, or scissors, as the case might be, from the cabin; and there were those who took an undue advantage of the circumstances, to beg, borrow, or steal all they could lay their hands on. One man was caught going over the side of the vessel with five caps as the results of his *loot;* they were unmistakably *forage caps.* Several individuals, whose packages had been very limited in extent in San Francisco, went ashore with quite a handsome collection of baggage, and were taken by the natives to be persons of much distinction. I am afraid that some liberal free-hearted members of our expedition, who returned to San Francisco, were considerably out of pocket in consequence.

In Plover Bay the whalers often succeed in capturing their prey in quiet water. We had opportunities of seeing their boats in pursuit of white grampus, and afterwards of true whale. Each boat is known by a distinguishing mark on

its sail, such as red stripes or a cross; they can then be told
at a distance by the vessels to which they respectively belong.
When the whale is harpooned, and floating dead in the water,
it is usual to plant a small flag in it.   After the leviathan is
towed alongside the vessel, it is cut up into large chunks,
and it is a very curious sight to witness the deck of a whaling
vessel covered with great masses of blubber.   Eventually it
is cut up into " mincemeat," in order that all the oil may be
extracted, and chopping-knives and even mincing machines
are employed for the purpose.   The oil is boiled out on
board, and, if not otherwise informed, a stranger seeing a
whaler a little way off with volumes of smoke and steam
arising from it, would suppose that the vessel was on fire.
On these occasions the sailors have a feast of dough-nuts
cooked in boiling whale-oil, whale-brain fritters, and *other
joints*.   My friend, Captain Redfield, a very successful whaler
well known in San Francisco and Honolulu, invited me, when
in Plover Bay, to witness the deck of his vessel with the
blubber lying on it, and gave me every chance of tasting
whale in various shapes.   I don't think that I wish to repeat
the experiment.

On the 20th we left Plover Bay for Norton Sound, Russian
America, arriving there on the 24th.   We anchored under
the lee of Whale Island, and later at an anchorage within
four miles of our destination, the Island of St. Michael's.
Norton Sound * is so shallow that vessels frequently touch

---

* Norton Sound was surveyed roughly by Captain Cook. It was named,
in the fashion of those days, after Sir Fletcher Norton, once Speaker of the
House of Commons (afterwards Lord Grantley), and a near relation of
Captain King, to whom Cook entrusted the exploration.

bottom at a mile or more from the coast. The wind, blowing off land, reduces its depth very perceptibly, and completely bares sand-bars at the mouths of the rivers entering it. The wind, too, very quickly raises a bad sea. On the night of the 28-29th a strong gale blew from the north-east, and our largest vessel, the 'Nightingale' (drawing 16 feet), touched bottom at stern or bows each time she pitched. Men on board were thrown off their feet, and out of their berths, and but for the soft mud bottom she must have sustained injury.

Here we met the explorers left the preceding season; and very shaggy and unkempt they looked, though, with one or two exceptions, in excellent health. But with the pleasure of meeting them was mingled one sad regret. Poor Kennicott had died suddenly at Nulato, on the Yukon, on the 13th May, 1866. His kind-heartedness, zeal, and earnestness, had endeared him to all of us who knew him, and it was believed that anxiety for the welfare and success of his party had accelerated his death.

Kennicott's name, by no means unknown in England, is much better known in the United States as that of an indefatigable traveller and collector. In 1859 he started on a prolonged exploration of the Hudson's Bay territory, and spent nearly four years in his favourite pursuit as a naturalist. The results of his labour have enriched the collections of the Smithsonian Institute, at Washington, and the Chicago Academy of Sciences. Through the former institution (which owes its existence to the bequest of an Englishman, Mr. Smithson), other museums, in both the old and new world, have benefited; and his services in the cause of Science entitle him to the grateful remembrance of his fellow men.

His party had followed out his instructions to the letter. Ketchum and Labarge had made the first trip through from the coast to Fort Yukon, and Ennis had explored the country north of Norton Sound as far as Port Clarence.

On the 1st October, we saw the last of the Telegraph fleet, and watched the 'Nightingale' till she was out of sight, knowing that for nearly a year our vessels could not return. The lateness of the season admonished us to make a rapid move for Unalachleet—the head-quarters of this section—as "between the seasons" there would be a period when travelling would be much impeded or wholly stopped. We therefore immediately commenced our preparations for leaving St. Michael's.

CHAPTER XII.

RUSSIAN AND INDIAN SETTLEMENTS.—NORTON SOUND.

St. Michael's — The fort and its inhabitants — The "Provalishik" — Russian steam-bath — "Total immersion" — The island — Incident of break-up of ice — Arrival of dead Indian sledge-driver — Steamboat trip — Steamer laid up — Russian post at Unalachleet — Malemute and Kaveak Indians — Skin clothing — Inter-tribal commerce — Trade with the Tchuktchis — Underground houses — Fishing through the ice.

REDOUBT ST. MICHAEL'S, or *Michaelovski*, the principal station of the Russian American Fur Company in this northern section of "Walrus-sia," deserves something more than a passing notice. It is not merely the best point* for a vessel to touch at, in order to land goods for the interior, including that great tract of country watered by the Yukon; but it has been, and is, to a great extent, a central post for Indian trade, and for the collection of furs from distant and interior posts. It has been already proposed—since the American occupation—to make it a military station; we may, not improbably, live to hear of a town springing up on the borders of the Arctic, and within 200 miles of Bering Straits.

---

* After what has been said about the shallow nature of Norton Sound, this might be considered open to doubt; the practical experience of our expedition proved, however, that both the mouths of the Yukon, or Kwich-pak, and the northern part of Norton Sound, were even worse, and St. Michael's was for over two years our base of supplies. Port Clarence was too far north for the goods intended for the Yukon, but is for certain parts of the country an excellent place for a station. See Appendix (IV.).

Fort St. Michael's, or Michaelovski.

St. Michael's is (on the authority of Zagoskin) in lat. 63° 28′ N., and long. 161° 44′ W. of Greenwich. It is situated on the south-east side of the island of the same name, and was founded in 1833, by Michael Tebenkoff, an energetic employé of the Russian Fur Company.

The station is built on the model of a Hudson's Bay Co.'s Fort, with enclosure of pickets, and with bastions flanking it. Inside are the store-houses and dwellings of the employés, including the "casine" (*caserne*), or general barrack, bath and cook-houses. These painted yellow, and surmounted by red roofs, gave it rather a gay appearance.

The inhabitants of the fort—all servants of the company— were a very mixed crowd, including pure Russians and Fin- landers, Yakutz, from Eastern Siberia, Aleuts, from the islands, and creoles from all parts. They were not a very

satisfactory body of men; in point of fact, it is said that
some of them had been criminals, who had been convicted in
St. Petersburgh, and offered the alternative of going to prison,
or into the service of the Russian American Company! We
found them—as did Zagoskin years before—much given to
laziness and drunkenness. Fortunately, their opportunity for
this latter indulgence was limited, usually, to one bout per
annum, on the arrival of the Russian ship from Sitka with
their supplies; whilst the "Provalishik," Mr. Stephanoff, the
commander of this fort, who had charge of the whole district,
stood no nonsense with them, and was ever ready to make
them yield assistance. His arguments were of a forcible character: I believe the knout formed no part of his establishment, but he used his fists with great effect! To this
gentleman we were all very much indebted, for enforcing the
orders of the Russian Company in our behalf; often to
the sacrifice of his own comfort, to say nothing of the skin
from his knuckles. The Russian American Company, however, gave these men salaries proportioned to their deserts:
1½ poods of coarse flour (about 60 pounds) per month, and
from 5d. to 10d. per day was the average allowance, and most
of them were hopelessly in debt to the Company. Fish and
game at this post were not reliable resources; and their pay
would barely keep them in tea, sugar, tobacco, and clothing.
The tea used was of a superior and expensive kind (worth 5s.
to 5s. 10d. a pound in the Company's store).

The true "Russian steam-bath" was always to be obtained
at these posts, as at every other settlement we visited, and it
was very popular among us. The bath-house consisted always
of two or more chambers, the first used for undressing, &c. The
inner room had a stone furnace, in which a fire was lighted

K

till it was intensely hot, and large barrels of hot and ice-cold water were always ready. Water was from time to time thrown on the heated stones, keeping the room full of steam, almost to suffocation. Entering, we invariably threw a bowl of cold water over our heads, and then reclined on shelves or benches provided for the purpose, till we were thoroughly steamed, then washed in hot water. On leaving the room it was very essential to throw cold water again over the head and whole person, or headache would result. The transition from the inner to the outer room, the latter sometimes having a temperature considerably below zero, was very sudden, and made us rub with great vigour, but we found ourselves much refreshed. The Russians invariably take a nap after the bath. Persons with apoplectic tendencies, or weak lungs, would probably suffer from their use ; I have seen men frequently sit or stoop down on the floor to get a cool gasp of air ; owing, perhaps, to the bath-house being too full of steam.

Outside the post, besides other buildings, there was a small chapel, in which, on " Prasniks," or holidays of the Church, and on each Sunday, a service was performed. A priest of the Greek Church, resident at the " Mission," on the Lower Yukon, comes down occasionally to baptize the natives. The Greek Church practises, it may be observed, *total immersion*, and when an infant is christened it is dipped bodily. In the case of Indians, they are baptized in the sea at this fort, and rumour says that some of them have been so christianized many years in succession, in order that they may obtain small gilt crosses, and other presents given them at such times. It becomes an interesting question, whether such a zealous convert, counts—in the missionary's reports—as *one* person, or as *four* or *five*, as the case may be ?

St. Michael's, though threatened by distant Indians, has never been seriously attacked. A small village of Indian houses—underground, or excavated in the hill—exists near the fort. A similar and larger village of natives of the same tribe will be hereafter described.

The Island of St. Michael's is mainly composed of a porous lava rock, riddled with holes (air bubbles?) innumerable. This formation apparently extends to the Yukon, and cliffs of a similar nature, but rather more crumbling in character, were observed by us at the station known as the "Mission" (*Missie*), on the lower part of the great river. Zagoskin says that the Indians have a tradition that St. Michael's was up-heaved from the sea—an occurrence at least possible. A large rocky island (in the chain of the Aleutian Islands), known by the Russians as the Bogoslov Volcano, rose from the sea in 1796. The same writer says that the spot where the fort now stands has been covered by the sea within the memory of Indians living at the date of his visit, 1842-3. The water of pools and creeks on the island is extremely nauseous, and our men always thought they could detect a sulphurous taste in it, probably from the decomposition of the rocks just mentioned. In fact, all the water used at the fort, in summer time, is brought from a spring on the mainland. The island is thick with moss, covering up, in some places, a bed of clay; berries in summer are abundant, and can be obtained fresh in winter by digging through their thick covering of snow. There are no trees whatever, and the fort is dependent on drift-wood from the mouths of the Yukon or Kwich-pak, which is fortunately landed in large quantities by the prevailing winds and currents, all over the shores of Norton Sound. A garden at the fort (perhaps 10 ft. by 3 ft. in size!),

which yields a few radishes and turnips, proves the practicability of growing something there.

The ice in Norton Sound forms early in October, but is
frequently broken up and carried to sea till late in winter.
On Christmas Eve some of the telegraph employés arrived at
St. Michael's from Unalachleet, having travelled on the ice,
sometimes at a distance of a mile or two from the coast. They,
as usual, were invited in at once by the Russians to "chi-
peat," or drink tea, &c. After this was over, they sauntered
outside the fort, to smoke their pipes, and look after the dogs.
What must have been their surprise to find that the ice, as
far as the eye could reach, that they had last travelled on, was
broken up, and gone on a cruise! Had they been half an
hour later, they would have gone with it, and would have
been floating about Bering Sea on a field of ice.*

On the coast, although the thermometer usually stands
rather higher than in the interior, the climate is really more
felt. Nearly all the cases of frost-bite among our men
occurred whilst travelling in and north of Norton Sound.
Again, whilst clear ice—that is, ice free from a covering of
snow—is scarce on the rivers, except very early in winter, it
is common for a long period on the coast. When your sledge
arrives at such ice, the dogs will often start off at a great
rate, although, but a few minutes before, they may have been
proceeding with difficulty. At such a time, it is usual to
jump on and take a ride, and you have to look sharp to do it.
Now, if there is much wind at such a time, however warm you
may be from previous exercise, you chill very readily. Under

---

* Norton Sound was not clear of ice till the third week in June,
1867.

exactly such circumstances as these, the Russians at St. Michael's were once horrified at the arrival of a sledge with an Indian on it—sitting erect—but perfectly dead. Unable to stop his dogs, the poor fellow had jumped on his sledge, and had probably frozen to death in a few minutes. Such incidents are rare; but it is common enough to find Indians with faces much disfigured, and having lost part of their ears or noses. It has been the universal testimony of Arctic travellers, that comparatively moderate cold, with wind, was more to be feared than the most extreme temperature without it.

By noon, on the 2nd October, we had loaded up a "baidarre," a whale-boat, and a little steamer, the 'Wilder,' left for our use, and, by detachments, we set off for Una-lachleet, a distance of sixty miles.

I took passage on the steamer, and found her crowded with freight and passengers to her utmost capacity. She was but sixty feet long, with a perfectly flat bottom, and a house of planks, covering two-thirds of her deck. Outside, the thermometer stood at about 10° Fahr.; inside the house we were at fever heat. We anchored at night off the Indian village of Taupanica, and early the next morning resumed our trip, soon reaching the sand-bars outside the Unalachleet River, immediately opposite Besborough Island, where we grounded, and the steamer had to be unloaded by Indians in " baidarres." The same evening she entered the mouth of the river safely, but it proved her last trip for the season.

On the 7th she was beached for the winter, about eighty telegraph men, Russians and Indians, assisted in hauling her high and dry. The river was almost completely frozen up, and our little craft a mass of ice from stem to stern. It was no

small work to break up and clear the space round her in
the river, before she could be moved.

At the mouth of the Unalachleet River, on the north bank,
is the most northern settlement on the coast, a Russian trading post, founded in 1840, and bearing the same name. It is
in lat. 63° 53′ 33″ N., and long. 160° 30′ 16″ W., and resembles
St. Michael's in being enclosed by a picket, but is otherwise
on a much smaller and poorer scale. The " bidarshik," or
head man, had but one room for himself and family. The
" casine " was occupied by several men with families, and by

Malemute Native.

an immense number of cockroaches, apparently with families
also! A large " pitchka," or oven, occupied an important
position in this establishment. The windows did not, as at

St. Michael's, aspire to the dignity of glass, but were of the
gut of fur seal, white and translucent, if not transparent.

To the N.W. of the post was a large village of Malemute
and Kaveak Indians, a race of tall and stout people, but in
other respects much resembling the Esquimaux. The men
very generally shaved the crown of the head, and wore the
ornaments known as the *To-took*, pieces of bone run through
holes on either side of the face, immediately below the
mouth. The women were generally tattooed on the chin,
and wearing ornaments of beads from their hair, and leaden
or iron bracelets. All adopted skin clothing; the true Male-

Female.   Male.

Malemute Skin Clothing.

mute coat or shirt is square cut at the bottom, is of but
moderate length, and has a hood almost invariably. The
woman's dress is longer, and has a rounded shape at

the lower part of it. Into the composition of these dresses many furs may enter; the hood is almost invariably wolf-skin, the long hairs of which shelter and half cover the face. Inside it is sometimes a lining of soft, white Arctic hare-skin. The body may be squirrel, mink, marten, seal, or reindeer skins, but, in point of fact, is nearly always of the latter. This, again, varies much ; it may be the thick cover-ing of an old buck, or the but half-developed *skin of a fawn that has never lived.* Zagoskin tells us how it is obtained, by practising a great cruelty : the poor doe, known to be with young, is driven from place to place by the natives, till her offspring is prematurely born. Then again it may be of the wild, or domesticated reindeer, shot by themselves, or imported from the Tchuktchis of the Asiatic coast, with whom they carry on a very extensive native trade. The Tchuktchis have large herds of tame reindeer (some of which I have mentioned at the Anadyr River, and elsewhere), whilst the animal is *never* met with in Russian America but in a wild state. I shall have to allude to this trade subsequently. The edges of coats and boots are often trimmed with strips of the much-prized wolverine-skin. This animal, the "carcajou" of the trappers, is well-known to be so wary and cunning that it is but rarely taken, and its fur is valued more highly than any other, without exception, by the natives of the whole coast and interior.

Pantaloons of seal or reindeer skin are worn by both sexes; the women's often have the socks attached, and in one piece. Their boots vary in length, and in the material used for the sides, but all have soles of "maclock," or seal-skin, with the hair removed. Fur socks, with the hair turned inside, are very common, and mits or gloves are made of all shapes and sizes. I have a pair made from dog-skin, two feet in length, and coming up far above the elbow.

These natives almost universally use a very unpleasant liquid for cleansing purposes.* They tan and soften the seal-skin used for boot soles with it.

The seal is perhaps their most useful animal, not merely furnishing oil and blubber, but the skin used for their canoes, thongs, nets, lassoes, and boot-soles. Their " baidarres," similar to the " oomiak " of the Greenlander, vary in size from those intended for three or four persons to others capable of holding fifteen or twenty persons. With them they go to sea, and cross the narrow part of Bering Straits. Their "baidarkes" are similar to the Greenland "kyack," but are more commonly constructed with three holes than with one. Both are admirably made; the frames light and strong, the skin covering sewn with sinew, and the seams rendered watertight by rubbing fat into them. The skin is prepared in the first instance, while yet the hair is on it, by spreading fermented fish-spawn over it, and allowing it to remain till the hair rots off. It is then stretched on a frame, and saturated with the liquid before alluded to, when it becomes translucent. The fat is removed with bone or stone knives, metal being considered likely to cut it.

In spite of the Russian posts in Norton Sound, a large part of the Indian trade was carried on with the American whaling vessels, who annually visited Port Clarence, Kotsebue Sound, and adjacent coasts, and paid much larger prices than the tariff fixed by the Fur Company. Another important part

---

* The scientific reader is referred to a paper by the author in the ' Transactions of the Ethnological Society ' for 1868.

of the commerce leaves the country by the hands of the Tchuktchis before mentioned, who cross from the coast of Siberia by the narrow part of Bering Straits, and generally meet the Kaveaks and Malemutes in Port Clarence. It is said that the natives from either side also meet on the Diomede Islands in the straits.

Inter-tribal commerce goes on to such an extent that clothing worn hundreds of miles up the Yukon, and in other parts of the interior of Russian America, is of Tchuktchi origin, and is made up by the women of the coast tribes, who sew better than those of the interior. This trade is principally for tame reindeer skins, of which the Tchuktchis have an overplus, and in exchange they receive bone, oil, and the furs of smaller animals. By constant inquiry I found that marten (American or Hudson's Bay sable of commerce), beaver, and fox skins, taken high up the Yukon, traded to the Co-Yukons, from them to the coast natives, and again from them to the Tchuktchis, eventually reach Russian traders on the Anadyr River, Eastern Siberia, or the American whaling vessels on the coast.

One object of Zagoskin's mission was to promote the establishment of an additional fort near Bering Straits, in order to put a stop to this trade, and he favoured the idea of placing it in Kotsebue Sound. This was, however, never accomplished, and from our party, who wintered in Port Clarence, I learnt that the larger part of the furs leave the country by *that* outlet. In spring several hundred natives meet there, and, in all probability, some station may now be formed in that neighbourhood by its American owners.*

---

* In 1867, Port Clarence was not clear of ice till the third week in June.

A large proportion of these natives have guns—both flint-lock and percussion-cap—obtained in trade. Guns, obtained as far off as the Hudson's Bay Company's fort at the junction of the Porcupine, find their way to the coast by inter-tribal barter. The smaller animals—hares, grouse, marten, &c.—are generally snared. The berries in summer are obtained in large quantities, and are eagerly sought. Varieties resembling blue-berries, huckle-berries, and a kind of dwarf raspberry (resembling in other respects the "salmon-berry" of Vancouver Island, &c.,) are all abundant. These mixed with seal-oil are considered a luxury, and are gathered in quantities for winter use. I have often obtained them in winter, from beneath the snow, and in almost as fresh a state as when they were first buried. Reindeer fat, *raw*, is always considered a treat, and an Indian cannot better show his esteem for a white visitor than by presenting him with a piece of buck-fat.

Their houses are usually underground, the roof only rising above the surface; the entrance is by a kind of tunnel or passage, by which you crawl into the room, and a hole in the roof lets out the smoke. This, when there is no fire on the floor of the room, is covered tightly with a skin. Nearly every dwelling has a stage for hanging furs or fish on, and a small wooden house or "cache" perched in the air on four poles, with a notched log for a ladder, is used to stow away supplies, and keep them safe from their dogs, or from wild animals prowling round the village. Canoes not in use are generally raised above the ground on trestles.

We frequently saw the Indians at this place engaged in fishing through holes made in the ice, catching quantities of a small kind of "white-fish." If we gave fish-hooks to the

natives, they usually tried to cut off the barbs; they took
the fish so readily that they could afford to lose a few from
the hook.   Involuntarily I thought of patient anglers by the
brook-side at home, waiting a day for a tenth part of the fish
caught there by an Indian in the same time, and could not
help coming to the conclusion that the Indian has the best
of it.   In windy weather, they frequently erect a screen of
skins, &c., and stakes.

CHAPTER XIII.

UNALACHLEET—NORTON SOUND.

Indian town-hall — Preparations for dance — Smoke-consuming Indians —
Feast — Dance — Chorus — The Malemutes and Kaveaks — The chiefs
— " Parka-mania " — Erection of quarters — Preparations for sledge
journey.

IN the village at Unalachleet, as in most others of the coast,
there are buildings set apart for dances and gatherings of the
people ; at other times, indeed, they are used for occupations
requiring space, as the manufacture of sledges or snow shoes.
These buildings may be regarded as the natives' town hall ;
orations are made, festivals and feasts are held in them, and
the passing stranger is sometimes accommodated in them, as
in an Eastern *caravanserai*.

I witnessed several of their public dances ; they are
constantly, indeed, held during winter, and it is surprising
to see how long and how much the older people are pleased
by such very monotonous performances.   In some of them
the actors imitate and burlesque the motions of birds and
quadrupeds, and of course here there is some scope for fun,
while some of their songs are said to have some meaning,
although on this point I cannot speak positively ; the only
ones I heard were the same words repeated over and over
again.

To one dance we were specially invited.   On arriving at
the doorway we found a narrow subterranean passage, two

and a half feet high, crawling through which we at last
reached the room, itself partly underground, and dimly
lighted by blubber lamps.

The Indians who were to take part in the dance, chiefly
young men, were engaged in dressing, and bathing themselves in the liquid *not* before mentioned. All were nude
to the waist, and wore seal, deer skin, or cotton pantaloons,
with the tails of wolves or dogs hanging behind, and
feathers and cheap handkerchiefs round their heads. The
elders sat on a bench or shelf, running round the entire
building, and looked on approvingly, whilst they *consumed
their own smoke,* as is the manner of the Tchuktchis, by
swallowing all they made, and getting partially intoxicated
thereby. Their pipe-bowls were on the smallest scale, and
they even diluted their tobacco by mixing willow shavings
" fine cut " with it.

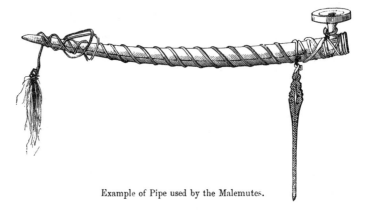

Example of Pipe used by the Malemutes.

Meantime the women were bringing in contributions of
berries and fish in large " contogs," or wooden bowls, varying
in shape from a deep dish to an oblong soup-tureen.

The performance commenced by the actors ranging themselves in a square, and raising these dishes of provisions to the four cardinal póints successively, and once to the skies with a sudden noise like "swish!" or the flight of a rocket. May-be it meant an offering to the seasons and to the Great Spirit. Then came the feast; and that over, a monotonous chorus, with an accompaniment of gongs was started. The gongs were made of seal-gut stretched on a circular frame, and were struck with a flat stick. The words of the song commenced, "Yung i ya, i ya, i ya!" and continued throughout "Yung i ya!" Then a boy sprang out on the floor, he was speedily joined by a second, then a third, till a circle of twenty was formed. Now they appeared violently attracted together, and now as much repelled; now they were horrified at one another's conduct, and held up their arms in warning gestures, and again all were friends and made pantomime of their happiness. In this performance there was nearly as much done by arms and bodies as with the feet. When there was a lull in the entertainment, small presents were brought round to all the strangers present; mine was a pair of boot soles of seal-skin.

So decided an odour at length pervaded the ball-room that we one by one dropped off from the festive scene; the Indians kept it up for hours afterwards.

The Malemutes and Kaveaks intermingle considerably, and have therefore been spoken of here as one people. Their habits, manners, and customs are identical, but they speak different dialects* and inhabit different parts of the country. The former extend from the Island of St. Michael's to Sound Golovnin, whilst the latter occupy a still more northern coun-

---

* For a brief vocabulary of Malemute words, see Appendix (V).

try adjacent to Port Clarence and Bering Straits. Although so much resembling the Esquimaux in habits, they are a larger, finer race, and it is by no means uncommon to find men of six feet in height; some, perhaps, over that standard. Nearly all the women are stout and blubbery in aspect, but have good-humoured features. Both sexes were employed in various ways by our expedition, and they were universally considered far above the average of Indians in every respect. The Malemute chief "Aleuyanuk" was a fine-looking old man, erect and soldierly, and wearing a moustache and imperial; his manners would not have disgraced a civilized assembly. "Comokin," the Kaveak chief, was as useful to us as he had been many years before to some of the expeditions engaged in the search for Sir John Franklin.

From our first arrival at Unalachleet, the men had very naturally a strong desire to obtain skin clothing for winter use, and also as curiosities, and, in the excessive competition for the limited supply in the hands of the Russians and Indians, prices went up about 200 per cent.! This was generally known as the "Parka mania" (from *parka*, Russian for skin shirt or coat) and was a great benefit to some of the more enterprising Russians, who set their Indian wives to work making up coats, boots, caps, and fur-socks in great variety, whilst they reaped themselves a harvest of five-dollar pieces. We all became extremely well informed on the different names and styles of furs. Of rein-deer alone, we distinguished three varieties: the ordinary thickly furred skin was in Russian simply * *Alany scoora; Nederist* was that of

---

* It is impossible to represent in English anything but the sound of a Russian word, as there are thirty-six letters in the Russian alphabet.

fawns of a few months old, while *Veperat* was the half-developed covering of the unborn young. We all acquired some little of the Russian language, or rather that *patois* of it spoken among the low-class Russians and half-breeds, many of whom had been born in Russian America.

During my stay at this station, all the men were employed in putting up quarters for winter use. A rude erection of earth and logs had been built for the Telegraph explorers the previous season, and now that a party of nearly forty were to winter there and commence the line, it was necessary to remodel the establishment. All hands then set to work with a will, and officers and men alike showed a determination to prove the energy of their race: besides, while some were shivering by night in tents, others were occupying the Russian employés' quarters, much, doubtless, to the disgust of the latter, although they took it philosophically.

The writer soon became *au fait* at building sod walls, and was consequently allowed to follow the natural bent of his genius, and each man, as far as possible, did that which he could do best. In consequence, we soon had a double-roomed house, well earthed round, and with a large *open* fire-place in one chamber. This fact is mentioned to show that an ordinary house on the surface, where, as in this neighbourhood, there is sufficient wood for fuel, can be successfully used in an Arctic climate. The other chamber, used as a kitchen, had an American cooking-stove; one of those excellent little institutions which will bake, boil, stew, fry, and broil, in the best manner, with the smallest possible expenditure of fuel.

The officers occupied (with the cockroaches) every avail-

able corner and bastion of the Fort, and several small rooms
were lined with deer-skins, making very cosy little places
of them.

During a portion of the time passed by me at this place we
had extremely bad weather, with strong N. and N.E. winds.
The thermometer invariably rose during the prevalence of
wind: it stood at points ranging between $+7°$ and $+32°$
during our stay.

Col. Bulkley, our Engineer-in-chief, had very kindly left to
me the privilege of selecting my own course of travel, with
due regard to the interests of the Company. I had the
previous year volunteered to accompany Major Kennicott;
but his party had been completely organized before I joined
the expedition, and my request could not be granted. I was,
however, determined to visit the unknown Yukon country,
which had been, from the commencement of our explorations,
more spoken about than any other. Ketchum, who had made
his very adventurous trip the previous summer, promised me
every facility, and kept his word. Indeed I can say, with
much gratitude, that I received every possible attention from
all the officers of the expedition, and am especially indebted
to Messrs. Ennis, Dennison, Dyer, Labarge, and the gentleman just mentioned.

We knew that early winter was not a favourable time for
travelling; the snow, but just fallen, is not "set" as it is at a
later period, and some parts of the rivers are not completely
frozen up. We, however, determined to lose no time, and
commenced our preparations. These included the selection
and purchase of sledges, dogs, harness, and skin-clothing, and
the division of the "spoil" that fell to our share, in flour, tea
and sugar, dried apples, bacon, beans, and rice. By the 26th

of October everything was ready for a start, and on the next morning we commenced our journey, by the shortest known route from the coast, to the Yukon River.*

---

* Captain Bedford Pim made—when engaged in the search for Sir John Franklin—a very adventurous journey through a country of almost identical nature lying between Kotsebue Sound, Unalachleet, and St. Michael's. Many of the Russians and half-breeds remembered his visit, and he had evidently left a very pleasant impression behind him.

CHAPTER XIV.

SLEDGE JOURNEY TO THE YUKON.

Routes to the Yukon — Sledges and dogs — Our start — Our party
— Unalachleet River — Brought to a standstill — Dogs desert — Ingelete Indians — Underground-houses, &c. — Beans *versus* rice —
Indian cleanliness — Medical aid — Ulukuk — The river — Indian
trading.

THE distance to that portion of the Yukon we were about to
visit is, by the mouths of the river, 700 miles, but a land route
to it is always employed in winter by the Russians travelling
from Norton Sound. By the latter route the total distance
from St. Michael's does not exceed 230 miles, and from
Unalachleet is approximately 170 miles.

The Russo-Indian form of sledge adopted by us was a very
light construction of birch wood, the knees alone sometimes
made of spruce, whilst it commonly had bone runners. Behind it were usually two guiding poles, and the general
appearance when loaded will be seen represented on our title
page. A lower and inferior kind, which may be regarded as
purely Indian, was occasionally used by us for very light
loads.

Although our expedition was well fitted out in the absolute
essentials of travel, no provision had been made with regard
to either sledges or dogs, it having been very naturally
supposed that the country itself was the best source from
whence to obtain these. We found, however, that the dogs
were neither plentiful nor of a good class. They were hardly

above the average of the sneaking, snarling Indian curs
of Oregon and British Columbia, and it was very difficult to
make them attached to you,—a proof to my mind that they
had as much of the wolf as the dog in them. I have always
succeeded in making a good dog my friend, and was much
chagrined at my want of success among these animals. They
are very hairy, are of all colours, iron grey predominating,
have wolfish features and short legs, but their immense bushy
tails make up for all deficiencies. Taking them all in all,
they did good service in transporting our goods, and with
them all of us made many lengthened journeys. Captain
Ennis twice made the trip from Norton Sound to Port
Clarence, Bering Straits; and the journey on the ice from
St. Michael's to Unalachleet was made a score of times, while
that to Nulato must have been made a dozen times during
the winter of 1866-7. The more remarkable journey of
Ketchum and Labarge will be mentioned hereafter.

On the morning of the 27th October, at eleven o'clock, we
bade adieu to our friends, some of whom persisted in accompanying us a little way on the frozen surface of the Unalachleet River, whilst the others honoured us with a grand, but
rather irregular volley of blank-cartridge from revolvers,
muskets, and the old battered cannon of the Russian post.
Our party comprised nine persons, as follows:—Captain
Ketchum and Lieutenant Labarge, his right-hand man,
Mr. Dall, a collector for the Smithsonian Institute, myself,
and Pickett, a man detailed for our service. Mr. Francis,
engineer of our little steamer, started with us on an excursion
trip, and three Indians completed our list. We took four
sledges, each drawn by five dogs, and very well laden
with a miscellaneous collection of boxes, barrels, tools, furs,

blankets, and snow shoes. Each load averaged 350 lbs.
weight.

The day was beautifully calm and clear, the temperature
just before starting was + 5° Fahr., but got much colder
during the day. As we had to run alongside of, or behind our
sledges, we soon found that the heavy fur clothing, so very
comfortable when stationary, was infinitely too much for us
when in violent exercise, and we accordingly divested ourselves of much of it. Many of our workmen wore ordinary
thick woollen clothing during the greater part of winter, but
native skin-boots were always adopted by us.

The record of this trip will be presented to the reader
mainly as it stands in my journal. We found the frozen river,
on whose surface we travelled all day, for the most part well
covered with snow. In a few patches the wind had bared the
ice, and there we could observe its true colours; sometimes
glassy green and transparent, so that we could see the pebbly
bottom of the shallow stream, in other places dark, opaque,
and colourless, with the shaded water underneath it giving
the impression of infinite depth. Some few parts of the
stream were not completely frozen; this generally occurred
on bars or small rapids, where the water ran swiftly. The
river was of moderate size,—as large as the Thames at
Hampton, but (excepting in the early spring freshets) even
more shallow. Within a few miles of the Russian station we
had just left we found spruce-fir and birch abundant on the
banks of the river, and a certain amount of drift-wood—the
wreck of larger trees swept from the skirts of the woods at
times of flood—is brought down by the swollen waters at the
break-up of the ice.

A few small accidents varied the day's travel, such as the

bone runners of our sledges cracking off, or the dogs getting loose and making a break for the woods. At four o'clock in the afternoon we stopped for a rest, raised a good fire of drift-wood on the surface of the ice, and then cooked our bacon and made some refreshing tea. We then resumed our trip by starlight, hoping to make the Indian village of Igtigalik the same evening. About six o'clock we came to a standstill ; a great patch of the river was entirely open, nor could we see a way round. Attempting to creep round the shelving banks our sledges were half-buried in the soft snow, and as the night was very dark, and we did not wish to risk losing our loads in the river, we came to the conclusion that we must camp. We unloaded the sledges, tied up the dogs, cleared a space in the snow at the top of the bank, and raised a magni-ficent log-fire. We spread a quantity of fir-brush on the ground, made up our beds on it, and slept closely packed together, with a large deer-skin robe covering us.

We had unfortunately relied on the next village for a supply of dog-feed. The Russian post we had just left was famous for " ukalee," an inferior kind of salmon dried for this purpose; but our men wintering there would, we knew, require so much of it that we had determined to obtain ours on the route. Our sledges, too, were otherwise filled to their uttermost capacity. The poor dogs passed a hungry night, howling dismally. We had to place everything eatable out of their reach, and as they did not object to skin clothing or old boots, and would readily devour their own harness, it was a somewhat difficult task.

28th.—In the morning we found that four of our dogs, disgusted and hungry, had deserted from our service, and we were sure that they had " made tracks " for the Russian post.

We made an early start in the brisk cold morning (temp.
— 6° Fahr.), and reached the village without any trouble,
after we had passed round the edge of the open water just
mentioned. There, however, the thin ice cracked beneath
the weight of our sledges, and we "kept moving," expecting
a ducking every moment.

On the right bank of the river we found a number of
Indian summer dwellings,—simply wooden shanties, built
above ground, with a small doorway, sometimes circular, and
a hole in the roof to let out the smoke. Behind them on
posts were the fish-houses, or "caches," as before described.

On the left bank were a few underground houses, intended
for winter use. These were simply square holes in the
ground, roofed in, and earthed over. The entrance of each
was always a rude shanty of logs or planks, passing into
which we found a hole in the ground, the entrance to a subterranean passage. Into this we dropped, and crawled on our
hands and knees into the room. "Amilka," the owner of one

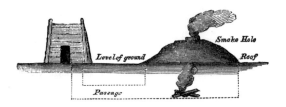

Diagram of Underground House.

of these houses, put half his floor at our disposal, and we
cleared it of dirt and encumbrances, and spread our skins
over it. A part of us stopped there some days, studying
the manners and customs of the people. Their manners
might pass, but some of their customs were decidedly nasty.

Igtigalik (known by the Russians as Nove, or New Ulukuk, to distinguish it from a neighbouring place of a similar name) was inhabited by a totally different tribe from that we had met at Unalachleet, and called the Ingelete people.   Although only twenty-five miles from the Malemute village, they speak an entirely different dialect, one—as we afterwards discovered— nearly allied to the Co-Yukon. These people were a fine stout race, with fair intelligence, and generally appeared to be very good humoured.   Many of the men were above the average in stature, and their general appearance much resembled the coast natives.   Polygamy exists, but not to any great extent, and occasionally a man discharges his wife and takes another, if the first proves barren, or disappoints with too many girls. Daughters are at a discount.

Their houses at this time were full of baskets for fish, traps, frames for snow shoes, and parts of sledges in course of manufacture.

The passage way into these houses was in wet mild weather nothing but a sewer.   The fire was built on the floor in the centre of the chamber, and when it burnt low the embers and sticks were always thrown out of the smoke-hole in the roof by the natives inside, and it was then covered with a skin.   This process effectually shut in all the warmth, but with it a good deal of smoke and carbonic acid gas.   The entrance hole was also usually covered with a deer skin, and the mixture of close smells inside the house, arising from more or less stale fish, meat, old skin clothes, young dogs, dirt and smoke, was very sickening.   The dogs scrambling and fighting on the roof above, sometimes tumbled through the smoke-hole on to the fire below, upsetting all the cooking arrangements, and adding a new smell to those above mentioned,—that of singed hair! It need not be said that they retreated with great alacrity, yelping and snarling as they went.

In place of soap these people use for cleansing purposes the liquid before mentioned as adopted by the Malemutes. The little children are plump and good tempered, suck a stick of ice as though it were barley-sugar, and are totally unacquainted with the use of the pocket-handkerchief. They seemed to be cowardly. If a strapping youngster tumbled down, and bruised or scratched himself, the women gathered round, gesticulating, and making a great fuss. If a few drops of blood appeared, they hid their eyes in their hands, as though it were something too terrible to behold.

Both men and women smoke ; the latter, however, do so only on occasions. Many, like the Malemutes and Tchukt-chis, swallow the smoke; and their pipe-bowls only hold a pinch of tobacco. They also use snuff, rubbing up the Russian leaf-tobacco in a kind of wooden pestle and mortar. This is simply a circular cup, roughly cut out from a knot of wood, and is held in the left hand, whilst the right grasps a stout round stick, the top of which is weighted with a stone. They have small oval-shaped wooden or bone snuff-boxes, and sniff the powdered tobacco into their nostrils through a small wooden tube.

At this, and other Ingelete villages, our goods lay un-guarded in our absence ; and I cannot recall a single case of proved dishonesty among them, although we found them gradually becoming more greedy in their demands for payment. Here we obtained a few Arctic grouse (ptarmigan) and dried deer-meat. We all became, from constant prac-tice, accomplished cooks ; nor do I think an epicure, especially after a day's travel in that appetizing climate, would have despised our "Telegraph" stews, flavoured and thickened at the right moment, with salt, pepper, and flour.

It was in Igtigalik that Francis and myself engaged in a great discussion—known afterwards as a *cause célèbre*—"beans *versus* rice." Francis, but recently arrived from China, was persuaded that rice was the staff of life, and that millions of Chinamen lived on little else. On the other hand, I contended that beans were more nourishing and glutenous, and that the miners and travellers of the Pacific coast swore by them as the most portable and satisfying of food. Francis pointed out the short time taken to cook rice; but I showed that beans, *when cooked*, were more inviting food. Beans fried *à la mineur*, baked *à la Yankee*, or boiled *à la clod-hopper*, were lively food, compared with insipid rice. We advanced our opinions with deep feeling and earnestness on either side, yet I fear left each other, and our listeners, exactly where they were before!

À propos of Indian cleanliness, a brief anecdote may be narrated. The previous winter an Ingelete had applied to Mr. Frederick Smith, a member of our expedition, asking him for medical assistance, stating at the same time that his chest pained him. A powerful blister was prescribed, applied, and left on all night. In the morning it was expected that his breast would be raw; but the only effect it had on his skin was to leave a clean space, the exact impression of the plaster! The man got better immediately.

A little Indian boy, playing with other children, received a gash in the cheek from a knife, and came to us for medical aid. A large piece of sticking-plaster was put over the wound, and the child was told that he must neither cry, talk, nor eat, as it would interfere with the charm of the application. The little fellow complied perfectly, would not utter a word, and starved himself for a week, so that his cut, being absolutely undisturbed, soon healed up, and our reputation was established. A small stock of simple medicines would be very useful to any future traveller; among them should be included pills, capable of acting powerfully, for natives who had over-gorged themselves. Healing ointments, for outward application, would, with sticking-plaster and lint, be of real service, as a great many of the natives suffer from skin diseases.

During our stay at the village, on October 30th and 31st, and on the 1st November, a thaw set in; the thermometer standing at points between + 32° and + 35° Fahr., and the wind south. Snow also fell. On the 2nd, Dall and Francis returned to Unalachleet, with the hope of recovering our dogs, several more of whom had left our service. Many of them had been borrowed from the Indian village, and very naturally preferred their lazy life there, to hard work with us. I saw no dogs in Russian America equal to the picked teams in Petropaulovski; but they had been selected from the best breeds of the whole peninsula. It was the intention of Colonel Bulkley to import a number from thence for our use, had the expedition continued for another season. Before leaving, Ketchum and myself purchased a small skin boat— which was subsequently used on my Yukon trip, and served for 1200 miles of river travel. We paid five dollars in American silver, and an axe worth two and a half dollars, so that it was not an expensive craft.

On the 3rd we started with four sledges for the upper

village of Ulukuk, a distance of fifteen miles. Our route
lay mainly on a " peronose " (as the Russians term a portage),
over land thickly covered with soft snow, in which our dogs,
sledges, and selves were half buried. On the top of an
ordinary sledge load we carried our skin canoe, and had no
small work in helping it along, more especially at snow
banks. We crossed many small streams, on which the ice
was not thoroughly formed, slipping into rather cool water
up to our waists. We carefully lifted our sledges over such
places to prevent wetting our goods. On some of the
tributaries of the river the route was like a well-made road,
with but a slight covering of snow, and we occasionally got a
few minutes' ride. It was, however, a luxury but rarely
attained. In the woods, through which our course partly
lay, the dogs invariably ran the sledges against the trees
and stumps, and there they would remain, till two or three
of us could clear them. Late in the day we arrived at the
Ulukuk River, which was still open. Rapids abound in it;
and there are warm springs in the neighbourhood, so that
this stream is but rarely quite frozen up. The Ingeletes
have availed themselves of this chance, by placing one of
their principal villages near it. They have large fish-traps
in the stream; and the village is very prettily situated on
an open space in the woods hard by the river. In the
distance is to be seen the range of the Ulukuk Mountains,
which are seen from the coast, and will be hereafter mentioned. Ulukuk is the paradise of this part of the country
in regard to salmon, salmon-trout, grouse, and deer meat;
and a larger number of Ingeletes congregate there than in
any other of their villages. There is no fear of your dogs
deserting from such a place.

The common native mode of cooking is roasting by the fire; some of them have, however, bought iron pots from the Russians. Salmon cooked on a stick placed near the fire, and occasionally turned till "done brown," is luscious.

On the 4th a terrible snow-storm occurred, with a strong N.E. wind. We were fortunately at that time in an underground house, exhibiting our treasures in magnetic compasses, pencils, note-books, &c., to an admiring crowd, and trading with them for dried fish for our dogs. It would be worth the traveller's while to take with him a small stock of toys and instruments of a simple nature, in place of so much of the conventional rubbish usually brought for Indian trade. Beads and bracelets are all very well, but burning-glasses, multiplying-glasses, kaleidoscopes, whistles, and small things in cutlery are novelties to them. Generally speaking, we found that the natives very sensibly preferred useful to ornamental things; and axes, knives, powder, caps, flints, and bullets were by far the best goods for trading. Yet, if they did become violently in love with a novelty, of however trifling a nature, there was no price they would refuse to give; and the traveller who has, above everything, to consider the portability of his goods, may, by selecting those small things which please even grown-up children here, save himself the trouble of transporting more unwieldy and less attractive goods. On several occasions we "astonished the natives" by lighting "Pharaoh's serpents," a novelty at that time even in San Francisco. A few small fireworks (packed in tin or zinc for safe transportation) would be much appreciated by the Indians, when gathered at their spring meetings.

CHAPTER XV.

SLEDGE JOURNEY TO THE YUKON.—*Continued.*

Cross the Ulukuk River — Walking on snow shoes — Ulukuk Mountains — Land travelling — Versola Sofka — Patent camp — Our frozen breath — Indian honesty — The use of snow shoes — Warm springs — First glimpse of the Yukon — Coltog — Old "Stareek"—Travel on the Yukon — Alikoff's "barabba" — Meet a Russian sledge-train — Arrival at Nulato.

On the morning of the 5th we turned our skin canoe to good account by using it to cross the Ulukuk River. By making several trips, we transported to the opposite bank our sledges, dogs, and goods. At Ulukuk I essayed my first pair of snow shoes, to the amusement of the natives, who wondered where a man could have been all his life who had not become familiar with their use!

Snow Shoe.

On the 6th we made a start, taking two sledges, an Indian man, and a boy; the latter we named "Tommy." We "cached" our skin-boat; it was to be brought up for us at a later period. The day was pleasant—temperature + 23° Fahr. ;—but the snow was fresh and soft, and all of our party wore snow shoes. After a little use, I became quite proficient. The only secret in wearing them is to strive to forget you have them on at all, and to walk exactly as you would anywhere else. The snow shoe then moves forward with the foot, but is not lifted much above the snow, and the lashings are so arranged that the toe remains fixed, while the rest of the foot moves up and down in the usual manner. Of course, the great object in using them is to diffuse your whole weight over a large surface, and they are usually of a good length, sometimes five and a-half feet long and upwards. An average length is four and a-half feet. All used in this part of the country are rounded and bent upwards in front, and pointed behind. They are made of birch-wood, covered at either end with a fine network of gut; the lashings for the foot are strips of hide.

We travelled N.N.E. magnetic, and followed pretty closely the base of the Ulukuk Mountains which in themselves are hills of inconsiderable altitude, not usually exceeding 3000 feet in height; they are, however, conspicuous landmarks in a country which is otherwise comparatively level. These mountains run north and south for 100 miles. One of their outlying hills, the "Versola Sofka," has a very graceful rounded form. To the west were hills and mountains of apparently greater altitude.

We occasionally stopped for a draught of ice-cold water. After breaking a hole in the ice of a creek, I noticed that our Indian invariably filled it up with loose snow before stooping down on hands and knees to drink. This was done to filter the water, and to prevent some little red worms, said to infest it, from being swallowed. Our route again lay through a "peronose," or portage, and presented alternations of open spaces, and light woods of spruce-fir, birch, and willow. At

4 P.M. we reached the base of the " Versola Sofka" Mountain, where we found a large frozen stream. We camped hard by it, and made a glorious fire and a bed of aromatic fir-brush; a screen of canvas, fixed behind our camp to the trees, and our snow shoes stuck in the ground, sheltered us from the only enemy we feared—the wind. We found from experience that tents were not in winter as comfortable as these open camps, as they could not be with safety placed sufficiently near the fire. After having arranged the camp, unloaded the sledges as far as necessary, and fed our dogs, we divested ourselves of our damp fur socks and skin boots, and hung them up to dry at a moderate distance from the fire. Our Indian meantime took the pots, and went to break a hole in the nearest frozen stream, to get the water for our tea. One of us sliced the bacon, got out a bag of " hard bread," or biscuit, or set to work concocting a stew of dried deer-meat or fresh grouse. Soon our meal was over, the ever grateful pipe smoked by one and all of us, and we turned into our blankets and furs, the stars looking down calmly upon us

> " Because they'd nothing else to do,"

and in a few minutes we were soundly sleeping. We woke in the morning to find our breath congealed in masses of ice on our moustachios and other hairy appendages. So great a nuisance was this, that many of our men shaved closely all winter. A merchant I had met the previous summer in Petropaulovski had once narrowly escaped suffocation from the ice forming in this way on his luxuriant beard and moustache. While travelling, he was unfortunate enough to wander into the woods, and lose his reckoning. He remained there a whole night, and in the morning, when

M

found by his anxious friends, the ice had almost completely glued up his nostrils and mouth. We always had to break up the clotted ice formed on our faces in this way, and then to perform our limited toilet by taking à little snow in our hands, and rubbing it over our faces,—a very refreshing operation. We then hastily cooked the breakfast, and were soon on our way again. We, once or twice, made a stew, and left it simmering all night at the camp fire.

We left the "Versola Sofka" on the morning of the 7th, and, finding the loads too great for our dogs under the circumstances, we raised an erection of poles, and deposited some bags thereon. I may here say, once for all, that our men often left goods, consisting of tea, flour, molasses, bacon, and all kinds of miscellaneous items—scattered in this way over the country, and that they remained untouched by the Indians, who frequently travelled past them. It would require some faith in one's species to do the same in St. James's Park! This day's travel was especially troublesome, the snow was deeper and softer than before, some little having recently fallen, and our sledges were perpetually upsetting. In order to make a track for our dogs, we frequently with the Indian, walked on a-head, returned, and again started forward, thus going over the ground three times. At night, after crossing a stream still open, we came to a small and very dilapidated Indian shanty, not much better than an open camp, known by the Russians as "Ivan's barabba" (house). It was a very wretched place, and we found it temporarily occupied by an Indian, with wife and child, whose apparent possessions no beggar could covet. Yet they appeared happy; for did they not know that on the morrow the hares and ptarmigan could be snared, the deer hunted with a little more exertion, and that if they were positively " hard up " they could get all they wanted for subsistence at the nearest village ? A little tobacco and a few trifles were given them, and from them we obtained a light sledge, standing no more than fifteen inches above the ground, to be used by us for transporting our blankets and light possessions.

On the 8th snow fell thickly, and travelling was so difficult that with our best exertions we did not make ten miles during the day. We camped thoroughly worn out. Although the use of snow shoes renders travelling possible, where otherwise it would hardly be so, they are very fatiguing in soft or soggy snow. The difference may be stated thus:—whereas without them you might sink in three or four feet, with them you only sink as many inches. But in certain conditions of climate the snow shoes get loaded with adhering snow and ice, and then every time you raise you foot you have to lift 10 or 15 lbs. extra. The shoes have to be constantly shaken, or otherwise cleared, at such times.

The morning of the 9th broke fine and clear, with a temperature of $+ 4°$ Fahr., and we travelled with greater ease through level country diversified by low rises from which we could see the break in the hills towards the Yukon. Our Indian, proceeding a good way a-head, shot several ptarmigan, and we made a fair day's journey of eighteen miles before camping. The next morning a north wind blew, and made us feel the cold very decidedly. It is wonderful how searching the wind is in this Arctic climate : each little seam, slit, or tear in your fur or woollen clothing makes you aware of its existence ; and one's nose, ears, and angles generally, are specially the sufferers. We passed this

M 2

day over a rather more hilly country (in a north-east direction), and in the valleys observed many warm springs which are said never to freeze in winter. I examined one, and found bubbles of gas rising to the surface. The temperature of the water was one degree above freezing, while the air was twenty-three degrees colder. Towards night it got down to zero, and the wind died out.

We made an early start next morning, travelling E.N.E., and later in a more northerly direction. About noon, from a slight eminence, we could see a faint streak of blue over the trees; we travelled hard to reach it, and at sundown broke from the woods, shot down a steep bank, and stood on an immense snow-clad field of ice,—the mighty Yukon! Hardly a patch of clear ice was to be seen,—all was covered by a wintry mantle. Large accumulations of hummucks had been in many places forced on the surface before the river had become thoroughly frozen, and even now the water was still open, and running swiftly in a few isolated and detached streaks. From bank to bank was not less than a mile, and several islands were visible in either direction. Let the reader think of a river 2000 miles long, and anywhere, at this part of its course, from one to four or five miles wide, one unbroken mass of snow-covered ice, from its source to its mouth, and he will then have pictured to himself the Yukon in winter. I had been prepared to see a large stream, but had formed no conception of the reality. Neither pen nor pencil can give any idea of the dreary grandeur, the vast monotony, or the unlimited expanse we saw before us.*

---

* The artist will understand me when I state that it would be necessary in a sketch of this river to make its width out of all proportion to its

OUR ARRIVAL AT THE FROZEN YUKON.

My first acquaintance with the Yukon, in common with several of my companions, was made sliding down the bank at the rate of "2.40" (to use an Americanism *), comfortably seated on my snow shoes. At such snow banks it is a very common thing for the sledge to shoot down faster than the dogs, who then get entangled in their harness, run over, and mashed in the snow. They frequently break loose at such times. The driver often throws himself down, and hangs on to the sledge to act as a drag. In Siberia, as I learnt from my friends who had wintered there, it is usual for the driver of a sledge, when riding on it, to have a pole or stake which he uses to impede its progress, driving it down into the snow every few seconds.

A quarter of an hour's travelling over this expanse of snow brought us to the Ingelete village of Coltog, where we again made a halt, and stopped in one of the largest underground houses we had seen; one inhabited by several families. The owner of this dwelling, old "Stareek," received us well, and produced white ptarmigan and berries. They were unfortunately short of dog-feed. This is one of the constant drawbacks in travelling, and stands much in the way of the transportation of large quantities of goods. The dogs, of course, weaken quickly without regular feed, and very naturally prowl about seeking something to devour. Provisions, even when packed up in boxes or barrels, are not safe where there are many dogs. The previous year they managed to burst open a keg of oil, and in a very short

---

height, and therefore as a picture it could not be satisfactory. This is my excuse for not reproducing more of my sketches of the Yukon.

* Two minutes forty seconds is the time taken by a high class trotting horse to run a mile.

time there was nothing left but a few scattered staves and hoops; on this trip one had gorged himself on half a ham, and was in consequence very unwell.

We stopped over the 12th and 13th at this village; both days being very gusty and stormy. Old "Stareek" harangued his neighbours by the hour together, and they brought us a fair amount of supplies. The poor old man—probably the "oldest inhabitant" of this district—with his shrivelled form, wrinkled face, long scattered hair, stubbly chin, and toothless mouth, wagging about in the most uncertain and eccentric manner, was a pitiable object; but we made his ancient heart rejoice by presenting him with cotton-drill, powder, and balls. Our teams, passing and repassing, would have to halt at this village constantly during winter. In "Stareek's" house several of the Indians slept on shelves or benches built round the walls, and by this means four or five families were packed into one room. When camped at these places, after taking our own meals, we invariably filled up the tea-kettle, and handed round to each of those natives who had done us any service, a cup of weak tea with a little broken biscuit floating on the top of it. Some of them have acquired from the Russians a taste for tea, but more especially for sugar. As these things were not articles of trade at the Russian Fur Company's posts, they rarely got a taste of either, nor do I believe that tea, *per se*, was much cared for by them, but that they simply liked it when hot and sweet.

We started up the Yukon on the 14th. An occasional patch of open water, running perhaps at the rate of three knots an hour, alone showed us that it was a river at all, and the dreary expanse of snow almost made us forget that we were on a sheet of ice. The river winds considerably,

and our course was often therefore from one point of land
to another.   We several times crossed from bank to bank to
cut off corners and bends, and, although we met with some
obstructions from masses of ice of all forms and shapes piled
wildly and irregularly around, travelling was on the whole
immeasurably easier than on the land portage.   Many cliffs
abutted on the river, and islands of sombre green forest
studded it in all directions.   We made about twenty-five
miles, then camped in a new but empty Indian house, known
by the Russians as "Alikoff's barabba."   The temperature at
sunset was − 2° Fahr.

On the morning of the 15th we rose early, and, after
travelling seven miles or so, met a large train of sledges
accompanied by several Russians and Indians.   They had
been sent down by the head man, or "bidarshik" of Nulato,
to transport their own winter supplies, and to assist us.   As it
was arranged that some of our men should make the return
journey to Norton Sound, a few days later, the Russians
turned round, and went back with us.   After about eight
miles' travel we reached Nulato, our destination, and made
a grand entry with much noise and fun, and the firing of
innumerable discharges.   All hands helped the sledges up
the incline leading up to the station, and a few minutes
later we were lunching at the "bidarshik's" table on raw
salt-fish and bread.   It need not be said that the "samovar"
had been prepared as soon as they sighted us in the distance.
The poorest Russian never neglects the sacred rite of hospitality, and we pledged each other in massive cups of strong
tea.   Later in the day we had something stronger.

Thus ended our trip to Nulato, a journey made by our
men later in the winter in much less time when the snow

was well packed, and when they could sometimes travel without snow shoes.

We found the quarters appropriated to our use—a low building forming one of the boundaries of the courtyard—to be large and reasonably comfortable. The place had been cleaned out, a large fire lighted in the "pitchka," or oven, straw laid on the floor, and, in short, everything done that was possible with the limited means at command. Later in the day we took a delicious steam-bath, and soon came to the conclusion that, after all, life in Russian America was perfectly endurable.

CHAPTER XVI.

LIFE AT NULATO—YUKON RIVER.

First explorers of the Yukon — Nulato — Our quarters — Water sledge — Fish traps — Winter sketching — Frozen provisions — Coldest day — Departure of a sledge train — Dinner party — Indian arrivals — Shortest day — Merry Christmas — Bill of fare — Aurora — Temperatures — Supplies — Principal winter trip of our explorers.

EMPLOYÉS of the Russian-American Fur Company were certainly the first explorers of the Yukon. Malakoff, in 1838, and Derabin, the following year, reached this portion of the river; the latter in the autumn of 1842 commenced the establishment of the post at Nulato, which, in consequence, long bore his name. In the early winter of 1843, Zagoskin, of the Russian Imperial Navy, arrived, having reached Nulato by the route just described, and he himself assisted at the building of the fort.*

Nulato is the most inland, and also most northern of all the Russian Fur Company's posts; on Zagoskin's authority it is in lat. 64° 42′ 11″ N., and long. 157° 58′ 18″ W. (of Greenwich). It is on the north bank of the Yukon, and is situated on a flat stretch of comparatively open land, bounded on the south-west by the Nulato River, a tributary of the Yukon,

---

* Zagoskin's work contains nearly all the information we possess on the Lower Yukon. It was translated by Mr. E. K. Laborne, the interpreter of our expedition, but was not printed. It exists in a German form.

—a stream one of whose mouths is at least seventy yards in width.

A smaller stream, also falling into the great river, bounds this open patch of land on the north-east. Trees of good average growth, and sufficiently large for building purposes, are to be found in the woods at a moderate distance from the fort, and the soil, a rich vegetable mould, with clay under-lying, though swampy in spring, might possibly be turned to some account. Luxuriant grass and innumerable berries grow up and ripen in the brief summer-time.

The post resembles those before described, and differs only in having two watch-towers. It is surrounded by a picket, and during our stay the gate was always shut at night, and Indians excluded when present in large numbers. Before our arrival a "watch" had been kept regularly at night, for reasons that will afterwards appear. The log building occu-pied by us formed a part of one side of the fort square. The windows of our room were of seal-gut, and, as the days were now about two hours in length, our light inside was none of the best. We slept wrapped up in fur-lined blankets and skins, on a platform raised about two feet above the floor, which latter we had caulked with moss and covered with straw and skins. Even then, although our room was gene-rally warm enough, the floor was sometimes intensely cold. I once hung up some damp cloth to dry ; near the rafters it steamed, within a foot of the ground it froze firmly, with long icicles hanging therefrom. The air near the floor has shown a temperature of $+ 4°$ when the upper part of the room was $+ 60°$ or $+ 65°$ Fahr.

Our supply of water was obtained from a hole kept con-stantly open—or as open as nature would allow it to be—

through the ice of the Yukon, at a distance of a quarter of a mile from the post. The "water-sledge" was one of the institutions of the place, and a large barrel was taken down and filled with water—and a good deal of broken ice—and brought back for the supply of the station. It was generally dragged by men, and sometimes by Indian women, as it would have taken more dogs than the place possessed to move it. It may very naturally be asked, Does not a river like the Yukon freeze to the bottom? and the answer is, most emphatically, "No; excepting only in extremely shallow places." We saw ice nine feet thick and upwards, but it was not produced by the natural process of gradual freezing and thickening, but had been forced up on other ice before the river was completely and firmly frozen. I think an average of five feet of ice will form where there is sufficient depth of water. Its universal covering of snow has, doubtless, the effect of preventing the formation of extremely thick ice; the current of the river has the same effect.

I have before mentioned the Indian mode of fishing through holes in the ice, but had not been prepared to see it practised on the large scale common on the Yukon. Early in the winter large piles or stakes had been driven down through the ice to the bottom of the river; to these were affixed traps, consisting simply of a wicker-work funnel leading into a long basket, not unlike the eel-pots to be seen on the Thames, but on a larger scale. Oblong holes above them were kept open through the ice by frequent breaking, and sometimes a great number of " white fish " and a large black fish (known by the Russians as *Nalima*) were taken, and we fell in for a share. The last-named is mainly used for dog-feed, but its very rich and oily liver was much eaten by the Russians, and was not despised by us.

Fish-traps on the Yukon.

In November and December I succeeded in making sketches of the fort and neighbourhood at times when the temperature was as low as thirty degrees below zero. It was done, it need not be said, with difficulty, and often by *instalments*. Between every five strokes of the pencil, I ran about to exercise myself, or went into our quarters for warmth. Several times I skinned my fingers, once froze my left ear, which swelled up nearly to the top of my head, and I was always afraid that my prominent nasal organ would get bitten. The use of water-colours was of course impracticable —except when I could keep a pot of warm water on a small fire by my side—a thing done by me on two or three occasions, when engaged at a distance from the post. Even inside the house the spaces near the windows—as well as the floor—were often below freezing-point. Once, forgetful of the fact (and it is a fact of which you do become forgetful), I mixed some colours up with water that had just stood near the oven, and, wetting a small brush, commenced to apply it to my drawing-block. Before it reached the paper, it was covered with a skin of ice, and simply scratched the surface, and I had to give up for the time being. One of our number going into a store-house to do some carpenter's work, put a large iron nail between his lips—to hold it for a moment— and, before he thought anything more about it, found them glued together, and had to go and thaw himself out by the fire !

The effect of intense cold on our stores in the magazine was a very interesting study ; our dried apples were a mass of rock, and had to be smashed up with an axe, our molasses formed a thick, blackpaste, and no knife we had would cut a slice of ham from the bone, till it was well thawed in our warmer room. Our preserved meats, would, with a continua-tion of those times, have been preserved for ever, and would have made, as Kane says, excellent "canister shot." After purchasing grouse or hares from the Indians, they would remain, uneaten, for a month or longer period, in as good condition as ever, and there was no fear of their getting too "high " in that climate.

Our coldest day for the whole season occurred in December. On the 26th of November the thermometer fell suddenly from the comparatively moderate temperature of $+ 2°$ to $-18°$, and continued lowering steadily—day by day—till it reached (on the 5th December) $- 58°$ Fahr., or *ninety degrees below freezing*. But the weather was lovely ; no wind blew or snow fell during the whole time, and we did not feel the cold as much as at many other times. Meantime the barometer rose rapidly, and stood at slightly above thirty inches on our coldest day.

On the 7th of the same month, the barometer fell considerably, the thermometer rose to − 24° and later − 16°, when snow fell thickly. The spirit thermometer used by myself (although by a San Francisco maker) agreed perfectly with a standard mercurial thermometer supplied by the Smithsonian Institute, as far down as − 40° (below which, as the reader doubtless knows, a mercurial instrument is of no further value): other thermometers showed a much lower temperature; one, in the hands of an explorer, then travelling up to Nulato, showed on the 5th a temperature of − 68°, but this was not a reliable instrument.

A few extracts from my journal will give—in perhaps the briefest form—an insight into some other of our experiences at this time :—

Nov. 18th (temperature at sunrise − 16° Fahr.).—Labarge, with Indians, started down to bring up another load from Unalachleet, and the Russians accompanied him. No less than ten sledges were employed, and the court-yard presented a lively scene, the men chattering with, or bidding adieu to their friends, shouting, and dragging their dogs to the "narta" (sledge); the dogs impatient, and ever and again trying to make a break for the frozen river. Here and there one was found who didn't want to go at all, and was seized by the scruff of the neck, and half carried, whining piteously the while, to his harness, which he then tried to chew to pieces. At last all was ready, and the fort gate opened; they ran down the incline made in the bank, and were soon lost to sight in the distance, their light loads enabling their drivers often to

ride, and make quick time. They would not return quite
so pleasantly.

19th (temp. − 32°).—Small supplies begin to arrive.
"Larrione" a Co-Yukon, and his brat, who carried a gun
twice his own length, brought us sweet fat melted into birch-
bark boxes and some Arctic grouse (ptarmigan), and we, of
course, returned the compliment, and both paid them and
gave them some tea and bread.

This day we gave a dinner-party to "Ivan," the bidarshik,
and his clerk "Iagor." Ivan, a half-breed, had been promoted to his present position from the fact that he was a
good trader; in other respects he was an ignorant man,
able neither to read nor write. We found him a pretty good
fellow. Our banquet of baked ptarmigan and fried ham,
pancakes (known, reader, by the poetical name of "flap-jacks")
molasses (known by us as "long-tailed sugar"), and coffee,
pleased our Russian friends well, but our tea was not to their
standard. They universally use a very superior kind. In
Petropaulovski, a merchant told me that he had once
imported a quantity of second-rate tea, and had to re-export
it, for the poorest Kamchatdale would neither buy it nor
take it as a gift.

17th December.—The first arrival of Indians from a distance; among them came an old chief from Nuclukayette,
240 miles up the river. He brought with him eight marten-
robes of twenty-four skins each, and was consequently a big
man with the Russians. We made him some presents—a coat,
a can of powder, and some balls, and a few trinkets—and he
harangued his companions in a peculiarly high-pitched voice,
as is the mode of the Upper Yukon Indians. Had we not
known that his speech was in our favour, we should have

supposed that he was making a war oration, in order to incite them to murder and revenge. He was not a bad featured old man, and our object in making friends with him was for the very good reason that we should afterwards—in the spring— pass his village, and probably be glad to get supplies from him. I tickled his fancy by slipping a plug of tobacco into his hand, when he had it extended in a theatrical manner in the middle of his speech, like Brutus pausing " for a reply." The reply was in this case satisfactory.

21st.—Our shortest day, the sun rose at 10·40 A.M., and set soon after 12·30 P.M. The *interval* is given correctly, but we had no " Greenwich time " to go by, and, therefore, it is only the duration of sun-light that is to be depended upon.

25th.—Merry Christmas! not the first by a good many that I had spent away from home and kindred. We all tried to be jolly, and were moderately successful, yet there was a slight " back current " of regret, and a tinge of melancholy in our proceedings. We decorated our room with flags and Indian trading goods, and spruce-fir brush, in place of holly; got out the newest and brightest of our tin plates and pewter spoons, raised a big fire of logs——in the oven! and Dall set to work vigorously in the manufacture of gingerbread and pies, but it could not quite put out of mind the dear ones at home, and what we well knew they were about. We, again, had our Russian friend Iagor with us, but the " bidarshik " was away on a trip. Our little company was composed of Ketchum, a jolly New Brunswicker; Labarge, a French Canadian, who had lived in the States most of his days, and was a gay free-hearted fellow, the favourite of all; Dall, a Bostonian, an enthusiastic collector and student of natural history, always ready to assist to the best of his power; and myself. Our Indian servant, Kuriler, might have passed for a Russian, as he had been brought up in the Fort, and spoke the patois of the employés better than his own tongue. He was over six feet high, very steady and good tempered, a pretty fair cook, and a good shot, and had only one failing. He could never resist shooting at anything where there was the most remote chance of hitting it, even though it were a crow or a gull. As long as his powder held out—and we were obliged to put him on allowance—he would blaze away at the slightest provocation, and, like the Indians of the whole course of the river, was very fond of saluting any arrivals at the fort with blank discharges from his flint-lock gun.

But I am forgetting Christmas. About five o'clock in the afternoon, the table neatly covered with cotton drill, and set out with the " plate " provided by the company, in the shape of iron mess-kettles, tin platters, and cups, was ready, and we sat down to a repast — to use a Californianism—of a " high-toned and elegant nature."

BILL OF FARE.

Soupe à la Yukon.
Arctic Grouse—roast.
Alaska Reindeer Meat.
Nulato Cranberry Sauce.
California (preserved) Peas and Tomatoes.
Dried-Apple Pudding.
Pies.   Gingerbread à la Dall.
Iced Cheese.
Coffee.   Tea.
Iced Water.

Winding up with a limited supply of rum punch, and pipes *ad libitum!*

N

Not a bad dinner of itself; the iced cheese was a novelty I can recommend; only the traditional pudding was missing.

We passed the evening singing and reciting. Dall read an original poem; and I brought out a MS. story (still there!), entitled the "Missing Mummy!"*

27th.—Just as we were turning in for the night a fine auroral display in the N.W. was announced, and we all rushed out to witness it from the roof of the tallest building in the Fort. It was not the conventional arch, but a graceful, undulating, ever-changing "snake" of electric light; evanescent colours, pale as those of a lunar rainbow, ever and again flitting through it, and long streamers and scintillations moving upward to the bright stars, which distinctly shone through its hazy, ethereal form. The night was beautifully calm and clear, cold, but not intensely so, the thermometer at + 16°. A second one was seen by us on the 13th January (1867), which had the arched form, but not of that exact nature which has been so often represented; and later we witnessed other displays, though not so frequently as we had expected.

The new year of 1867 began cold, and with some variations in the interval, reached as low as − 49° on the 15th. January was our coldest month, and included three days in which the thermometer showed a temperature below the freezing-point of mercury; but although the *mean* temperature of the month was lower, the exceptional days in Decem-

---

* Our men at Unalachleet organized some private theatricals, and an original piece, called ' Roderick Doo, and how He was Done,' was played with great success.

ber had been even more intensely cold. In December there were *six* days in which the thermometer fell below the freezing-point of mercury; eleven such days occurred during the winter.

Our supplies from the resources of the country, though very variable, were not at times inconsiderable; occasionally we were down to flour "strait," but more commonly got enough of either Arctic grouse, hares, or fish. Very little deer meat came in for several months. We carefully preserved the white soft skins of the hares to cover our blankets; and all of us there luxuriated in such by night. It takes forty to cover an ordinary blanket. Our indefatigable quartermaster, Mr. Dyer, looking a-head for the future, got together at the end of winter about 800 of these skins. It must not, however, be supposed that our small party had eaten that number of hares! The larger part of them were purchased from the Indians, who were ready enough to sell us the skins, but preferred to eat the meat themselves.

Many an excursion on the frozen river was made by us, many a visit to the fish-traps, or to the snares set in the woods by the Indian women of the Fort. The river at Nulato is, by measurement, *from bank to bank, a mile and a quarter*, and to an island opposite the station 1000 yards; and often did we cross it in pursuit of health, exercise, natural history specimens, our daily food, or for sketching purposes. A large log building was put up at a mile from the post, and was intended to serve as a telegraph station; we all, more or less, took part in the erection of this building. Some future traveller may reap the benefit.

The principal event of the winter was, undoubtedly, the trip made by Ketchum and Labarge from Nulato to Fort

Yukon. On the 2nd March, Labarge arrived from Unalachleet, bringing with him twenty-two dogs, and "ukalee,"
or dried salmon, enough for twenty-five or thirty days' use.
As it was necessary to keep all of this for the trip, it was
no easy matter to feed so many hungry dogs; nevertheless,
we were determined they should start in good condition.
We therefore got together every eatable thing that was
available, and made a soup for them, as the Russians also do
at times, of oil, fish, scraps of meat, bran, and rice. We
even sacrificed our last beans for their benefit, and found—.
contrary to Dr. Kane's experience—that they *would* eat
them, when properly softened. This concoction was stewed
slowly on a moderate fire, and when ready, was allowed to
cool partially; it was then turned into a long wooden trough,
round which the dogs scrambled and fought, until the last
morsels and drops were licked up. It evidently suited them;
they fattened on it.

Two Ingelete Indians, who had promised to accompany
Ketchum, backed out at the last moment, doubtless afraid of
travelling so far from their own villages; and their place
was filled by Co-Yukons, with the addition of two boys,
one of whom proved the best of the batch. At last, on the
11th, all their preparations were made, and they started
with four sledges; one of these being exclusively filled with
dried fish, and another with the lighter necessaries. We
all feared that the trip had been attempted too late; snow
had but recently fallen, and the surface of the river was
in as soft a condition as it had been in the early winter.
We gave them a good start, helping the sledges through
the soft snow; while Dyer almost brought down one of the
old watch-towers, by firing off a rusty unused piece of

artillery which he found lying there.   The result of this trip
I must leave to its proper place in the narrative.

In place of interspersing the numerous references to
Indians among other matters, as in my journal, I have
massed them together in the succeeding chapter.   As
Indians come to Nulato, even from a distance of several
hundred miles, we had much opportunity of intercourse
with them.

CHAPTER XVII.

THE CO-YUKON INDIANS.

Co-Yukon tribe — Fashions — The Nulato massacre — Incidents of the attack — Indian murders — Mourning observances — " Wake " — Four-post Coffins — Superstitions — " Corralling " deer — News travels fast — Furs and trading — Indian women — Indian "goggles."—Children's dolls.

THE Co-Yukon is the largest tribe on the Yukon River, and extends virtually from the confluence of the Co-Yukuk River to Nuclukayette at the junction of the Tanana with the Yukon; for, although some of the' intervening tribes have local names, yet they speak one dialect, and may fairly be considered as one people. They also inhabit the banks of the Co-Yukuk, and other interior rivers.

In general appearance they somewhat resemble the In-geletes before mentioned; but have a wilder and more ferocious cast of feature. The true Co-Yukon dress is a double-tailed coat, one tail before, and one behind. If the reader will imagine a man dressed in two swallow-tail coats, one of them worn as usual, the other covering his stomach, and buttoned behind, he will get some idea of this garment! Owing to inter-tribal commerce, Male-mute clothing is much seen on the Yukon; but the style just mentioned is regarded as a Co-Yukon fashion, and, with various modifications, is adopted by the other tribes on the upper Yukon for at least a thousand miles of its course. The women's dress is more squarely cut; and they adopt very much a long ornament of Hy-a-qua shells

(*Dentalium*), obtained from both the trading companies on the river. This is worn on the nose, and runs through a hole made in the cartilage between the nostrils. Strange to say, higher up the river, as will be mentioned hereafter, it is the men exclusively who adopt this ornament. The Co-Yukon winter dwellings are underground, the same as those already described.

These people are much feared by surrounding tribes, and gave the Russians much trouble in the early history of Nulato. Behind the post there is a small burial-ground, where lies one brave Englishman, a lieutenant of our Navy, and a member of Captain (now Admiral) Collinson's expedition, who, in the search for Sir John Franklin, met his death at the hands of these Indians. The narrative of this occurrence, as learnt from the Russians, is as follows :—

Lieutenant Barnard was landed at St. Michael's on October 12th, 1850, and remained there till the Commander of the post at Nulato came down in the early winter. He then accompanied this Russian up to the Yukon, travelling there by the route used by ourselves. Mr. Adams, an Assistant-Surgeon, R.N., and one seaman, were left at St. Michael's. On arriving at Nulato, Lieutenant Barnard despatched one of the employés of the Fur Company and an Indian to Co-Yukuk to make some inquiries. The Russian, on arrival there, fell asleep on his sledge, and in the absence of his Indian servant, was killed by the Co-Yukons. The Indian, who had but gone a little way to obtain water, on his return found his master dead, and immediately ran away affrighted. The others beckoned him back, saying they had no intention of injuring *him*. He, believing them, returned, and as he approached, was shot by arrows, and killed also.

The murderers—numbering, it is said, more than a hundred men—then started down for Nulato. About forty Nulato Indians were congregated in some underground houses, near the mouth of the Nulato River, and not more than a mile from the post. The Co-Yukons surrounded these dwellings, heaped wood, broken canoes, paddles, and snow shoes over the entrance and smoke-holes, and then set them on fire. All of the unfortunate victims below were suffocated, or shot in attempting to escape. Only five or six solitary Nulatos are now in existence.

Early the next morning the Co-Yukons swarmed into the court-yard of the fort, which then had no picket fence surrounding it. A fatal security reigned among the Russians, and they had not even secured the doors ; it is said that an Indian woman in the fort knew of the occurrence of the night before; but was afraid to impart her knowledge to the others. Finding the commander outside, they stabbed him in the back repeatedly. He lived for a few minutes, only just managing to stagger into his own doorway. The Indians then rushed into the room where Barnard and another man, an interpreter, were still lying on their beds. They jumped up and grasped their guns and pistols. The Englishman fired several shots, but without much effect, and a powerful struggle ensued. His double gun was afterwards found broken in the stock. At last, numbers overpowered him, and they threw him on the bed, stabbing him repeatedly. The interpreter was also severely wounded.

As they came out from this house a Russian shot at them from the building opposite through a hole in one of the gut windows. Instantly an Indian raised his bow and arrow in position, when the Russian again fired and shot him so dead that he fell with the bow and arrow stiff in his grasp. The others immediately dispersed.

An Indian "Lofka" was at once despatched to St. Michael's with a letter for Mr. Adams, the surgeon there. This native put the paper in his skin boot, and was on the road confronted by the Co-Yukons, who examined his blankets and clothes; they, however, overlooked his boots, and did not therefore discover his *ruse*. Mr. Adams at once started up; but arrived too late to be of any assistance. The cross and inscribed board on the grave, put up by this gentleman, were last summer (1867) in good preservation.

The Commander of Nulato is said to have ill-used these Indians; but their reason for this wholesale butchery is involved in mystery. Admiral Collinson very kindly put his notes of this transaction at my disposal, and I found no essential difference in the two versions of this sad story, excepting only as to whether the Indian murders preceded *or* followed those of the white men.

We heard of recent brutal murders among themselves; and although we got along well enough with them, they are, undoubtedly, a wilder and more savage race than those of the coast. In the autumn of 1865, an Indian of this tribe went hunting in the mountains with two men, brothers, inhabitants of the same village as himself. In the woods he got them apart on some pretence, and succeeded in killing both. He returned to the village, seized their possessions in fish and furs, and bullied the widow of one of them into living with him. Some of the murdered men's relatives came from a distance to punish this monster; but he learnt of their approach in time, and escaped to the forest, taking the woman with him; up to the time of our leaving he had not been caught, but will eventually meet his reward, as the Indians round were much exasperated at his villany.

These tribes mourn for the dead one year, and the women during that time often gather together, talking and crying over the deceased. At the expiration of that term, they have a feast or "wake," and the mourning is over. One such entertainment took place at Nulato during our stay, and by special request was allowed to be held in the general barrack of the fort. It was to commemorate the death of a Co-Yukon child, and was a queer mixture of jollity and grief.

The poor old mother and some of her friends wept bitterly, while the guests were gaily dancing round a painted pole, on which strings of beads and some magnificent wolf skins were hung. They kept up singing, dancing, and feasting to a fashionable hour of the morning; and one little savage, who had been shouting at the top of his lungs for hours, got up the next day without any voice at all—a case of righteous retribution. The decorations of the pole were divided among those who took part in the "wake." So vigorously did they dance, that the old oven, used in warming the building, shook to its foundations, and part of it fell in.

They do not inter the dead, but put them in oblong boxes, raised on posts, sometimes decorated with strips of skin hanging over them; sometimes with the possessions of the deceased (as a "baidarre," or other canoe, with paddles, &c.) on the top of the box. Small possessions are often put inside with the corpse. The tomb cannot be better described than as a four-post coffin! These are common to the coast tribes also.

They have certain superstitions with regard to the bones of

animals, which they will neither throw on the fire nor to the
dogs, but save them in their houses or caches.   When they

Co-Yukon Four-post Coffin.

saw us careless in such matters, they said it would prevent
them from catching or shooting successfully.   Also, they will
not throw away their hair or nails, just cut short, but save
them, sometimes hanging them in packages to the trees.

The mode of fishing through the ice practised by the
Russians is much in vogue with them, and they also have an
ingenious mode of catching reindeer in the mountain valleys.
A kind of corral, or enclosure, elliptical in form, and open at
one end, is made on a deer-trail, generally near the outlet of
a wood.   The further end of the enclosed space is barricaded;
the sides are built of stakes, with slip-nooses or loops between
them.   Herds of deer are driven in from the woods, and,
trying to break from the trap, generally run their heads into

the nooses, tighten them, and so get caught, or are shot, whilst still bewildered, and running from side to side. Near the opening it is common to erect piles of snow, with "portholes," through which natives hidden shoot at the passing deer.

It is surprising, in this thinly inhabited country, how fast news of any kind will travel from tribe to tribe. Should a vessel call at St. Michael's, in a week or two it will be known on three parts of the Yukon. During winter false rumours reached our men at the coast station that we had been attacked by Indians, and Captain Ennis immediately sent up, offering assistance. On the other hand, reports, equally false, reached us with regard to the coast parties; all being probably caused by some petty disagreement, exaggerated from mouth to mouth.

We once said, jokingly, that if supplies did not come in faster, we should have to eat up the plump babies of the settlement. Before many days elapsed, it was spread all over the country that we were cannibals, and devoured children wholesale! and many a serious enquiry was made about it. Generally speaking, we found it answered our purpose to joke, sing, and affect gaiety with them, but we had to be very careful what statements we advanced. We told them confidently, however, of the expected advent of a big steamer for the Yukon, as, indeed, we ourselves believed at the time; but, unless some private individuals do what our Company proposed to do, I am afraid the Indians will think us terrible liars. Many of them went down to see our little steamer, then at the mouth of the Unalachleet River, and it excited a good deal of interest, as they spread the news throughout the country. Few individuals, even of the Co-Yukons, have ever

A CO-YUKON DEER CORRAL.

tasted "fire-water." How long that happy state of things will last, remains to be seen. Their smoking habits are the same as those of the coast peoples, modified, of course, by the introduction of pipes of a larger growth, introduced by the trading companies and ourselves.

The women are often passably pretty, and when living in the forts often improve in habits. They are there sometimes allowed a "steam-bath." They are very fond of playing together, behaving at such times like children, snow-balling each other, rolling each other in the snow, or sliding down banks on sledges or snow shoes. I think they treat their children well, and the young mothers are certainly very fond of their first-born.

One day in summer, Dall gallantly presented a wild rose to a young Indian damsel. She accepted it graciously, but did not appear to know what to do with it. He put it up to her nose, when she turned away with a "puh!" as contemptuous as Hamlet's! It will not, perhaps, do to put this down as a national trait. Of the furs obtained by them, a portion only reached the Russian forts. Some were accumulated till spring, when at Nuclukayette they could trade them to their neighbours, or to the Hudson's Bay Company. Another part of the trade reaches the coast, and eventually the Tchuktchi natives, as before mentioned.

Still, in one season at Nulato, the Russians have taken 5000 marten, and large quantities of beaver, with an occasional black or silver-grey fox. They did not trade guns or ammunition on the Yukon, and the Indians were very dissatisfied with both their tariff and goods. Our powder and balls, with some additional supplies contributed by Dall, were invaluable.

With regard to beads, it was required that they should
not be fragile—a strong large porcelain bead was the correct thing; combs were much desired, and looking-glasses
were not bad things for trade; cotton, of various kinds, was
much in demand, while trinkets went for very little. They
commonly tested beads by rapping them sharply on wood, on
the table, &c. If they were not broken, all was well. Flints
and steels, knives, and scissors, were all in demand, and
soaps and matches would both have been, could we have
spared any. Our needs were chiefly confined to the purchase
of supplies and skin clothing; special services were paid for
by larger rewards, guns, blankets, or clothing.

The Co-Yukon dialect is—with slight variations—spoken
by the tribes of the middle and lower Yukon, for several
hundred miles of its course. The Ingelete dialect, as before
mentioned, is closely allied to it. It appears to be *totally
distinct* from those of the coast peoples. In the brief
vocabularies of Co-Yukon and Malemute words to be found
in the Appendix (V.), there is hardly a word which seems to
have a common origin. That the coast natives of Northern
Alaska are but Americanised Tchuktchis from Asia, I myself
have no doubt; but where shall we look for the stock from
which the Yukon Indians came? They appear to be more
nearly allied to the true North American Indian. These
natives very constantly reminded me of Catlin and the older
writers, and they almost appeared like old friends.

In spring, the Co-Yukons, in common with all the surrounding tribes, adopt wood "goggles" when hunting or
travelling. These are used to prevent the glare of the sun-
light on the snow from producing blindness. These " specs "
are made of many shapes, all having a narrow slit through

which the wearer can see with sufficient distinctness. We wore coloured glasses for the same purpose.

For the amusement of children, the women manufacture dolls, often very fair copies of themselves or the men, in dress and general appearance. But the children soon develop into men and women; and, at ten years old, a boy may possess and know how to make good use of a gun, while a girl, at fifteen, may have a husband, or, at all events, be setting snares for one!

Co-Yukon Goggles.

CHAPTER XVIII.

CANOE JOURNEY.—ASCENT OF THE YUKON.

Spring — Thaw — Break-up of the Yukon — Preparations for journey — Our canoes — Start — Dangerous condition of river — Its size — Current — Perilous navigation — Submerged islands — Co-Yukuk — Birch-bark fleet — Sachertelontin — Lagoon — Newicargut — Purchase of supplies — Tooth-brush experiences — Medicine-making — Indian dissipation — Child's birch-bark chair.

ALTHOUGH snow covers the ground, and the rivers are frozen, for nearly eight months of the year in Northern Russian America, winter can hardly be said to exist for that time. As early as April 5th, a thaw occurred, and, though it again got cooler, it proved to us that spring was fast approaching. On the 9th, flies made their appearance, the court-yard of the post became a swamp, and, on the 10th, I found the willows and smaller trees budding. The Russians at last became convinced that winter was over, and commenced clearing the fast-melting snow from the roofs and yard. The houses leaked much, and trenches had to be dug in the enclosure, and round the fort. It was amusing to watch the lazy employés of the Fur Company : their mode of proceeding was somewhat as follows. One Russian shoveled a few pounds of snow on to a hide. Two others then—with great appearance of fatigue—dragged it slowly to the edge of the bank and dropped it over. This unparalleled exertion rendered it necessary for the trio to sit down and smoke. After an interval of repose—and the " bidarshik " making his appearance

—with great zeal and alacrity they started to work again. The "bidarshik," satisfied that they were indefatigable servants of the Company, went in himself to take a nap, or to play a game of cards with his clerk. They repeated the process, and cleared up a few inches more; it was then time to "chi peat" (drink tea), and they adjourned for the purpose. Their mode of working was on economical principles, each doing as little as he could; the Company paid them in exact proportion.

From the 11th to the 25th of April, the weather got cooler, with slight falls of snow. After the latter date, however, the thermometer rarely fell below freezing point, and, by comparison with our winter experiences, it seemed quite warm. On the 28th of the same month, the first goose from the south arrived, and "Kuriler" was in his element. He frequently scrambled across the opening and fast-thawing ice of the river, to the island opposite our station, remaining there all night, and never returning empty-handed.

On the 5th May, the Nulato River made a decided break-up; it had shown many signs of it before, but its ardour had been nipped in the bud. This time it burst in good earnest, and on the 12th it opened still more, and ran out on the *top of the Yukon ice*, for more than a mile *up* the great river. In many places the rain had bared the ice from its usual covering of snow; it is, without doubt, a powerful agent in breaking up these great rivers. The general effect was mess and confusion; the ice dirty, and mixed with logs and débris, and the water, in tortuous streams, running all over its surface. Several persons belonging to the fort, who had been shooting on the island opposite, had much

difficulty in getting back; and Ivan, the "bidarshik," almost
came to grief, getting wedged in between loose ice, and
up to his neck in water. He was rescued by canoes from
the fort. Indians have been carried away, and drowned by
an unexpected break-up of the river, and the fish-traps are
invariably swept away.

On the 12th, musquitoes made their first appearance,
and on the 13th the swallows arrived, and were flitting
round the fort, or building under the eaves of the roof. The
indefatigable Kuriler bagged six geese, and, the following
day, ten more. The weather was now so warm and sunny,
that we felt enervated and oppressed by it.

19*th*.—First real break-up of the Yukon, the ice coming
down in a steady flow at the rate of five or six knots an hour.
For several days afterwards this continued, and was an excit-
ing scene after the monotony of the winter. A constant
stream of broken ice passed the station, now surging into
mountains as it met with some obstacle, now grinding and
crashing on its way, and carrying all before it. Whole trees
and banks were swept away before its victorious march,
and the river rose some fourteen feet above its winter level.
On the 22nd, a quantity of "black ice," *i.e.* ice discoloured
by some very dark-looking earth, went by. By the 24th, the
river was beginning to clear.

The varied conditions in which we found the ice would
make a very interesting study. Some of it was beautifully clear, representing perfect ice, whilst a larger proportion seemed to be in a sodden, half water-logged state.
One variety appeared to be riddled or honeycombed, whilst
a very common kind appeared to be in a rotten, *yet* crystalline
condition. When this struck against a second floating lump,

it cracked into a thousand fragments, and there was a constant sound as of the smashing of glass. As before stated, much dirt, and that of many shades, was mingled with the ice, and the water was as discoloured as that of the Thames at London. Much well-packed snow still remained on the miniature floating bergs; and trees, whole or in fragments, came down imbedded in them. The Russians often dragged quantities of this drift-wood ashore, and kept it for fuel and building purposes. Our man Pickett was set to work in the same way, and succeeded in collecting a good quantity.

All was now activity: the Russians preparing for their spring trading excursion, Dall and myself for our projected trip, and Mr. Dyer for his journey down the river to its mouths, where he expected to meet Mr. Everett Smith—a gentleman of our service, employed in taking soundings there. Provisions and goods had to be selected, weighed out, and packed: guns and pistols cleaned: and oars and paddles manufactured by the dozen.

The skins from our "baidarre" and Mr. Dyer's three-holed "baidarke" were taken off their frames, re-patched in rotten places, soaked in water, &c., and then again put on, well oiled, and fat rubbed into the seams. By the 25th we were all ready and anxious to get away. Although it was raining hard on the morning of the 26th, at 7 A.M.. Mr. Dyer, with two Indians, left us to descend the river, and by eight o'clock the Russians and ourselves made our start up. The Russians, with Indian workmen, numbered eight persons, under the direction of our friend "Ivan," the head man and trader of the Nulato Fort. Their skin boat was of large size, had a rudder, mast, and large square-sail: it carried over two tons of goods and provisions. Our craft was a much

smaller skin boat, yet carried five persons, a tent, blankets,
cooking utensils, and guns, two bags of biscuit (100 lbs.),
150 lbs. of flour, with smaller packages.   Our crew comprised
Kuriler, as steersman, and two Indians,—one a representative
of the Ingeletes, the other, of the Co-Yukons.   Dall and
myself paddled usually, while the others rowed: we also
carried a sail, but no rudder; Kuriler steered us with a
paddle, and helped us along at the same time.   The river was
still full of ice and drift-wood, and navigation was difficult.
The only way of ascending the stream was by keeping near,
generally *very* near the banks.   We had frequently to cross
and recross the stream to get into quieter water, and at such
times exerted ourselves specially, so that we might not lose
much by the operation.   As it was, we usually drifted down
half a mile or so.

How shall I, in few words, describe this immense stream,
one that our men were wont to compare with the Mississippi!
At Nulato, which is 600 miles above its mouths—as before
stated,—it is from bank to bank one mile and a quarter
wide, while in other places it opens out into lagoons, four
to five miles in width, studded with innumerable islands.
Our explorers have travelled up it 1800 miles.   Its tributaries—to be hereafter mentioned—would be large rivers in
Europe, and I can therefore understand the proud boast
uttered by a native of its banks, and translated for our
benefit,—" *We* are not savages, we are Yukon Indians!"

About a mile above Nulato, steep cliffs abut on the west
side of the river, showing a sandstone formation, with shale
intermingled, and with numerous plants and ferns growing at
their base.   About noon we stopped for tea; a fire was soon
made on a very shelving bank, not selected from choice, but

THE YUKON IN SPRING: BREAK UP OF THE ICE.

from necessity. A small creek of limpid ice-cold water was near it, and we enjoyed a simple lunch, and then resumed our trip.

We had proceeded but a short distance when we came to turns of the river, round which logs and ice, and drift-wood, were sweeping at a great rate. It was absolutely necessary for one man at this time to stand in the bows of the canoe, with a pole shod at one end with iron, to push away the masses of ice and tangle of drift wood, lest a collision should ensue. We saw large trees pass *under* the Russians' canoe, and positively lift it for a moment out of the water, although it weighed at least three tons and had eight men on board. This can be understood by taking into consideration the great momentum that a floating mass acquires when sweeping at the rate of six or eight miles an hour, and itself somewhat sunken by the rapidity of the current. Had the same logs struck the canoe broadside, or directly in the bows, in all probability a serious disaster would have occurred. We could often *feel* the ice and logs rolling and scraping *under* the keel of our canoe, and it was a very uncomfortable sensation. It was not the thickness of a *plank* between us and destruction, but simply that of a piece of seal-skin, an eighth or a tenth of an inch thick. Still a skin boat has its advantages; the tough flexible skin will *give* for several inches without necessarily tearing. It is in such a river infinitely safer, and will stand more wear and tear than the cedar canoes of British Columbia; and birch-barks— at least while there is yet a flow of ice in the water—are evidently very unsafe craft. On the other hand, we found that the seams where the skins were sewn together were very liable to rip,—especially on the flat bottom of the

canoe,—when passing over logs and ice, or stones and
" snags," in shallow water.

At one of the above-mentioned bluffs so difficult was it
to proceed, that the Russians, after vainly struggling against
the current, gave in, drifted down a little way, and then
camped. Our steersman grinned, and asked whether we
also meant to turn back, or whether we would run all
risks, and try to cross the great torrent into quieter water
by the other bank. We immediately saw a brilliant chance
of distinguishing ourselves, and told him we would proceed.
The Russians had rather pooh-poohed the notion of Dall
and myself—both comparatively young men—ever reaching
Fort Yukon; so we were on our mettle, and paddled and
rowed with great vigour. We had many a close shave
with the floating ice and wood, and sometimes had to stop
and drift down to let some more than usually cumbersome
mass pass on its way; but by Kuriler's excellent steering
we crossed safely, and then travelled along the bank for some
distance a-head of our Muscovite friends. Nothing could
exceed the glee of our Indians, and they could not understand how Dall and myself could show no more excitement
about it, overjoyed as we evidently were. We at length
came to a comparatively dry spot on some low ground, and
made our camp. It was on the east side of the river, and the
land was level for some distance back. It terminated at a
distance of thirty miles in the snow-capped range of the
T'Kitske Mountains. We had included a tow-line in our
apparatus, but no tracking was possible for a week after this
date; many of the lower banks and islands were submerged.
We erected our tents, and indeed needed them, as it rained
incessantly.

27th.—Started at 3 A.M., and proceeded with rather less difficulty, finding the water comparatively quiet between the numerous islands. Many of them were entirely submerged, and we floated over some of the lesser tree-tops. At noon, we arrived at the Co-Yukuk village and river: stopped at the home of our Co-Yukon boatman, and bought a large pike there—a not uncommon fish on the river. Hard by was an Indian four-post grave-box inclosed with rails, and a flag waving over it.

Near this spot the "Co-Yukuk Sofka," or mountain, terminated on the river in a very grand and steep sandstone bluff of castellated appearance, perpendicular strata taking the place of the more usual horizontal formation. Round its rugged base the water swept with terrific force, and we had again to cross the river, which at this point makes a great bend to the eastward.

We passed several small encampments of Indians, and were accompanied by a fleet of canoes, their owners all bound for the annual trading meetings at Newicargut and Nuclukayette. Their canoes were of birch-bark, covering a well constructed and light frame of willow and birch, and varied in length from eight to sixteen feet, according as they were intended for one or three persons. The seams of these frail barks are sewn with the finer roots of spruce-fir, and are caulked with spruce-gum. When a leak is discovered, they go ashore, light a small fire, warm the gum,—of which they always carry a supply,—turn the canoe bottom upwards, and rub the healing balm in a semi-fluid state into the seam until it is again water-tight. Single paddles are usually adopted ; double ones, like those used by the Greenlander in his "kyack," are occasionally seen.

It is a common thing for them to use no paddles at all in shallow water, but simply stakes or poles (like small stilts) in either hand; and they will sometimes stand up when progressing in this way.

Each man had some little dried meat, but trusted mainly to finding something by the way. They surrounded our camp with hungry looks; our plan was to give to those only who worked for us. Occasionally we allowed our Indians, when fatigued, to change with some of the owners of these birch-barks, and so kept our crew fresh. Steady exertion is foreign to them, and they made a great fuss over any trifling blisters raised on their hands in the unaccustomed exertion of rowing. Still, they behaved better than I had expected, and little Mikeshker, our Ingelete, was a capital fellow, the first to volunteer in anything that was to be done. Some of the Indians travelling up with us had cotton-drill tents made by themselves in imitation of the Russians; our own men usually rigged up our sail into a shelter tent.

Ivan, in the evening, gave us some wild-duck eggs he had obtained in trading; they were not plentiful at this part of the river. We camped on the east side of the river, after a long search for a spot of dry land.

28th.—Made an early start, 1 A.M., and crossed the river three times, once where it was two miles wide. A light breeze enabled us to use our sail with fair effect. We found at this part of the river some tall straight poplars, all, however, with a curious bend, or "kink," near the top. We passed several Indian graves and camps. The Russians, on nearing any Indian locality, announced their arrival by firing a large flint-lock gun, something of the calibre of a

whaling gun. We camped about 2 P.M. on a steep bank.
Rain fell in the evening, and it was almost welcomed, as
it kept off the musquitoes.

On the 30th we waited over a whole day in camp to
regrease our "baidarre." The Russians did the same, and
our Indian friends also, so that there was a large encampment. It rained incessantly.

31st.—We passed the fishing-village of Sachertelontin.
From this point I kept a constant running survey (bearings
and apparent distances). Our only authority—the map of
Zagoskin—terminates about this point. (With many wind-
ings, the general direction to Fort Yukon is N.E. magnetic ;
and so little does it vary from this that my notes contain
little else but points ranging from N. to E.)

1st June.—We arrived at a large opening or lagoon on
the river, about eight miles long, and five wide. It ran
in an easterly direction, and had several large islands in it.
At its termination the river again narrowed. Sandstone
bluffs and some crags of conglomerate bordered the lagoon.
Within three days we obtained one heron, two or three
ducks and geese, and a few eggs; also some beaver-meat.
The heron was decidedly tough eating; the beaver-meat was
very musk-like in flavour; the tail alone excepted, which is
the trapper's greatest luxury, and was really delicious.

The natives here, when very short of supplies, eat the
flesh of marten, owls, hawks, &c., but it is from necessity
rather than choice. They "ken eat crow, tho' they don't
hanker arter it." In point of fact, I noticed these luxuries
generally fell to the lot of the old people, who do not have a
very pleasant time of it, if they happen to get feeble or
decrepit. They are not ill used, but simply neglected.

At this part of the river's banks, we found the spruce-fir unusually large, and the river itself was full of great natural rafts of trees and drift-wood, which came whirling down with great rapidity in the ever varying current. Now they would seem to be gliding along steadily, when, all at once, they got into an eddy and spun round, so that you could not answer for their course. They frequently scraped and jarred against our canoe, and steering had to be an ever watchful operation.

2nd.—Large mountains to the N.N.E.,—the Suquonyilla range. We reached the mouth of a large stream, the Melozecargut River, which enters from the N.W. (the termination *cargut* simply means "small river" in the Co-Yukon dialect; be it observed that the Melozecargut is only small by comparison with the Yukon). We passed a large log of maple lying on the beach; our men found none growing below Fort Selkirk, so that it must have travelled from some point very near the head-waters of the Yukon. The afternoon was so intensely warm that we slept for several hours on the bank, resuming our trip in the evening, and travelling till 2 A.M. on the 3rd. On this latter day we started early, and camped with the Russians, in the early afternoon, opposite Newicargut, one of the most important halting-places on the river. The chief came over to us in the night, and invited us at once to the village, and we broke camp, and returned with him. On the S.E. side of the Yukon, we found a comparatively narrow opening, leading into a kind of bay, into which the Newicargut River empties itself. The Russians and ourselves saluted the village with a miscellaneous discharge from revolvers, carbines, and shot guns, as is the delight of all the Indians of the country, and they returned the compliment

INDIAN SUMMER ENCAMPMENT, NEWICARGUT; YUKON RIVER.

with great zest. Our man, Kuriler, blazed away, until we had to threaten to take away his powder-flask.

Here we met about 150 Indians, of a highly decorated and painted kind, wearing almost universally the double‑tailed coat, much ornamented with bead trimmings, and elaborately-worked fire‑bags, knife-sheaths, and belts. They were almost all of them living in either cotton-drill tents made by themselves, or in open booths, constructed of poles set up and tied together, roof fashion ; a few green boughs, pieces of birch bark and skins covering them. Little fires were burning everywhere, to keep off the musquitoes. The weather was intensely warm, the thermometer standing at 72° in the shade.

Yukon Fire-bag, Knife and Sheath, &c.

While the Russians were busily trading for beaver, marten, and other furs, Dall purchased about 250 lbs. of dried deer and moose meat and fat, and also a kind of native pemmican. He very kindly undertook this part of the performance, my line of business was exclusively managing the crew and the travelling arrangements. An extra canoe was bought, and two Indians engaged to navigate it; it was a sort of tender to our craft. We were not well provided with trading goods, and both Dall and myself had, in common with many of our men elsewhere, to find a good deal for the necessary payments, presents to chiefs, &c. Spare shirts, socks, pocket or sheath knives, and other possessions, gradually melted from our gaze. At this place, the Newicargut chief asked me for my towel and soap, and as he had been useful in whipping up supplies for us, I let him have them, knowing that Dall was pretty well provided in this matter. But here it did not rest, he saw me with a tooth-brush, and wanted that also. I need not say he did not get it; but the future traveller should either cut down his own kit to the lowest standard, *or* take all the little luxuries of life by the dozen. Much the same sort of thing once befell me in an airy board-and-shingle "hotel" in Cariboo, where I found a miner (evidently from Pike County, Missouri) who was engaged in cleaning up quartz specimens with my tooth-brush, of the use of which he was totally ignorant. Seeing a just perceptible shade of annoyance flitting over my face, he asked me whether I wanted it? I assured him I had done with it for ever.

In the evening of the 4th, "Larrione," a Co-Yukon, made medicine over a sick man. A group of Indians encircled the invalid; in the midst of them burnt a dim fire. A monotonous chorus in an undertone was kept up, whilst Larrione went through an elaborate performance, some details of which would be unfit for the reader's perusal. Now he appeared to draw the evil spirit from the sick man, and, wrestling with it, throw it on the fire, and then repelled, ran wildly from it with mock terror and affright. Now it had possession of him, and he gesticulated, groaned, and frothed at the mouth—the whole accompanied by a recitative, artistically managed in connection with the chorus. The affair was not unlike a weird scene in a sensation drama, taking into consideration the accessories—the overhanging trees, the twilight, the dim fire.

At last, the performance assumed a gayer tinge, the chorus grew louder and livelier; the man was supposed to be dispossessed, and he hobbled from the scene. I should imagine that the Indians were very divided in opinion on Larrione's skill; some, from the expression of their faces, were apparently impressed, others seemed to laugh his pretensions to scorn, and to look on the whole thing as a farce.

The Indians on the river had, in the summer time, a peculiarly haggard appearance, caused apparently from incessant dissipation! They were constantly dancing, singing, or eating, and slept but little. The perpetual daylight of the short summer has a wakening tendency, except when one is thoroughly fatigued, and the natives seemed to feel it.

I saw at this village, and elsewhere on the river, small chairs composed of birch-bark, intended for the use of children. The engraving explains their shape, and shows the arrangement of a piece of wood so placed that the child's limbs are not likely to become bow-shaped! The infant sits comfortably on a layer of moss, and is often carried on the maternal back on such a contrivance. The sketch is respectfully dedicated to the mothers of England, and any enterprising Oxford-street baby-jumper or rocking-chair maker is welcome to the idea.

If birch-bark is not to be obtained, let him substitute *papier maché* or gutta percha. Through the child's nose will be seen a miniature ornament, like that already described in connection with Indian children of a larger growth. In this case also "all rights are" *not* "reserved."

Indian Child's Birch-bark Chair.

CHAPTER XIX.

CANOE JOURNEY (*continued*)—ASCENT OF THE YUKON.

Meet a deserter — Indian taste for "Nigger" minstrelsy — Tracking —
Lagoon — Piles of drift-wood — Nuclukayette — Unsophisticated Indians
— Ceremony — Leave the Russians — The Indian's head — Mountain
gorge — Indian dogs — Canoe leak — The rapids — The "Ramparts" —
Moose-hunting — Islands — Overhanging banks — Shallows — Shortest
night — First English Indians — Porcupine River — Fort Yukon.

June 5th.—WE got off about 5 A.M., and travelled till the
noonday heat compelled us to camp for a time. The evening
and early morning are the only times for travelling in this
country during the brief summer. Few would believe that here,
almost in the latitude of Bering Straits, it was nearly 80° in
the shade, and the effect was nearly doubled by the fact that
this heat followed so closely on the intense cold of winter.
We wished, as far as possible, to accompany the Russian
traders, or we would long ere this have travelled exclusively
by night; but they preferred the day, for reasons best known
to themselves. After we left them we followed our own ideas
in this matter.

In the cooler afternoon we again started, and were proceeding steadily, when we were surprised to see—a little
way ahead—a large fire on the beach. Indians rarely make
such, but prefer to sit—even in winter—shivering over a
few sticks, and we felt sure that it must be the camp of a
white traveller or travellers. We landed, ran up to the

place, and found standing there a deserter from the Hudson Bay Company's fort. He had, with one Indian, descended the river thus far, when his canoe had upset, and his few worldly possessions, including his gun, had gone to the bottom. He and his companion had managed to get ashore, clinging to the canoe, and were now calmly drying their clothes, waiting for something to " turn up." We of course fraternised, and supplied them with a few necessaries. The " white man " —very slightly the whiter of the two, by-the-bye—declared that our supper that night beat anything he had eaten for years. Ivan, who camped near us, immediately asked him to " chi peat," and gave him a blanket. We tried to induce him to return with us, which he would have done willingly enough, but for the fear of being treated as a deserter. Poor fellow, he had experienced a hard life for many years, and some real or fancied grievance at Fort Yukon had caused him to take this step. He had been in the Company's service for a long period, and had entered it when quite a youth.

We learnt subsequently that he made his way to St. Michael's, and got away on a vessel touching there. As he had been through a large part of the Hudson Bay and Russian American Companies' posts *from the Atlantic to the Pacific*, he had certainly made the " North-west-passage " by land with a vengeance.

6th.—Bidding adieu to the stranger in the afternoon, we travelled steadily till 4 A.M. on the 7th. There was no darkness whatever—night was no night : a subdued twilight stood in its place, and the sunset glow never left the horizon till it merged in sunrise. The Indians worked steadily *for Indians ;* we did our best to keep them in a good humour, and they were specially fond of harmony. I will guarantee that any future traveller on the river, within the next few years, will hear snatches of "nigger" minstrelsy which we taught them. They readily acquired simple tunes; their great favourites were "Marching through Georgia," and "Excelsior." The latter, with its insane chorus of *Upidee-idee-ida!* is well adapted for any nation, people, or tongue.

The water had now fallen several feet, and we began to get a good deal of tracking. Our Indians were sometimes barefooted, but more commonly wore the water (or summer) boots of the country, *i. e.*, boots made entirely from seal-skin well greased, and waterproof, and varying only in length. The work was no joke; now they were floundering in slimy mud, now climbing over logs or round small rocky bluffs, with the line fixed to their shoulders, and the current making the canoe drag on them. The steersman had enough to do to keep the boat off shore or out of too shallow water. We again entered a lagoon of the river, running in a northerly direction for twenty-five miles, with high bluffs on the east side, and, as usual, full of islands. Rounding one of these appeared an interminable journey, and Dall seriously asked me to turn the canoe round; he considered we were in some tributary of the Yukon! We at last reached the main stream, however; the island was fifteen miles in length.

On the 7th we passed low swampy land, whose principal production appeared to be musquitoes, and early on the 8th reached the mouth of a large stream entering from the W., and known by the Indians as the Towshecargut River. At the confluence we found an immense pile of drift-wood, perhaps fifty feet high, the accumulation of ages. We lighted our fire near it, took our regular dose of tea, and then proceeded on our journey. We again got a favourable

P

breeze for a short time. The river there was very wide, with
many islands. In the evening we made the junction of the
Tanana River and the Yukon, between which, on a tongue of
land, Nuclukayette, an Indian trading ground of importance,
is situated. We purposely passed it by nearly two miles, and
then, with the Russians and a whole fleet of Indian canoes,
crossed the river, so that with drifting down we should just
make the village. On arrival the Russians fired their large
gun, and we kept up a running volley from our miscellaneous
collection of arms.

This place is the furthest point ever reached by the
Russian traders, and is about 240 miles above Nulato.
Within the last two or three years some of the Hudson
Bay Company's men have also come down with trading
goods to this village. Hither come Indians from all quarters.
Co-Yukons, Newicarguts, Tananas, and even the Kotch-á-
kutchins from Fort Yukon. On some occasions their gatherings have numbered 600 persons. The Tananas had not
arrived, but we met a number afterwards. I believe them
to be the most unsophisticated Indians to be met with at the
present day. They were gay with painted faces, feathers in
their long hair, patches of red clay at the back of their heads
covered with small fluffy feathers, double-tailed coats and
pantaloons of buckskin much adorned with fringes and beads,
and elaborately-worked fire-bags and belts. They reminded
me of the ideal North American Indian I had read of but
never seen.

On landing at this village a ceremony had to be gone
through, possibly to test whether we had "strong hearts"
or not. The Indians already there, advanced, whooping,
yelling, and brandishing their guns till they reached us, and

TANANA INDIAN.

then discharged them in the air.   We, with the Indians just arrived, returned the compliment, and then the chief whose acquaintance we had made during winter came forward and welcomed us.   This man had treated Ketchum and Labarge very well in their trip in the winter, and they had left a letter for us, asking us to give him powder, &c.   We found this place almost bare of provisions ; the Indians dancing and singing all the same with empty stomachs, knowing that the season for moose-hunting was at hand.   The chief and some others brought us small quantities of sweet fat.

We had expected to meet Antoine Houle, a half-breed interpreter from the English fort ; but he had left the day before we arrived, having traded all his goods.   He had virtually been starved out of this village.   We despatched an Indian "express" after him, to ask him to wait and bear us company ; but the man returned without succeeding in reaching him, having delayed by the way to shoot two moose.

9th.—We rested here till half-past three o'clock in the afternoon, and then bade adieu to our Russian friends.   We hired an Indian from the Nuclukayette village, in place of one of those from Newicargut ; and he proved a good, sturdy, steady-going native, with an intimate acquaintance with the great river.   Several canoes again accompanied us, each with a wooden bowl or birch-bark basket of embers on board, the smoke from which kept off the musquitoes, and enabled the travellers to raise a fire ashore at camp time, or when their craft required repairs.   Among our Indian escort at this time were some Tananas.   I have spoken of the patches of red clay stuck on the back of their heads, and their purpose, which is one of adornment.   But when they are not in full dress, when the feathers have tumbled out and left a mass of fluff

and dirt in the hair, it has a very disagreeable appearance.
The first time I observed it I supposed the man had some
terrible head disease, and offered him a small piece of soap,
requesting him at the same time to keep out of my tent till
he had washed himself. He took the soap, smiled at my
ignorance of the fashions, and went away. I suspect his
head is unwashed to the present day. It is a question
whether he had ever before seen soap.

Immediately above Nuclukayette the river narrows, and is
shut in by wooded hills and craggy heights. From this
point we travelled exclusively by night, or by what stood in
its place. As we had two men navigating our birch-bark tender, we were able to change our crew occasionally, and keep
all pretty fresh. Birch-barks are so easily navigated that I
should adopt them exclusively if travelling in that country
again. The dogs belonging to the Indians with us went the
larger part of the journey *by land,* and often had a good deal
of trouble in getting round the cliffs jutting into the river.
When we crossed the stream—an event of constant occurrence—they swam after us through very swift rapids, and
where there was a width of half or three-quarters of a mile.
These dogs had a better time of it, though, than those at
the Russian forts, where it was usual in summer to let
them forage for themselves. Here they always got something given them, and often fed luxuriously. They proved
of a good deal of use, as they constantly scoured the woods
for something eatable. In the evening they found a
young moose, which they surrounded till the Indians were
enabled to kill it. We travelled this night about twenty-six
miles.

Early in the morning of the 10th we found our skin

boat leaking badly from having touched on rocks. We immediately went ashore, and found too large slits ripped in the seams. Fortunately, Indian women among those accompanying us were ready to sew the places for a consideration of a (penny) looking-glass, and a few trifles, to which we added a cup of tea with a little broken biscuit floating on the top of it—a *ruse* worthy of the traveller's notice whose supply may be limited. The biscuit swells considerably, and looks imposing, while it serves to disguise the weakness of the tea !

10*th*, 11*th*.—Started about 2 P.M., and again tracked the larger part of the distance. Travelled generally in a N.N.E. direction. In the evening we came to the " Rapids;" an exaggerated account of which, derived from the Russians, had made us fear that we might find great difficulty in passing them. The river here is comparatively narrow, and a long island of rocks, at that time submerged, makes an obstruction, and the water boils, fumes, and frets around them. But there is a clear channel on either side ; that on the west side is especially good. There were other rocks more or less submerged, and the water was very strong, running perhaps seven knots. For the greater part of the way we tracked from rocks on the west side, occasionally having to take our Indians on board, and paddle with great vigour. It would be easy to make this a sensational affair, but in truth we passed them without great difficulty. A steamer could go through them, except perhaps for the first fortnight in June, when the water is at its strongest. A good deal, however, depends on the height of the water. Ketchum, the previous year, found it ten feet higher, and therefore could not track from the rocky bank. The water had fallen at this time at least twelve feet (from its highest point of the season).

The heights surrounding the gorge we were now passing through are known (at Fort Yukon) as the "Ramparts," from crags and rocks of castellated structure which tower grandly above the river.

The Indians brought Dall a fossil tooth of a large size, and there is little doubt that some interesting collections might be made in this direction.   See Appendix (VI.).

A small stream enters the Yukon about six miles above the "Rapids" on the west side, known as the Klakin-ikot River.   The dogs found a porcupine, and one of the Indians shot it.

We camped at 4 A.M., finding wild gooseberry and currant bushes on the bank.   I had previously seen a quantity of wild rhubarb, which the Indians gather in quantities, and it really was very little inferior in flavour to the cultivated kind.   The wild rose was everywhere abundant.

11th, 12th.—We made a start at half-past 4 P.M., still passing through a mountain gorge, but of a more open nature.   About 9 P.M. found we had again damaged our canoe, and stopped to repair it.

This part of the river abounds with moose.   At this season the musquitoes in the woods are a terrible scourge, and even the moose cannot stand it.   He plunges into the water, and wades or swims as the case may be, often making for the islands.*   This is therefore a favourite part of the Yukon for the Indian hunter.   The moose are scarce below

---

* In some cases the Indians in numbers surround an island known to have moose or reindeer on it, and a regular *battue* ensues.

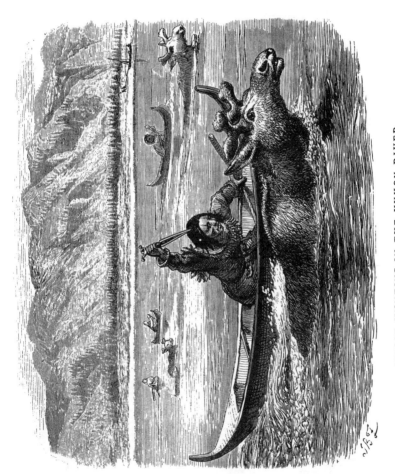

MOOSE HUNTING IN THE YUKON RIVER.

Nuclukayette, and never known as low as Nulato.   They
must, however, be abundant on the smaller rivers; as, for
example, on the Newicargut, where the meat obtained was
nearly all of this animal.   In winter, it is said, the Indians
can, by following them on snow shoes, tire them out, and
so get near enough to kill them.

Later in the evening the dogs found one near the river,
and fastened on him, and he was soon despatched.   In the
water he is a very clumsy animal.   The meat is excellent;
far above deer or even reindeer meat, and its nose, properly
stewed down, is a great luxury; better to my mind than the
other extremity of the beaver, its tail, which is everywhere
considered something specially delicious.

But for the occasional excitement of hunting, our trip
on this part of the river would have been very monotonous.

On the 13th June the dogs again routed a moose out of
the woods, and we easily shot it.   Early the next morning
we shot a second.   On the evening of the 15th we were
proceeding steadily when we saw a cow-moose with a calf
following her, swimming for the very bank that we must
pass, and paying no attention whatever to us, although we,
made a good deal of noise.   I instantly jumped ashore,
and ran along the beach, but the mother was too quick
for me, and managed to get into the woods.   I shot the
calf, with some qualms of conscience, I must admit.   It
proved the very finest meat we had tasted ; others were shot
subsequently by us, and one was killed in the water by the
knife of an Indian.   The natives do not always waste powder
and shot over them, but get near the moose, manœuvring
round in their birch-bark canoes till the animal is fatigued,
and then stealthily approach and stab it in the heart or

loins.   When full grown they weigh 700 lbs. and upwards, and *have* been obtained 1200 lbs. in weight.

Yukon Indian's Knife.

As long as we were among the "Ramparts" we tracked constantly from the beach, but on the 15th we emerged from the gorge, and found the river again opening out into lagoons and shallows with innumerable islands. The banks are much worn away and undermined by the current. It is no uncommon thing to find trees growing with their roots dangling in the air, and only supported by a little moss-bound earth. These are, of course, frequently falling in. It was sometimes difficult to avoid getting our canoe half-filled with loose earth which was slipping from these "leaning" banks, and the edges of the river were much obstructed by half-sunken trees and logs. We frequently tracked from the water, our men proceeding carefully for long distances in apparently interminable shallows. Our baidarre seams ripped frequently, and needed constant sewing; and travel was therefore somewhat harassing.

19th, 20th.—The water alternately strong and shallow, sometimes both together. Early on the 20th a terrific rain cloud burst over us: at last we gave in from sheer fatigue, drenched to the skin. We soon made all right by raising a gigantic fire near a pile of driftwood. On other American rivers wood for a steamer is sometimes a matter of difficulty ; here it is ready, only requiring to be cut into lengths.

21*st*, 22*nd*.—We knew that we could not be far from our destination, and travelled hard to make it. This was the shortest night of the year : the sun setting at a few minutes after 11, and rising about a quarter to 12. How near we were to the Arctic circle I leave to those who thoroughly understand the subject ; suffice it to say, the sun was absent from our gaze not over forty-five minutes.

Towards 7 o'clock in the morning we met the first of the Upper Indians, a branch of the Kotch-á-kutchins. They were camped by a " slough " of the river, engaged in drying fish, some of which they were glad to trade for our tobacco— the supply at Fort Yukon having been exhausted. They were apparently better provided with guns, clothing, and tents, than the " Russian " Indians. They were cleaner, and better mannered. In the course of the morning their chief—" Sakneota " (known as " Senitee " at the fort)— arrived, and immediately made us a present of moose-meat, and we returned the compliment in some trifles.

22*nd*, 23*rd*.—We determined this night to make our destination, and let nothing stop us ; and therefore halted twice for rest and refreshment in place of once as heretofore.

We travelled very steadily, refusing to listen to our Indians, who were very fatigued, and wished to camp ; and a little before noon we made the mouth of the Rat or Porcupine River, entering the Yukon from the North. Half a mile's paddling brought us in sight of Fort Yukon, and we gave vent to our jubilant feelings in a volley of fire-arms, which was immediately answered from shore. As to Kuriler,

he blazed away till we were all deaf, but for once we let
him have his way. Landing, we found two young Scotch-
men, and a French half-breed, the sole occupants of the
Fort, the commander and many of his men being absent
on the annual trip for supplies. A large crowd of Indians,
awaiting their return, were camped outside. We shook
hands with everybody—including the Indians—and were
soon installed in a room of the Fort. Thus ended a journey
of 600 miles, occupying twenty-nine days; twenty-six of which
had been engaged in actual travel.

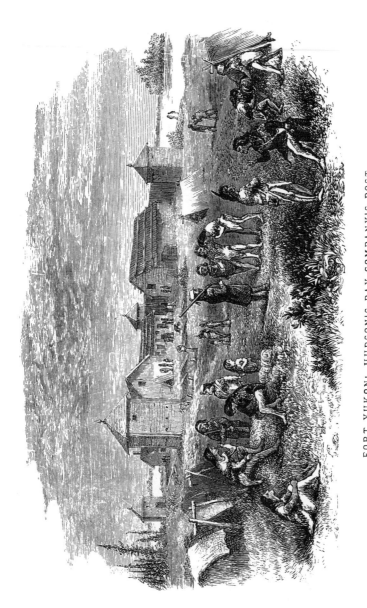

FORT YUKON; HUDSON'S BAY COMPANY'S POST.

CHAPTER XX.

FORT YUKON.

Return of the Commander and Missionary — Information received from
them — Mackenzie and the Yukon — The Indians — Numerous tribes —
The furs — Fictitious black fox — Missionary work — Return of our
explorers from the Upper Yukon — Fort Yukon sledges, &c.

ON the 26th June the commander—Mr. MacDougall—returned, and with him the Rev. Mr. MacDonald, a missionary
of the Church of England stationed there. Both of these
gentlemen welcomed us warmly, and in their society we
spent many pleasant hours.

Their news from the outer world was later than ours.
Copies of ' The Nor-wester,' a paper published in Red River
Settlement, and of dates up to the end of 1866, told us of the
successful working of the Atlantic cable, and many other
events of the day.

Our new friends did all that was possible to make our
stay agreeable, and as they had just brought in their season's
goods, we fared luxuriously for such an out-of-the-world place.
Our stores, too, were of some assistance; yet we had a taste
of the kind of life they endure year after year. Moose-meat
boiled, varied by boiled moose-meat, alternating with the
meat of moose boiled, was our staple diet! This fort is so
inaccessible that little else but trading goods are brought in.
The commander, and one or two of the men, get a small
allowance of flour, and all get a few pounds of tea, but

the quantity is so small, that it does not hold out more than two or three months, and for the remainder of the year they return to the eternal moose. Everything brought to this station is transported through the whole series of forts from York Factory in Hudson's Bay; the men of each post contributing something towards their transmission. The employés of Fort Yukon fetch their goods* from La Pierre's house, a small post on the upper part of the Porcupine River, a distance of 600 miles. The trip occupies them twenty days ascending the Porcupine, camping regularly, and but five or six days descending it without camping. Between La Pierre's house and the Peel River, a tributary of the Mackenzie, mountains intervene, and a long *portage* of eighty miles has to be made, over which the goods are packed on men's shoulders for the greater part of the distance. The nearest station on Peel River is Fort McPherson, which is situated thirty miles above its confluence with the Mackenzie. The nearest fort on the Mackenzie is Fort Simpson, distant 1500 miles from Fort Yukon.

The Porcupine or Rat River is undoubtedly that mentioned in Mackenzie's 'Voyages.' When on the great stream that now bears his name, he was told of a river " in comparison of which," he says, " that on whose banks we then were was

---

* I took the measurements of the boats used for this trip, thinking that it might prove an item of importance to some future expedition. The boats, when loaded with a hundred " pieces," or packages of an average weight of ninety pounds, draw only 2 to 2½ feet of water, and are of the following dimensions :—

Total length ..   41 feet.
Length of keel   29 „
Depth from gunnel to keel 3 feet 2 inches.
Width of beam 9 feet 6 inches.

but a small stream, that the natives were very large and
very wicked, and kill common men with their eyes," that
they were "adorned with wings," and that they could eat
"a large beaver at a single meal." His informants also described it as falling into a great lake or sea. Now the Porcupine, with its virtual continuation the Yukon, answers well
enough to this; but it need hardly be said that the people
—as we found them—were comparatively commonplace
after this description.

Fort Yukon was founded in 1847. The present erection
was, however, commenced in 1864, and was in an unfinished
condition last year (1867). The older fort was built a mile
higher up the river, but the bank on which it was placed
had been gradually undermined by the strong current, and
the process of destruction had almost reached the gate of the
station. It may fairly be considered as the most remote of
the Hudson Bay Company's Forts, and is in approximately the
high latitude of 66° N. It is well known to be within
the boundary line of Russian-America, and the Hudson's Bay
Company did for a time, at least, pay the Russian-American
Fur Company for the privilege of trading within their
territory.

After our experience of the rather dirty Russian forts, it
was quite a relief to find newly plastered walls, glazed
windows, capital floors, open fire-places, and a general appearance of cleanliness. In addition to the dwellings of the
commander and men, there were magazines, stores, fur room,
fur press, ice and meat wells.

The river near the fort has no less than five distinct
channels, and intervening islands prevent your seeing from
bank to bank.

After a few days the Indians mustered very strongly; canoe after canoe arrived, and there was a constant blazing of musketry, as though the fort was in a state of siege. Over 500 natives were at one time congregated outside the station. They erected tents, open booths, and "lodges;" the latter being constructed of poles and moose-hides, and usually placed two together, the doorways facing each other, with a small fire burning between them. Each male, on arrival at the fort, received a present of a small cake of tobacco and a clay pipe; and those who were out of provisions drew a daily ration of moose-meat from the commander, which rather taxed the resources of the establishment. Indian hunters are attached to the fort, and some of the canoes brought in large loads of fresh and dried meat.

There was a decided difference between the Upper and Lower Yukon forms of clothing. At this place we saw quantities of buck-skin dresses; and mocassins were commonly worn. The leading men of the tribes assembled wore mock uniforms, presented to them by the Company; old "Red Leggings" in particular, one of the Kotch-á-kutchin chiefs, was gorgeous in one with immense gilt epaulets, brass buttons, and trimmings, and had as many coloured ribbons hanging from his cap as would stock ten recruiting sergeants for life. Many had "capotes," shirts, and coats of civilized appearance, purchased in the store. In winter these people wear moose-skin shirts or robes, with the hair turned inwards.

We here met the representatives of many tribes. The Kotch-á-kutchins* (or lowland people) are the Indians of

---

* In the Appendix (V.) will be found a full vocabulary of the Kotch-á-kutchin dialect made by the late Major Kennicott, whose death whilst

the immediate neighbourhood. Higher on the Yukon (or
Pelly as it has been long marked in our maps) dwell two
tribes, the "An Kutchins" and the "Tatanchok Kutchins."
The former are known by the "voyageurs" of the Company
by the flattering epithet of *Gens de foux*, and the latter bear
the name of *Gens de bois*. Some of the *Gens de bouleau*, or
Birch River Indians, and *Gens de rats* or Rat (or Porcupine)
River Indians were also present. Large numbers of the
Tanana Indians, *Gens de butte* (or knoll people), the original
"mountain men," mustered on this occasion, and were, as I
have before stated, undoubtedly the most primitive people
we met. Their clothing was much be-fringed with beads,
and many of them wore through the nose (as did most
of the other Indian *men* present), an ornament composed of
the Hya-qua shell (*Dentalium entalis* or *Entalis vulgaris*).
Both of the Fur Companies on the river trade with them,
and at very high prices. These shells* were formerly used,

---

engaged in our service I have already recorded. It was compiled long
before, during his visit to the territory in 1859-62, when he passed through
the larger part of the Hudson's Bay Company's posts. He never lived to
make the trip nearest his heart—that from the Pacific (Norton Sound,
Bering Sea) to Fort Yukon, the journey above described. His lengthened
journey just mentioned was made from the *Atlantic* States, and Fort
Yukon was the furthest point he reached.

* See the 'Proceedings of the Zoological Society of London,' March 8th,
1864, where specimens, brought home by J. K. Lord, Esq., are commented
on by Dr. Baird. Mr. Lord says, speaking of their use among the inhabitants of Vancouver Island and British Columbia and adjoining coasts,
"The value of the *Dentalium* depends upon its length. Those representing
the greater value are called, when strung together end to end, a 'Hi-qua;'
but the standard by which the Dentalium is calculated to be fit for a
'Hiqua' is that twenty-five shells placed end to end must make a fathom,
or six feet in length. At one time a 'Hiqua' would purchase a male

and still are to some extent, as a medium of currency by the natives of Vancouver Island, and other parts of the north-west coast. I saw on the Yukon fringes and head ornaments, which represented a value in trade of a couple of hundred marten skins.

Of the great river on which the Tanana people dwell we know nothing. From information derived at Fort Yukon I infer that its upper waters are not far from the Upper Yukon. The Tananas sometimes cross to Fort Yukon by a land route. From the diminished volume of the Yukon water *above* the confluence of the Tanana River, the latter must evidently be a very grand stream.

The women of all these upper tribes dress more simply than the men, and wear few ornaments. They do more drudgery than the females of the Lower Yukon and coast of Russian-America. They adopt a loose sack garment very plainly cut, with large loose sleeves. In the fort some of the Indian women wore European clothing.

It is said that some of the chiefs and "big Injiens" of these tribes, have large piles of beads—of which they make no use —secreted miser-like in the woods. They had bought them, not knowing how better to invest their capital, after acquiring all the guns, blankets, knives, and pots they needed. Generally they appeared to thrive under the auspices of the Hudson's Bay Company, who I believe treat them better

---

slave, equal in value to fifty blankets, or about 50*l.* sterling." These shells are generally obtained from the west coast of Vancouver Island.

Although I have, in the above quotation, followed Mr. Lord in his method of spelling the word "Hiqua," I must lean to my own mode printed in the text as conveying a closer approximation to the usual pronunciation of the word.

than they do their own employés at these inaccessible posts. The first Indian who brings furs can get anything there is in the fort: the men can only draw a fixed amount of clothing and tobacco, and get the poorest kind of provisions. I am well aware that this is not the case in the larger forts and factories, but at a place like Fort Yukon—which must be, by the way, a profitable station—no provisions worth speaking of are brought in at all, although large quantities of heavy goods, hardware, guns, &c., are transported thither.

The fur room of the fort was a sight not to be witnessed every day; thousands of marten skins hanging from the beams, and huge piles of common furs lying round. They also get a very respectable number of silver-grey and black foxes. *À propos* of the latter I once heard an anecdote, bearing rather heavily on the Hudson's Bay Company. A man in their service purchased—in the hurry of trading—a fictitious black-fox skin; one that had been originally white, but that had been dyed by Mr. Indian, perhaps as a grim joke on the Company. Of course the fraud was eventually discovered, but it did not end there. The *full commercial value* of the fur was charged against the salary of the unfortunate trader, who thus paid more pounds than it had cost shillings at the time of purchase. If this be true, comment is superfluous.

The wolverine is specially valued by all the Indians, on account, doubtless, of the difficulty in capturing it. These furs—in commerce nearly worthless—are yet bought by the Hudson's Bay Company, who then entrust them to Indians well known at the forts, to trade at a distance for marten or other skins. Mr. Red-skin is allowed half profits.

The tariff fixed for Fort Yukon was rather higher than that of the Russian posts. A gun nominally worth about forty shillings brought twenty "skins." This term is the old one employed by the Company. One "skin" (beaver) is supposed to be worth two shillings, (!) and it represents two marten, and so on. You heard a great deal about "skins" at Fort Yukon, as the workmen were also charged for clothing, &c., in this way. If we asked the worth of a pair of unmentionables, we were told six "skins:" a pair of common mocassins represented one skin, and so on.

During our stay, the Rev. Mr. MacDonald, who is a representative of our Church Missionary Society, held several services with the Indians, addressing them sometimes directly, and sometimes through the fort interpreter, Antoine Houle, —a man who speaks French, English, and any number of Indian dialects. They listened with apparent attention, and joined in some singing. This gentleman has taught some of the younger people to read English, and his influence is doubtless good. I could not, however, help thinking, that with an audience of Indians, representing half-a-dozen different tribes, speaking as many dialects, it must be very questionable whether they all understand the missionary's words. As in other places, so here, there is a general jargon called "broken slavee," used for purposes of intercourse; but such a bastard dialect will barely express the language of common life, how much less then the figurative language of the Bible! * One of the great difficulties in Mr. Mac-

---

* We find in our own land that the Oriental tinge, the metaphors and parables of the Bible, render it somewhat hard to be understood, though we are addressed by teachers of our own race, who have a perfect command of our own language. The missionary, with at the best a foreigner's knowledge of a strange tongue, *addresses those who have no collateral education to assist them,* and who know little of anything but their own immediate

Donald's way in this place, is that the Indians are for the larger part of the year scattered all over the country, hundreds of miles apart. Of the gentleman himself, I can only speak in the highest terms; he is an undoubtedly earnest and zealous missionary, and he has one point in his favour, that so far, no whisky trader has come in to interfere with the good work in which he is engaged, and that no rival sect—so far as Fort Yukon is concerned—is present to unsettle the minds of his converts.

It is worthy of mention that minute specks of gold have been found by some of the Hudson's Bay Company's men in the Yukon, but not in quantities to warrant a "rush" to the locality.

On the 29th June, Ketchum and Labarge returned from their trip to Fort Selkirk. It will be remembered that in the winter they left us at Nulato, and were to proceed on the frozen Yukon to the Hudson's Bay Fort. This trip they had performed, but with great difficulty. It had occupied them nearly two months, owing mainly to the softness of the snow, and insufficient dog-feed. The river, too, commenced its break-up before they reached Fort Yukon, and their journey lay through rotten ice and water.

As soon as the river broke up fairly, and at about the same time that we started for Fort Yukon, *they* started for Fort Selkirk (always known as Mr. Campbell's Fort), now

---

surroundings. I have shown before how a phenomenon of nature had no name in the Chinook jargon, and that the phrase "children of the forest" could only be translated in a manner to excite the Indian's laughter. It is not, then, difficult to understand how the poetry of the Bible might become the subject of a jest, and its imagery be wholly unintelligible.

an abandoned station. Great difficulty had been experienced by the Hudson's Bay Company in keeping that fort supplied with trading goods; and Indians coming from a distance, and unable to sell their furs, had threatened the garrison on several occasions. After it was deserted, the natives had burnt it down; Ketchum brought us a piece of its blackened remains.

He found the Upper Yukon running for the most part through mountain gorges, but navigable for the whole distance (600 miles). Their supplies of meat and game had been good, the Indians everywhere peaceable and desirous of seeing more of the white man: their trip had been made in twenty-nine days, ascending and camping every night, and four days descending the stream (without camping). The general course of the river agreed with that laid down on Arrowsmith's maps. Ketchum gave me two fir-cones, brought from Fort Selkirk, which Dr. Hooker kindly examined, and determined to be *Pinus contorta*—a variety never observed by us on the lower course of the Yukon, much of which is, be it observed, in a higher latitude.

I had, in conversation with the Rev. Mr. MacDonald, learnt that the Indians from the Chilcat River (N.W. coast of Russian America, about lat. 59° N.) sometimes came across to the Yukon, at Fort Selkirk, in fifteen or twenty days. Ketchum's enquiries elicited the same fact, which has been confirmed since my return to England by information obtained from Captain Dodd, of the 'Beaver'* by Admiral

---

* The old 'Beaver,' now temporarily used as a surveying vessel on the coast of British Columbia, was the first steam-vessel on the Pacific. She

Collinson, C.B., who has very obligingly laid before me
extracts from his private journal (kept on H.M.S. 'Enterprise'
when engaged in the search for Sir John Franklin).   Up
to the present time, I believe, no white man has ever made
the journey.   Mr. Campbell used, by means of the natives,
to communicate with Captain Dodd on board the 'Beaver'
in Lynn Canal.   A copy of a chart, rudely drawn by the
natives, was obtained by Admiral Collinson.   This sketch-
map showed a river, emptying into the *West* branch of
Lynn Canal, which the natives ascended, and then made
a land journey to a lake which itself was the source of
the Lewis River, a tributary of the Yukon.   The *return*
journey occupied them fifty days, much of it being against
the stream.

The Rat Indians (the natives on the Rat or Porcupine
River, who trade at Fort Yukon) also communicate—
mainly *viâ* the Mackenzie River—with the coast natives.
In an extract from Admiral Collinson's journal (July 24th,
1854, Camden Bay), I find the following note.   Speaking of
some delay, he says, "It was so far fortunate as it enabled
our Baxter Island friends (the Esquimaux) to pay us
another visit, and we soon found out that they had several
strangers with them, the chief of whom produced a paper
on which was written, 'The printed slips of paper delivered

---

was taken out in 1835 (*viâ* Cape Horn) by the Hudson's Bay Company,
and this fact deserves to be recorded, as it was not till 1838 that the 'Great
Western'—the pioneer of our ocean service to America—made her first trip
across the Atlantic.   The "Beaver" is now commanded by Lieut. Pender,
R.N., who has been so often honourably mentioned in connection with this
survey by Sir Roderick I. Murchison, in his annual addresses to the Royal
Geographical Society.

by the officers of H.M.S. "Plover," on the 25th April, 1854, to the Rat Indians, were received on the 27th June (of the same year), at the Hudson's Bay Company's establishment, Fort Yukon.' The Rat Indians are in the habit of making periodical trading excursions to the Esquimaux along the sea-coast. They are a harmless, inoffensive, set of Indians, ever ready and willing to render every assistance they can to whites." This paper was signed by Mr. Hardisty, then clerk in charge of Fort Yukon, now commander of the whole district (Mackenzie River, northern department). These facts may be of some value to the future traveller in that country.

The sledge used at this fort, and generally through the Hudson's Bay territory, at this part of the continent, is perhaps the simplest in the world. It is nothing but a plank twelve to sixteen feet in length, one end bent upwards, in a prowlike form, having been softened by steam for the purpose. Thongs keep the curved end in its place, and a few cross pieces and lashings complete it. It is a kind specially adapted for soft snow. Runners are occasionally, but by no means universally, added. The snow shoes commonly adopted were shorter than those employed by the Russians, and were pointed at either end.

Fort Yukon Sledge (loaded).

CHAPTER XXI.

DESCENT OF THE YUKON.

Drifting down the stream — Yukon salmon — Arrival at Nulato — Overdose of arsenic and alcohol — Trip resumed — Indian music — Anvic —
The mission — Earthquake *on the water* — Andreavski — The mouths of
the Yukon — Smith's observations — Pastolik — St. Michael's — Progress
of the telegraph — Frozen soil — Scurvy — Arrival of our barque —
Plover Bay — Return to San Francisco.

On the 8th July, our " baidarre " having been repaired, we
took two additional birch-bark canoes, and all started down,
determined to travel day and night to Nulato. Bidding
adieu to our friends, who honoured us with a grand salvo of
musketry, we pushed out into the stream, and soon found we
should have little need to exert ourselves. The current took
us at the rate of 100 miles a day (of twenty-four hours); and
usually our canoes were all lashed together, with sometimes
a rude awning erected over all three, under which we smoked
and dozed. We slept and ate our frugal meals on board,
only going ashore twice or thrice a day, to boil our tea and
fry our fish. This was indeed a holiday excursion, and all
the more appreciated after our experience of ascending the
stream. All that was necessary was for one man to steer;
and, except when we drifted out of the current, or stuck on
a bar, our trip was made without trouble of any kind. I do
not, of course, propose to narrate the incidents of our return
journey to Nulato, as it was over the same part of the river

that we had already passed over. On the 10th we arrived at the "Rapids" above Nuclukayette, and found the island of rocks looming out of the water very distinctly, and the current much less strong than before. Early on the 11th we reached Nuclukayette; the Indians had separated, and only a few remained on the opposite side of the river, drying fish.

The Yukon salmon is by no means to be despised. One large variety is so rich that there is no necessity, when frying it, to put fat in the pan. They are taken all down the river in weirs set in shallow places, in hand-nets of circular form, and by spearing. We saw the very pretty sight of a whole fleet of birch-barks, proceeding together as regularly as a company of soldiers. At a given signal the owners of each dipped his round hand-net into the water, and if, on raising it, a big salmon came up struggling to get away, there was a general shout of derision. I saw so much harmless fun and amusement among these Indians, and they evidently find so much enjoyment in hunting and fishing, that I could only wish they might never see much of the white man, and never learn the baneful habits and customs he is sure to introduce.

There are at least two, and I think three, varieties of Yukon salmon.* The larger kind sometimes measures five feet. I have seen boots whose sides were made of the tough skin; they are, however, not common, and are confined to the Lower Yukon and coast. On the 13th we arrived at

---

* Two varieties of Yukon salmon (obtained through the Hudson's Bay Company), *Salmo consuetus* and *Salmo dermatinus*, are described in the 'Zoology of the Voyage of H.M.S. *Herald*.'

Nulato. Our journey had occupied but five days twenty hours for 600 miles.* Here we received an indefinite communication with regard to our company ; one part of it was however plain,—that every thing portable was to be brought to St. Michael's.

In our absence P——, a workman, had stolen some arsenically prepared alcohol, intended for the preservation of natural history specimens. Wishing to ingratiate himself with the Russians, and, as we charitably presumed, believing the alcohol to be pure, he gave some of them a good drink. The result can be imagined. Our poor Muscovite friends suffered severely from inward gripes and colic ; had it not been for the large quantity they had taken they would have been killed. The overdose saved them.

Before leaving we obtained a larger skin boat and two extra Indians, and at half-past eleven of the evening of the 15th July we made a start down the great river, determining to travel as before without camping. Before six o'clock next morning we passed Coltog, the point where we had in our sledge journey first struck the Yukon. This, a distance of forty-five miles, was made within seven hours, a result due partly to our vigorous rowing, partly to the swift current. We passed many Indian villages, at which the Ingeletes were drying fish. Our Indians, as well as ourselves, made the hills and river-banks echo with songs; all of us feeling "gay and festive," as the Americans say, and cheerfully looking forward to seeing our ships. I could not help

---

* It will be remembered that the same distance had taken us twenty-six days *ascending* the stream.

remarking the air of an Indian chorus sung by our boat-
men—usually in unison—which is here presented to the
reader, a "song without words."

It was said to be an obsolete song, for the words were not
intelligible to the present people of the Yukon.

On the 17th, at 3 A.M., we reached Yakutzkelignik, an
Indian village then uninhabited, and later in the day we
passed several small villages, among the principal of which
was Shaglook, which is situated on the western bank, opposite
the mouth of a river of the same name, and where a great
"slough" of the Yukon exists. At several of the villages we
obtained salmon, dried and fresh, and one white swan, which
proved very tough eating. In the evening we came to
rapids, of which the Russians had given us a very exaggerated
account. A steep bluff abutting on the river, and no beach,
makes "tracking" from the bank difficult, but the current is
simply unusually strong, and we saw no falls whatever.

On the 18th a head wind impeded us, and we stopped at
the village of Anvic, at the mouth of the river of the same
name. It is one of the largest Indian settlements of the
Lower Yukon. There we saw native pots and jars of clay,
well fashioned, and used by the Indians for cooking purposes.
The natives there, and generally on the lower river, were
of miserable appearance and badly clothed; they see less of
traders than even the upper Indians. They were very easily
satisfied with our payments for fish, &c. For five needles,
or less than that number, we could buy a thirty-pound

salmon, and tobacco went further than we had ever known it do before. Glazoonav, the first Russian explorer of the Yukon, reached this point from the northern mouth of the river in 1835.

19th.—Head wind. We passed three villages, at one of which the wooden bowls, or "contogs" used all over the country, are manufactured. The tribe inhabiting this part of the country is known as the "Primoske" people. On the 20th, at half-past four in the morning, we reached the " Missie," or Mission, once exclusively what its name implies, but now both the residence of a priest of the Greek Church and the sole Russian trading post on the lower river. We met the priest, or "pope," as the Russians term him, afterwards at St. Michael's, and a very saintly and heavily-bearded individual he was, but said to be by no means averse to the bottle. The inferior clergy of the Greek Church generally are, as far as my experience goes, a convivial and social set of men. At Petropaulovski, on one festive occasion, the most inebriated person present was one of these representatives of the Church. It struck us as a very curious thing to hear the foreign merchants at the above town speaking of Madame ——, the "pope's wife," although we were well aware that the Greek clergy were allowed to marry. I had the honour of dancing, on one occasion, with the "pope's" daughter.

The Russians had centralized their forces at the Mission, and had withdrawn them from Andreavski—to be hereafter mentioned—and from the Kolmakoff Redoubt on the Koskequim River. From this place they made periodical trading excursions.

Most of the Russians were absent on their annual trip

to St. Michael's, but those remaining—three in number—
soon placed the "samovar" on the table, and we went
through the indispensable rite of drinking tea together.
They had experienced a shock of earthquake the night
before ; we had felt it on the water as though our canoe had
suddenly come into collision with a rock or "snag." The
cliff at the Mission is of rock, riddled with holes—like that of
St. Michael's—but of a more crumbling nature. The settlement comprises a chapel with two buildings attached, the
property of the priest, and three log houses appertaining to
the Fur Company. There is no fort or enclosed space.
Immediately adjoining is a Primoske village, with houses
on the surface, much resembling those we had seen at
Sitka.

We stopped there about three hours, and then resumed
our journey, passing more Indian houses and one village like
that just mentioned. The Indians brought alongside our
large boat, fish, ducks, and geese, and always appeared
contented with what we paid them, asking for no presents—
a circumstance that surprised and gratified us, as we were
nearly out of trading goods. All were poorly clothed, and
rich in nothing but fish, their staple diet summer and winter.
It is so abundant that they rarely hunt, although the country
looks like a good locality for deer. It is wooded, with hills
more or less bare.

We travelled almost exclusively on the west side of the
river from Nulato downwards. The night of the 20-21st we
drifted into a heavy fog, so that we could not see the bows
of our canoe, and trusted ourselves entirely to the current.
The morning broke fine, and cleared up for a hot day, 76°
Fahr. in the shade. The banks of the lower river are much

wooded. Long stretches of uninviting country, islands,. and
"sloughs" innumerable, made our travelling monotonous.
The current was more sluggish, yet certainly averaged three
knots an hour. In spring it is much more rapid. A steamer
of good power, capable of going ten or twelve knots, and
built in the American manner, as most suitable to a swift
shallow river, with flat bottom and stern-wheel, could proceed 1800 miles on the Yukon, and sap the entire fur-
trade of the country. Such an experiment has been projected by traders in San Francisco. If the United States
Government would—in the interests of exploration—under-
take this, a comparatively inexpensive survey of the whole
Yukon and surrounding country might be very easily accomplished.

On the early morning of the 22nd we reached the abandoned fort Andreavski (*Andreas Adanotchke*), and found
there one solitary white man with an Indian. He was—
for a Russian—in a very deplorable plight—he was quite
out of tea! and, as we were enabled to supply him with a
little, we made his heart rejoice. He soon busied himself
in getting out some coarse bread and raw salt-fish. This
place had a regular enclosure, but had no bastions. Two
old cannon were lying rusty and unused in the yard.

We borrowed the Russian's sole companion to show us
the opening to the "Aphoon," or northern mouth of the
Yukon. The course followed was approximately N.N.W.
to the sea, but the other mouths trend much to the W. and
S.W. At half-past 8 o'clock, on the morning of the 23rd,
we entered it. This mouth is distinguished from the others
by willows and larger trees on its banks; the other openings
are larger, and more shallow, and have little vegetation on

the islands and banks.   The Aphoon mouth is a passage of a
narrow and intricate nature; streams enter it, and passages
from the Kwich-pak mouth.   There is water enough for
a clumsy sloop or "barkass" brought up annually by the
Russians.   It has a tide.

Mr. Everett Smith—a sailor by profession and a member
of our expedition—very carefully examined the Kwich-pak*
or Yukon mouths, and from his notes, obligingly put at my
disposal, I glean the following information.

Mr. Smith found that while the "Koosilvac" mouth gave
soundings of from two and a half to nine fathoms, a vessel
could only enter it by going out first some distance to sea.
The intermediate mouths were too shallow, and he came
to the conclusion that the Aphoon mouth was the only
available one.   His sketch map (which I have incorporated
with my own) shows innumerable passages running between
the mouths.   He found them blocked with ice till the
1st of June.   Generally the water outside was extremely
shoal; Smith found it fresh ten miles out at sea, and there
is little doubt that this is true for a greater distance.
The Indians drive the "balouga," or white grampus, into
the shallow water of the Kwich-pak, and there spear them.
On native authority, it is said that whales from Bering Sea

----

* Kwich-pak (pronounced Kwif-pak) is the name given to the river by
the Indians of the neighbourhood, and the term was adopted by the
Russians. On the upper river the Co-Yukons and other natives call it
"Yukona," and the Hudson's Bay Company adopted their name. Both
signify "big river." Perhaps "Yúkon" would better represent the true
pronunciation of the word. It has not yet become a familiar name to
geographers, and, in consequence, may be found spelled in all ways—
Yukon, Yucon, Youcon, and *Youkon.*

go into the mouths to calve. Geese and ducks are for a season extremely abundant; some breed there, but a larger number take their flight to the Arctic. Smith, in three days, shot 104. My friend, Mr. Dyer, our Nulato quartermaster, who accompanied Smith for a part of the time taken up in this examination of the mouths, told me that wild fowl and geese eggs were so plentiful, that he could purchase from the Indians ten for a needle! and obtain them by the hundred.

23rd.—We reached Pastolik, a village on the coast at the outlet of the Aphoon mouth, sixty-five miles from St. Michael's, and, for the first time after leaving Nulato, slept ashore. This place is celebrated for the manufacture of skin boats, and among the natives we saw a number of small bone carvings, some of which we purchased for needles, &c. On the morning of the 24th we hired a second and more sea-worthy "baidarre," and, dividing our crew, sailed in company; passing the Magemute village of Pikmigtalik, we reached in the evening the "canal" (as the Russians term it, and it is really little more) which separates the island of St. Michael's from the mainland. We tracked through some parts of it, and proceeding without camping at night, arrived at Redoubt St. Michael's at 3 P.M. on the 25th. Our journey of nearly 1300 miles had occupied us but fifteen and a half days (i.e. nine and a half days from Nulato, added to five days twenty hours from Fort Yukon to Nulato).

Our friends of the expedition gave us a warm reception, and informed us that Major Wright had called at St. Michael's in the barque 'Clara Bell' to give us notice to get ready for an immediate departure—that the Telegraph Enterprise had been abandoned.

Our men during winter had been employed in building telegraph, and camping out for weeks together at temperatures frequently below the freezing point of mercury! In such a climate this work was no joke, and the simple process of digging a hole to receive the telegraph pole became a difficult operation when the ground was a frozen rock with five feet of snow on the top of it, and where the pick and crow-bar were of more use than the spade or shovel. Frequently the snow drifted over these holes lightly, and many amusing incidents had occurred of men tumbling down into them head first, or slipping in and getting half buried in holes that they had dug themselves. Their depth was usually three feet, varying somewhat with the nature of the soil; to dig six such, and clear the over-lying snow, was considered a good day's work. In the autumn of 1865, Colonel Bulkley visited both sides of Bering Straits. In Grantley Harbour, Port Clarence (Russian America), he found that the ground, covered with a heavy growth of moss in detached bunchy masses, was *itself* only thawed to about ten inches beneath the surface, and below that was frozen solid. Light soil on the Yukon was, we found, in summer thawed to fifteen or eighteen inches, whilst on the Siberian side of Bering Straits the loose broken débris of rocks was thawed to a depth of three feet. The latter was almost devoid of vegetation.

Then, again, our men had found that their axes and other tools constantly lost their edges, when used on frozen wood or soil, and cracked to pieces from the influence of intense cold. Yet they had persevered, and had put up a large piece of the line; and I can sympathize with the feeling that prompted some of them at Unalachleet, Norton Sound, on hearing of the withdrawal of our forces, to hang black cloth on the telegraph-poles, and put them into mourning!

Some few of the workmen had suffered from frost-bite and scurvy. *À propos* of the latter terrible scourge, it is to be remarked, that our men at Port Clarence, the worst fed of all our parties, who had lived for a long time on a native diet of walrus and seal blubber, had not suffered from it at all, while those in Norton Sound, who got a fair amount of flour, &c., from the Russian posts, suffered severely from the disease.

On the 18th August, after many a false alarm of a "ship outside," the 'Clara Bell' arrived, and on the 29th of the same month we were all gathered once more in Plover Bay on the opposite Asiatic shore, awaiting the arrival of our largest vessel, the 'Nightingale.'

In Plover Bay were now encamped 120 men who had wintered at places as widely apart as the Anadyr, Plover Bay itself, and Russian America; and Major Wright and Captain Norton, of the 'Clara Bell,' deserved great credit for the energy with which they had accomplished the task of collecting them. To most of the stations they had paid two visits; the first, of course, to give notice to the employés in the interior. Of the men who wintered in these almost Arctic spots, but one had died, while a second, smitten by the charms of some lovely squaw, had determined to remain —a voluntary exile in Eastern Siberia! Captain Kelsey, who had charge of the Plover Bay station, did all in his power to make the parties comfortable in their temporary camps. Rude erections of canvas, sails, poles, and planks,

R

lined the shores of the little harbour, and our stay at "Kelsey-ville" (as it has been already inserted on a map issued by the Department of State at Washington) will not soon be forgotten by us. During our stay, Captain Redfield, of the 'Manuella,' arrived ; and, after he had got through his trade with the natives, gave them a display of fireworks and blue lights—a thing frequently done by the whalers. The exhibition took place on a lovely evening, and the calm water of the bay gave double effect to the scene.

Whilst stopping in Plover Bay, some of our men found a keg of specimens preserved in alcohol, belonging to one of our Smithsonian collectors. Having had a long abstinence from exhilarating drinks, the temptation was too much for them, and they proceeded to broach the contents. After they had imbibed to their hearts' content, and become "visibly affected thereby," they thought it a pity to waste the remaining contents of the barrel, and, feeling hungry, went on to eat the lizards, snakes, and fish which had been put up for a rather different purpose ! Science was avenged in the result, nor do I think they will ever repeat the experiment.

I was informed by my friends, Bush, MacCrea, and Farnham, that at the Anadyr River blinding snow-storms had been prevalent during winter, and between log houses no more than a hundred yards apart, it had been found necessary to stretch a guiding rope for the men. One of our barques, the 'Golden Gate,' had been wrecked in Anadyr Bay the previous autumn, in the following manner. She had grounded on a sand-bar, and the ice had formed round her before she could be got off. At a later period, a gale of wind raised a bad sea, and the ice, smashing up round her, stove in an immense leak, and she was eventually much broken up in the hull. All her stores, rigging, and sails were stripped from her, but fortunately no one was lost or injured by her wreck. They had obtained supplies of meat in quantities. On one occasion they purchased 150 head of reindeer, and preserved the venison frozen for several months. The herds belonging to the Tchuktchis of that part of Siberia were numbered by the thousand.

On the 6th September, Colonel Bulkley arrived in the 'Nightingale,' and, as soon as everything and everybody was on board, we set sail for San Francisco, and made an excellent run there in twenty-two days.

CHAPTER XXII.

THE VALUE OF ALASKA. — THE ORIGIN OF THE ESQUIMAUX
OF NORTHERN ALASKA AND GREENLAND.

The value of Alaska — The furs and fisheries — The purchase, an act of
justice to Russia — The Aleutian Islands — Volcanoes — Bogoslov Island
— The Asiatic origin of the Esquimaux — The Tchuktchis — Sea-going
canoes — The voyages of two Japanese junks — The connecting links
between the Tchuktchis and the Esquimaux — Language — Degeneration
of the Esquimaux — Community of goods — The "Schaman" and the
"Angekok."

THAT Russian America is likely to prove a bad bargain to the
United States Government, I cannot believe. The extreme
northern division of the country may, indeed, be nearly
valueless; but the foregoing pages will have shown, that,
in the more central portions of the territory, furs are abundant, and that the trade in them, which may probably be
further developed, must fall into American hands. The
southern parts of the country are identical in character
with the neighbouring British territory, and will probably
be found to be as rich in mineral wealth; whilst the timber,
though of an inferior growth, owing to the higher latitude,
will yet prove by no means worthless.

The fisheries may become of great value. There are
extensive cod-banks off the Aleutian Isles, and on many other
parts of the coast. Salmon is *the* commonest of common
fish in all the rivers of the North Pacific, and is rated accord-

ingly as food only fit for those who cannot get better. In Alaska, as in British Columbia, the fish can be obtained in vast quantities, simply at the expense of native labour. To this add the value of salt (or vinegar), barrels and freight, and one sees the slight total cost which would be incurred in exporting to benighted Europe that which would there be considered a luxury.*

There is a further reason why the United States have done well to purchase this territory. It is an act of justice to the Russian Government. For the past twenty years the whalers in Bering Sea and the Arctic—who are mainly Americans—had traded at certain parts of the coast, and had thereby considerably reduced the profits of the Russian American Fur Company. Although nominally whalers, they were nearly all traders also. The Russians, albeit always hospitable, were naturally very averse to these vessels putting into their ports, and may-be trading under their very noses. A large part of the whaling captains had consequently never visited many of the larger Russian settlements, such as Sitka, Ounalaska, St. Paul's, or St. Michael's. Now, all these and many other ports are perfectly open to them, whilst the

---

* In Petropaulovski a merchant told me that he had made in this way 6000 dollars in one season, at no more trouble to himself than that incurred in a little superintendence of the natives employed. The enterprising American is the last man to neglect this source of profit.

A recent newspaper "Correspondent" expresses surprise at the latest news from Sitka, which states that the carcass of a deer may still be purchased there for three or four dollars (12s. to 16s.); a grouse or a salmon for 25 cents (1s.). But they are worth no more at this day in Victoria (V. I.), in the towns of the Columbia or Fraser rivers, and, at the date of my visit to Sitka, were to be obtained for a castaway coat, a string of beads, or a few charges of powder.

cargoes of furs, walrus tusks, oil, &c., will enter San Francisco, or any other port in the United States, duty free—an important consideration to them.

The chain of the Aleutian Isles, comprising four groups (the Fox, Andreanoff, Rat, and Blignie islands *), is a valuable part of the new purchase. The world owes their first discovery to Bering (in 1741). Almost immediately after this (from the year 1745) Russian merchants of Siberia commenced trading on them, and to them we owe the discovery of the larger part of the chain.

It tells us plainly how valuable were the cargoes of furs, &c., then obtained, when we find that out of eleven recorded voyages † from 1745 to 1778, five were decidedly unfortunate, either ending in shipwreck or in the murder of part of the crews, and that, nevertheless, the Russians persevered in the trade. Now-a-days the Aleuts are often to be found serving as sailors on whaling and other vessels in the North Pacific. Until recently, they were looked upon as the immediate subjects of the Russian-American Fur Company, and each male was required to pass three years in its service. The Company had several stations on these islands, the principal of which was Ounalaska.

The Aleutian Islands, besides having some commercial importance, yielding, as they still do, the furs of amphibious animals to a large amount, have many points of interest. On nearly all of them active or passive volcanoes exist, and on

---

* Sarytscheff (who accompanied Billing's Expedition in 1791-2) determined the geographical positions of many of these islands. Cook, Kotsebue, Lütke, and others, have all done more or less towards the same end.

† Coxe's ' Russian Discoveries.'

one or two, geysers and hot springs have been discovered. There are records of very severe shocks of earthquake felt by the Russian traders and natives dwelling on them. It is more than probable that large deposits of sulphur, as in Sicily, may be found there. On the following islands of the group, large volcanic mountains, &c., exist:—

OUNIMAK. (See p. 85.) The volcano of Chichaldinskoi (this mountain emits smoke). A second near it, apparently unnamed hitherto. The Pogrommoi volcano.

AKOUN. One (smoking) volcanic peak: hot springs.

AKOUTAN. One active volcano. (See p. 86.)

OUMNACK. Vcevidovskoï and Toulikskoï volcanoes: geysers.

BOGOSLOV ISLAND (Joan Bogoslov). (See p. 131*).

AMOUKTA. Extinct volcanoes.

SEGOUAM. Smoking mountains: hot springs, &c.

ATKHA. Several, among which are the Korovinskoï and Klutchevskoï mountains.

KANAGA. Smoking volcano.

TANAGA. Extinct (?) volcanoes.

GORELOY. Volcano of the same name, said to be the highest on the chain of the Aleutian islands.

SEMISOPOCHNOI. Several volcanoes.

The authorities for the above list will be found cited in

---

* "To the northward of Oumnack is a long reef stretching for twenty-six miles in a nearly north (*true*) direction, at the outer point of which is the *Ship Rock*. It was so named by Cook, and is in the form of a tower.

"At 200 fathoms within the *Ship Rock* is the small island of Joan Bogoslov. It is of volcanic origin, and did not appear till 1796, after an earthquake. The length of this small island, from N.W. by N., to S.E. by S., is 1¾ mile. Its breadth is about the half of its length. A chain of rocks projects two miles beyond its N.W. extremity, and another a mile beyond its N.E. point. According to the observations of Captain Wassilieff, the peak in the centre of the island is 2240 feet high. This island, as before stated, is connected with Oumnack by a reef of rocks, which doubtless owe their origin to a similar cause; for, in 1778, Cook, and, thirty years later,

Findlay's 'Directory for the Navigation of the Pacific Ocean,' and comprise, among the number, the works of Krusenstern, Lütke, and Cook.

It need not be said that the Aleutian Islands, lying as they do so closely together, could be very easily examined by a scientific traveller who should take up his abode on one of them for a year or two. That they deserve such an examination can hardly be doubted.

The allusions to the Tchuktchis, to the trade across Bering Straits, and to the coast peoples of Northern Alaska, scattered at intervals throughout many of the previous chapters, serve,

----

Sarighscheff, sailed between the Ship Rock and the island of Oumnack." Baranoff (the founder of Sitka) furnished Krusenstern, in 1817, with some account of this phenomenon, which the latter has recorded in his celebrated 'Mémoires Hydrographiques.' It is briefly as follows:—In 1806 the peak just mentioned was first observed; and, on May 1st in that year, "a violent tempest from the north occurred, and, during its force, a rumbling noise, and distant explosions, similar to thunder-claps, were heard at Ounalashka. At the commencement of the third day the tempest abated, and the sky became clear. They then observed, between Ounalashka and Oumnack, to the north of the latter, a flame jetting out of the sea, and soon after, smoke, which continued for ten consecutive days. After this, a white body, of a round form, was observed to rise out of the water, and increase rapidly in size. At the end of a month the flame ceased, but the smoke increased considerably, and the island kept on increasing. On June 1st, 1814, they sent a baidär to examine it, but they could scarcely land, on account of the violent currents and the pointed rocks. The island was formed by precipices, covered with small stones, which were being continually ejected from the crater. In 1815, a second expedition found the island very much lower than in the previous year, and its appearance entirely changed. The precipices had fallen, and were continually crumbling away."—*Findlay's* 'Directory,' &c.

at least, to confirm the observations and theories of many previous travellers and authors.

Scientific men are now agreed on the Asiatic origin of the Esquimaux, even of those who have migrated as far as Greenland.* Of the Mongolian origin of the Tchuktchis themselves, no one who has seen individuals of that people would for a moment doubt. A Tchuktchi boy taken by Col. Bulkley (our engineer-in-chief) from Plover Bay to San Francisco, and there educated and cared for in the family of a kind-hearted lady, was, when dressed up in European clothes, constantly taken for a civilised Chinaman ; and two of our Aleutian sailors were often similarly mistaken. This happened, it must be observed, in a city which is full of Chinese and Japanese. That the Aleuts, also, are of an Eastern stock, is to my mind undoubted.

The inter-tribal trade carried on so regularly every year *viâ* Bering Straits (which is likely now to receive a decided check from the American traders, who will crowd into the country) proved with how little difficulty a colony of " Wandering Tchuktchis " might cross from Asia and populate the northern coasts of America. Open skin canoes, capable of containing twenty or more persons with their effects, and hoisting several masts and sails, are now frequently to be observed among both the sea - coast Tchuktchis and the inhabitants of Northern Alaska. I have seen others that might be called " full-rigged " canoes, carrying main, gaff, and sprit-sails, but these were probably recent and foreign innovations.†

* See Markham " On the Greenland Esquimaux," ' Journal of the Royal Geographical Society,' 1865.

† In a recent number of ' Harper's (New York) Magazine,' my friend

I may be excused if I here allude to two well-authenticated and oft-quoted facts. In the years 1832-3, two remarkable and unintentional ocean voyages—one of them terminating in shipwreck—were made from Japan to the north-west coast of America,* and to the Sandwich Islands, by *junks*.

Mr. Knox—who accompanied us across the Pacific in 1866—tells us that he heard, during his stay in Siberia, of a peculiar mode of effecting marine insurance, which is said to be in vogue amongst the Tchuktchis, and which, says he, "I do not think will ever be popular among American sailors." In crossing Bering Straits, the captain and owner of the boat—bearing in mind the Dutch proverb " zelf is de man "—when a storm arises, throws his crew, one by one, overboard, reserving his goods to the last. They allow themselves to be drowned with a complacency unknown to Christian nations. I will not vouch for the story, nor would, I think, Mr. Knox.

* See Washington Irving's 'Astoria;' also Sir Edward Belcher's 'Voyage of the *Sulphur*,' (quoted by Findlay), wherein he says :—"We received from the officers of the Hudson's Bay establishment several articles of Japanese china, which had been washed ashore from a Japanese junk, wrecked near Cape Flattery. Mr. Birnie knew little of the details of the event ; but in the Appendix to Washington Irving's 'Rocky Mountains,' vol. i., p. 240, is the following account of it, in a letter from Captain Wyeth :—'In the winter of 1833, a Japanese junk was wrecked on the N.W. coast, in the neighbourhood of Queen Charlotte's Island, and all but two of her crew, then much reduced by starvation and disease, during a long drift across the Pacific, were killed by the natives. The two fell into the hands of the Hudson's Bay Company, and were sent to England. I saw them on my arrival at Vancouver in 1834.' Mr. Birnie states that it was at Cape Flattery, and not as above ; and on this point, his local knowledge makes him the best judge. 'There were,' he says, 'two men and a boy purchased from the natives. As soon as it was known that some shipwrecked people were enslaved among the natives, the Hudson's Bay Company sent their vessel "Lana," Captain M'Neil, to obtain them by barter ; and there was some trouble in redeeming the boy. They were subsequently sent to England, and then home, but their countrymen refused to receive them.' Further my informant could not acquaint me."

The last mentioned is known to have been ten or eleven months at sea, and had nine Japanese on board, who nevertheless arrived safely, anchoring in the harbour of Waialea, Oahu. The Sandwich Islanders (Hawaians, or, as they are called in California, &c., "Kanakas"), when they saw these strangers, much resembling themselves in many respects, said, "It is plain, now, we come from Asia." How easily, then, could we account for the population of almost any island or coast in the Pacific.

Such facts as these—the passage of comparatively frail vessels, blown away from their native coasts by typhoons or other unusually violent gales, buffetted about for lengthened periods, yet eventually reaching foreign coasts thousands of miles from their own—should, I think, make us very cautious in our ideas on the limitation of native migrations.

At what time, or by what route, the adventurous, discontented or rebellious Tchuktchi, Onkilon, or Tunguse, first wandered, sledged, or paddled on his way to Greenland, it behoves not me to say. The subject has already engaged the consideration of able and travelled writers, and no one has more clearly treated the subject than Mr. Markham ('Journal of the Royal Geographical Society,' 1865). He has shown us that the native migrations, which have peopled the coasts of northernmost America and Greenland, commenced at the period when Togrul Bey, Zengis Khan, and other chiefs of less celebrity, troubled Asia with their lust for conquest. "Year after year the intruding Tartars continued to press on. Sheibani Khan, a grandson of the mighty Zengis, led 15,000 families into these northern wilds, and their descendants, the Iakhuts (? Yakutz) pressed on still farther north, until they are now found at the mouths of rivers falling into the

Polar Ocean." Neither were *they* the first inhabitants of the country along the banks of the Kolyma or Anadyr. Other and older people, who have now disappeared, have left their traces (ruined *yourts*, &c.) in the whole of that country as far north as Bering Straits and Cape Chelagskoi.*

Mr. Markham believes, in common with a large number of our best Arctic authorities,† in the existence of land round or near the Pole, and which may nearly connect Siberia with Greenland, and sees in that land the route probably taken by the adventurous wanderers. Between the traces of former life found at Cape Chelagskoi, and those observed on the Parry Islands, a gap of 1140 miles indeed intervenes, in which no such have been observed; but this is, in all probability, simply owing to our ignorance of those latitudes.

The Greenlanders may indeed have taken such a route, but the natives of Northern Alaska doubtless crossed by the "direct short-sea" passage, *viâ* Bering Straits.

In comparing notes with my brother, who was pursuing his researches in Greenland during a part of the time that I was in Alaska, &c., we have noticed many points of similarity between the Esquimaux, on the one hand, and the Malemutes or Tchuktchis on the other. Some resemblances are, of course, simply on the surface, are obvious at first sight, and have been discussed before. Their food, costume, houses, implements, and weapons are closely allied in character, and the resemblances could well enough arise from identity of wants, and from the similar nature of the countries they inhabit. Were

---

* Von Wrangell (Mrs. Sabine's translation), p. 372. See also p. 89 of this work.

† See Captain Sherard Osborn's Paper in the 'Proceedings' of the Royal Geographical Society, May 7th, 1868.

we to transplant a colony of Europeans to such countries, and shut them off from foreign and outside supplies, in a generation or two they would be living much as these natives do. These superficial points can never, therefore, prove much. Many of our older Arctic explorers, and our more recent telegraph explorers, have been in those countries more or less clothed, fed, and housed in native fashion.

It is rather to physical characteristics,—languages (genuine and not imported) customs, and tribal practices—that we must look for information. The Tchuktchi language is said to have a great resemblance to that of the Greenland Esquimaux. On this point I will say nothing, as my visits to the Siberian coast were hurried, and of short duration, while the subject has been already discussed by those who are excellent authorities.*   But I would call the attention of those interested in this matter to the very close similarity of some of the words in my Malemute (Northern Alaska) vocabulary, to be found in the Appendix, with those in the best Esquimaux vocabularies which we possess.†   Thus :—

				Malemute.					Greenland Esquimaux.
I -	-	-	-	Wounga -	-	-	-	-	U-anga.
He	-	-	-	Oona	-	-	-	-	Una.
We	-	-	-	Wurgut -	-	-	-	-	U-agut.
You	-	-	-	Itlepit	-	-	-	-	Iblet. Illipse.
Man	-	-	-	Inuet	-	-	-	-	Angut. Innuit.

---

* Billings (quoted by Wrangell, p. 372, Mrs. Sabine's translation), also Wrangell elsewhere.   Hooper's 'Tents of the Tuski.'   Markham ('Journal of the Royal Geographical Society' for 1865).   Balbi's 'Atlas Ethnographique,' and Klaproth's 'Sprach Atlas,' quoted in Washington's 'Esquimaux Vocabulary, &c., for the use of the Arctic Expeditions.'

† My brother reminds me that the Greenland Esquimaux vocabularies were often acquired through Danish media, and that they have, therefore, been written in English with a foreign accent.

		Malemute.					Greenland Esquimaux.
Woman	-	-	Achanuk -	-	-	-	Arnak.
Day	-	-	Oblook	-	-	-	Utlok.
Sun	-	-	Sickunyuk	-	-	-	Sekkinek.
Water -	-	-	Imuk	-	-	-	Imék (salt water, Imak'.
Snow -	-	-	Kanik	-	-	-	Kannik.
Ice	-	-	Seko	-	-	-	Sikkó.
Head	-	-	Neakuk -	-	-	-	Niakok.
Face	-	-	Keenyuk	-	-	-	Kenak.
Mouth -	-	-	Kanuk	-	-	-	Kánnek.
Teeth -	-	-	Keeutik -	-	-	-	Kigutit.
Wood -	-	-	Kushuk -	-	-	-	Kessuk.
Canoe -	-	-	Omeuk-puk	-	-	-	Oomiak.

And so on. I am fully aware that attention has been called to this point before, but a *special* vocabulary of Malemute (Norton Sound) words has never been before published, although we have those of neighbouring dialects—that of Kotsebue Sound, &c.

That the Greenland Esquimaux has somewhat degenerated —in both physical and mental characteristics—I can well believe. The average height of the Greenlander of to-day is under the European standard, while many individuals, at least, of the Tchuktchis, are over it. This point is of itself of no importance whatever. Greenland, may-be, is not a worse country than Northern Siberia; but who knows what these races endured on their way thither—especially if they went by Mr. Markham's North Polar route!—and how far less food, and intenser cold, than they were accustomed to, with untold hardships superadded, may have stunted and dwarfed them? I am told that they are excessively simple and child-like, that they live in much harmony, quarrel rarely, and have many other good features; and the reader has only to turn to Hooper's 'Tents of the Tuski' to find the same thing stated with regard to the Tchuktchis, and some of my previous pages to find similar statements with regard to the Alaskan peoples.

My brother says much of the community of goods enjoyed amongst them, how the industrious hunter supplies the whole village crowd, as a matter of course, taking and getting no credit for it; and how the more he gets, the worse he is off. This, which is more or less a feature of all the coast tribes in the North Pacific, is specially true in Northern Alaska, on the Yukon, and in Norton Sound, where the chiefs, who are invariably good hunters or fishermen, often attain and keep their position by periodical distributions of their effects. They are themselves often the worst clothed and worst fed members of their own villages. Generosity is among them the rule, and not the exception. No man, woman, or child among them goes unfed, unhoused, or unwarmed, if there is food, dwelling, or fire in the settlement.

The " Schaman " (pronounced exactly like our word " showman," a very appropriate title!), the conjuror-priest, the " medicine man " of the Tchuktchis (and also of the North Alaskan peoples, who use the same term) was, and apparently still is, represented in Greenland by the " Angekok," who held similar powers, and was reverenced or feared accordingly. My brother says " the Danish pastors and missionaries believe that the Angekok is extinct. Publicly, he appears to be so, but the natives are known to hold secret meetings, about which, strange to say, none of the Danes are able to learn details, and at these it is believed Angekokism is still practised." Their profession, besides including medicine and exorcism, made a prominent feature of rain and wind making.

In Greenland, the former Esquimaux practice of burying

the dead under a pile of stones, has been abandoned, and they have adopted Danish customs.   At the Anadyr River I saw Tchuktchi graves which were covered by piles of reindeer horns.   The "four-post" coffins, described in connection with the Northern Alaskan peoples, and which are probably a later inspiration, have been perhaps adopted for this reason:—stones are less common—at least in Norton Sound, Port Clarence, and on the Yukon—than soil; whilst the latter is frozen at a few inches beneath the surface at all seasons.   Hence the real difficulty of making a grave—superadded to their natural ·indolence—has caused a new form of sepulture to be adopted.

That some future North Polar Expedition will clear up every mystery hanging over the route taken by these wanderers from one desolate clime to another, I, for one, cannot fail to believe, but the question has more of interest about it than of importance.

CHAPTER XXIII.

W. U. TELEGRAPH EXPLORATIONS IN ASIA.

Major Abasa appointed Chief — Arrival in Petropaulovski — Travels in
Kamchatka — Ghijega — The town, &c. — Route between Ghijega and
Ochotsk — The explorations of Mahood and Bush — Nicolaiefski, Mouth
of the Amoor — Travel to Ochotsk — Reindeer riding — The Tunguse—
Ayan — Ochotsk — MacCrea and Arnold's wanderings among the Tchuk-
tchis — Anadyrsk.

THE explorers of our W. U. Telegraph service made many
important and interesting journeys in Asia, which certainly
deserve to be recorded. I cannot pretend to narrate their
experiences fully. The following brief account of their travels
may, however, be depended upon : it has been derived
directly from themselves, with some additions from the
published articles of my friend Mr. Knox, of New York,
who, it will be remembered, accompanied us in 1866.

In 1865, Major Abasa—a very cultivated and energetic
Russian gentleman, who had travelled much, especially in
the United States—was appointed chief of the Asiatic explorations proposed to be made by our Company. On the
8th August, of the same year, that gentleman, in company
with Messrs. Kennon, Mahood and Bush, arrived at Petropaulovski, on the brig 'Ochotsk' from San Francisco, our
headquarters. The two latter explorers were immediately
despatched, by sea, to the Amoor River, whilst the Major,
Mr. Kennon, and a third *employé* of the expedition, made

S

their preparations for an early start—their destination being
Ghijega (Ghijinsk on old maps) at the head of the Ochotsk
Sea.   This they proposed to reach by land, *viâ* Kam-
chatka.

Major Abasa and his companions left Petropaulovski on
the 25th of August,—a month which in Kamchatka is often
extremely warm, and when there is no snow whatever on
the lowlands.   They followed the eastern shore of the peninsula till, at the village of Sharon, they reached the Kamchatka River,—a tortuous stream of no great size, which has
been already mentioned in connection with the narrative
of Bering's life.   Their route so far was principally over
undulating plains, covered by much moss, grass, and underbrush, but with a limited amount of poorly grown timber.
It is one of the peculiarities of Kamchatka that the forests
get thicker and the trees larger the farther north you proceed.
It is, moreover, constantly stated, and apparently believed
also by the foreign residents in the country, that the soil
is warmed by the volcanic fires beneath, and that the cultivation of grain in the brief summer is thereby rendered
impracticable, as it sprouts before its time.   It is known
that, in winter, the snow, in places, sometimes melts where
it is in contact with the earth, while a foot or so above it
there is the usual wintry covering.   This snow, undermined
as it were, frequently tumbles in when travellers are passing
over it, and they "find their level" a little lower than they
expected.

After following for a short distance the Kamchatka River,
the party turned westward, to cross a much more rugged
country, in order to reach the village of Tigil, on the coast of
the Ochotsk Sea.   Here they met with many difficulties.

The route was an alternation of rocks and swamps, with much rotten snow overlying them, and even the sure-footed little Siberian pack-horses, which were well loaded with the personal effects, &c., of the party, were constantly in trouble. Now they were stuck in sloughs of unknown depth, now they were half carried away by the swift mountain-streams they were attempting to ford, and now and again they came down on their knees or haunches when attempting to clamber over the slippery rocks. But at length they reached Tigil, which, by the route they had travelled, was 1200 versts (800 miles).

From Tigil, Major Abasa wrote to the " Ispravnik " (Civil Governor) of Ghijega, notifying him that he was on the way, and asking him to issue orders to the inhabitants under his jurisdiction to render every assistance. The letter was sent to Sessnoi, the last Kamchatdale village on the route, and from there passed from one tribe of Koriaks to another, until it reached its destination. Abasa had taken the precaution to send on word that he would " remember " any natives who had facilitated the delivery of his message, and the letter therefore reached Ghijega very quickly. The Ispravnik immediately issued the necessary orders.

From Tigil to Sessnoi, the party travelled by or near the sea coast, and reached the latter place successfully. North of Sessnoi the route was known to be extremely difficult; they therefore divided their forces, the Major and one of his men (with natives) proceeding in a whale-boat and skin canoe by sea, whilst Kennon attempted to take the pack-train, &c., across the mountainous coast. They, however, were unfortunate at this part of the trip; the party on the sea experienced bad weather, whilst Kennon found the lately fallen snow too soft and deep for his horses. They therefore returned to Sessnoi, to wait till the season became a little more advanced, and employed their time in purchasing dogs from the natives, and in the manufacture of sledges, &c. They found great difficulty in inducing the Kamchatdales to part with their dogs. A sum of 200 silver roubles (over £30), for a team of ten dogs, was often refused.

While in Sessnoi, Major Abasa had some very interesting interviews with chiefs of the Koriak and Tchuktchi tribes. It was the period of their annual migration southward, when they go to hunt the sable on the plains and in the mountains of Kamchatka. In January they gather around Tigil, to exchange their furs for tea, sugar, coffee, powder, lead, &c. Bad weather detained the party in Sessnoi, and by a judicious distribution of presents they succeeded in making them communicative. They advised the Major in proceeding from Sessnoi not to follow the sea-coast, but to incline to the eastward and pass through a country comparatively little known to the whites. Everything being ready, the party left Sessnoi on the 20th of October, passing over the mountains and finding a very bad road. Four days later they reached Bodkaguernaya, having found the temperature at night from forty to forty-five degrees below zero. North of Bodkaguernaya the mountains gradually diminished, and the country was found to be cut up into plains covered with moss, and ridges on which there was a growth of low bushes that sometimes attained to the dignity of small trees. Viewed from an elevation, the whole region had a very desolate appearance. The country was found to be inhabited by the Koriaks, some of the tribes wandering from place to place, and the others remaining in fixed localities. The wandering

Koriaks were kind, hospitable, and peaceable, but the settled Koriaks were the reverse. A stronger and more efficacious representation of the Russian Government was needed among them. The Koriak country and the Ghijega and Anadyr districts are all supposed to be under the direction of the Ispravnik at Ghijega, who has only twenty-five Cossacks under him, and neither time nor ability to visit a hundredth part of his immense territory.

Major Abasa exchanged his dogs for reindeer at the first Koriak camp, a hundred versts from Bodkaguernaya, and travelled with the latter animals to Kammenoi, where the party arrived on the 16th of November. The Major wished to go to Anadyrsk from this place, but the natives refused to take him there; they were willing to go to Ghijega, and in fact had received orders from the Ispravnik to go there if the party desired it. The Russian traders were at Kammenoi, on their way to the coast of Bering Sea, and the Koriaks were anxious to accompany them, but were ordered not to do so until after Major Abasa had proceeded on his way. They, at length, after a harassing journey, reached Ghijega on the 22nd of November, where the Major established permanent quarters. He had thus traversed the whole peninsula of Kamchatka.

This insignificant village, of two or three hundred people, has a little more importance than its size would lead us to believe. It is, first, the seat of local government; it is, next, a centre with regard to the fur trade of the district; and it is, lastly, the only place for several hundred miles round, where the poor Russian settler, or semi-civilized Kamchatdale, can get any tea, sugar, or *vodka* (whisky). As *vodka is occasionally* to be got there, it need not be stated that a vener-

able "pope" (priest) of the Greek Church stops there
permanently.

Ghijega is situated on the river of the same name, about
eight miles from the coast of Ghijinsk Gulf,—an arm of the
Ochotsk Sea. Mr. Knox does not describe it as a terrestrial
paradise. Speaking of his visit, in the summer of 1866, he
says, " the flat plains or *tundras* were covered with water
in many concealed and unconcealed holes. Every little
bunch of moss was like a well filled sponge. I returned
from a pedestrian excursion with my top-boots as thoroughly
soaked as if they had been used for water-buckets. There
was not a wheeled vehicle of any kind, and there were but
three horses for fifty miles. There was no steamboat on the
river, and balloons had not been introduced."

Major Abasa, having despatched Kennon and Dodd to
Anadyrsk, to meet and co-operate with MacCrea, turned his
attention to the but-little-known country lying between
Ghijega and the town of Ochotsk. In winter the intercourse
between Ghijega and Ochotsk is quite limited. The yearly
mails, and a dozen sledges with goods for a few Russian
traders, are the only passengers over this distance, and there
is, consequently, no regular road,—travellers following no
track, but going in certain directions, guided by the position
of the mountain-streams and forests. Sometimes snow-
storms and fogs conceal the signs which guide the traveller,
and force him to remain stationary for days, and even for
weeks at a time. No means have been taken by the
inhabitants to make the road practicable. They themselves
know very little of the country within forty or fifty miles of
their homes. The settled population of the few villages
along the coast consists of a mixture of Russians, Koriaks,

and Yakutz. There is a floating population, known as Tunguse, who wander through the mountain and forest regions from Kolyma nearly down to the Amoor. These tribes rarely use sledges, but perform their migration on the backs of reindeer, of which they have not a very large number, barely sufficient for their necessities. The Koriaks are much more wealthy, some of them owning from one to two thousand deer.

The Tunguse have therefore been unwilling to let the Russians know the best routes through the country, and have maintained secret paths of their own. Major Abasa did not find them badly disposed toward the Telegraph enterprise, but fearful that it might impair the value of their hunting grounds. He succeeded in establishing friendly relations with them, and convinced them that the damage, in that respect, would be more than made good by the supplies they would be enabled to obtain by the establishment of the Company's forts among them. Their indolence and carelessness operated only in a negative manner, in preventing them from being actively useful in building the line.

On the 22nd of February (1866), Mahood and Bush—who, it will be remembered, had been despatched to the Amoor River—arrived in Ochotsk from Nicolaiefski.* The com-

---

* Nicolaiefski, a town of very modern growth, is at the mouth of the Amoor,—a river with which, thanks to the published travels of Atkinson and others, we are somewhat familiar. " It is," says Mr. Knox, " emphatically a government town, three-fourths of the inhabitants being directly or indirectly in the service of the Emperor. It has a ' port ' or naval establishment, containing dock-yards, machine-shops, foundries, and all the odds and ends of sheds, warehouses, and factories necessary to the functions of a naval station." " All the houses in the town are of wood . . . . . the great majority are of logs, either rough or hewn." " Going back from

mander of the sea-coast provinces of Eastern Siberia, (Governor Fulyhelm) had given them all the assistance in his power, but the route from the Amoor, northwards, had been one of the most rugged character. Captain Mahood, moreover, struck out a new and more direct line for himself than that usually followed by the Russians, having in view the requirements of the Telegraph service.

Governor Fulyhelm sent to the Tunguse, a hundred versts to the northward, ordering them to procure reindeer for Captain Mahood's expedition. Those were to be forwarded to Orelle Lake, north of the Amoor, and to this point the party proceeded when all preparations were completed. There they found the Tunguse, who were awaiting them with twenty deer. After a little delay in arranging the loads, the expedition started; each of the men riding a deer, while twelve of the animals were required to carry the baggage and provisions. The saddle for a reindeer is placed on the animal's withers, the back not being strong enough to sustain the weight of a man. The saddle is a mere pad, and has no stirrups, so that it requires constant care to retain one's balance—a novice in this kind of travelling being sure to get many tumbles before he learns to manage his new beast of burden. The deer is guided by a halter and a single line.

---

the river, the streets begin grandly, and promise a great deal that they do not perform. For one or two squares they are all good, the third square is passable, the fourth is full of stumps, and when you reach the fifth and sixth, there is little street to be found. I never saw a better illustration of the road that commenced with a double row of shade trees (à la boulevard) and steadily diminished in character until it became a squirrel-track and ran up a tree."—'Harper's Magazine' (New York), *August,* 1868.

There are now a large number of steamers on the Amoor. The season when the river is open is limited to about half the year.

One is required to exercise considerable dexterity to mount a reindeer without the assistance of stirrups. A staff is always used to assist one in mounting. The pack-saddle is placed on the shoulders of the animal and the reindeer will carry a load of from seventy-five to one hundred pounds in this way. A Tunguse rides one deer, and leads a pack-train of four to a dozen animals; the halter of each deer being fastened to the one that precedes him.

Between the Amoor and the Ochotsk there is not, nor has there ever been, any kind of a road; but the guides and travellers follow whatever route they think proper, always keeping their general course in view. The reindeer go through the forest, over hills and along wide stretches of barren land. The rivers are forded where shallow, and when too deep for this, rafts are built for men and baggage, while the deer are forced to swim over. In winter the ice affords a secure foothold, and, for this reason, travelling is much better in the cold season than in summer. Reindeer food grows on most parts of the route; so that, in summer or winter, it is only necessary to turn them out at night, and they will be found well fed in the morning.

Captain Mahood's journal makes frequent mention of crossing rivers, climbing over mountains, and traversing forests and *tundra*, or long stretches of barren land. Several times he was delayed by being unable to procure a sufficient number of deer for his purposes, some having "given out," and the term for which others were employed having expired. Sometimes guides were lacking, and it was necessary to send a considerable distance to obtain them.

At Ayan it was found that the Russian-American Company, which formerly maintained a post there, had departed, having given up all business on this coast. The agent of the Company still remained, with a single clerk; both of whom, with the officials, were ready to lend all assistance. The former sent at once to the "sartost" of Nelkan, ordering him to have deer and men ready to assist the party on its way to Ochotsk, where they at length arrived, as above stated.

Ochotsk is a place of which the glory has somewhat departed, owing principally to the establishment of the newer town of Nicolaiefski. It is said to have about 500 inhabitants—if you count the dogs, who outnumber the human part of the population. Its most interesting associations are those connected with the narrative of Bering's voyages.

The third, and last, journey undertaken in our service which I am enabled to record, is that made in 1865-6, by Messrs. MacCrea and Arnold, from the mouth of the Anadyr River to Anadyrsk and Ghijega. Some brief mention has been already made of the camp established at the Anadyr by the former gentleman.

After MacCrea and his party had erected temporary quarters at the mouth of the Anadyr, they began immediately to prepare for their exploration. About the 1st of November there was sufficient snow for sledging. Captain MacCrea hoped to set out soon after, and attempted to purchase reindeer for that purpose. The Tchuktchis have a superstition about selling live reindeer, though they have no hesitation about killing them and selling their carcasses. Captain MacCrea was, at first, unable to purchase deer, but finally negotiated with one of the native chiefs for transportation to Anadyrsk by way of the Tchuktchi villages south of Anadyr Bay. After some delay, this personage took Captain MacCrea and Lieutenant Arnold to the great Deer Chief, who invited these gentlemen to join the Tchuktchis in a winter excursion to Anadyrsk. As there was no other way to make the journey they accepted the proposition, and, after some delay, moved away. The progress was slow,—about eight miles a day,— the Tchuktchis having no particular appreciation of time, and not understanding how any one can ever be in a hurry. The journey occupied forty-two days, in addition to twenty-two consumed in reaching the Deer Chief's camp; making sixty-four days that MacCrea and Arnold passed among the Tchuktchis. They were kindly treated, though the accommodations were not of the finest character, and the *cuisine* was not suited to civilized tastes. Added to the slow mode of travelling, the route was very circuitous, and thus the journey was made longer than it would otherwise have been.

There are two large villages, about twenty versts apart, and three smaller ones in the neighbourhood, all known by the name of Anadyrsk; the former being designated the Crepass (fortress), and the second, farther up the river, the Markova. When Captain MacCrea reached the Markova, he found there the other members of his party, who had been brought up from the mouth of the river by the direct route.

From there MacCrea and Arnold proceeded to Ghijega. Above the Markova, the Anadyr is well wooded.

It will be remembered that Kennon and Dodd left Ghijega for Anadyrsk; and it was on this trip that the former discovered a river, named the Myan, which, rising in the mountains near the Penjinsk River, eventually forms one of the principal tributaries of the Anadyr. Mr. Bush, as before mentioned (p. 119), who also travelled from Ghijega to the mouth of the Anadyr, was enabled to make a longer direct

journey than any others of our explorers,—that from
Nicolaiefski to Anadyr Bay.   Later, in 1866-7, many of the
gentlemen just mentioned, with others, went over various
parts of the same country, but their journeys were made
more with reference to the business of the Company, the
transportation of goods, &c., than with a view to exploration.

I have simply recorded the outlines of these Asiatic
journeys: it is for those engaged in them to give us a fuller
narrative, or narratives; and I trust that some of them may
yet do so.

CHAPTER XXIV.

CALIFORNIA.

California in 1849 — To-day — Agricultural progress — Wine manufacture — Climate — Lower California — San Francisco — No paper money — Coinage — Growth — General prosperity — Scarcity of labour — Hiring a domestic — Luxuries of the land — " The Mission " — Hotel *carte* — Home for the Inebriates — Immigration desired — Newspapers — Chinese population — "John's" status — John as a miner — Dead Chinamen — Celestial entertainment — Merchant's pigtail.

TWENTY years ago, California, one of the richest and most fertile countries of the globe, was lying absolutely unheeded, with but a few indolent Spanish settlers, and a still smaller number of Americans, scattered at long intervals over its surface.   Now it has a population of half a million, and the cry is " still they come."

When the gold excitement* in 1849 broke out in full force, it called attention to the country ; and thousands, drawn there by the universal magnet, remained to become prosperous and permanent settlers.   There are few who know California who do not become warmly attached to it, and, in the country itself, it is a well-known and oft-remarked fact, that most of those who, after a lengthened sojourn, leave it for their old

---

* It is well known that the first gold discovery of importance was made in 1848 by Marshall, a man in the employ of Captain Sutter, a Swiss who first settled there in 1839.   But Californians usually date the rise of the country from 1849.

homes in other parts of the world, soon return to their "first love," finding no other like it.

An impression prevails in England that we know all about this happy land, because, in its early history, book after book issued from the press, telling of the gold, of the restless spirits who gathered from all points in its search, of the lawlessness that prevailed, and of the unheard-of prices of the necessaries of life. Some there were, too, who told us of the natural wonders of the country, of the geysers, of the grand Yosemite Valley, and the "big trees" of Calaveras and of Mariposa. All admitted it was a fruitful land, but we then heard little or nothing of the chances of its ever becoming a grand field for agriculture.

Yet, although at the present time, gold, silver, mercury, and coal all yield abundant returns, they are eclipsed by the more solid progress of the country in the cultivation of the soil. So much grain is raised, that not merely does it help to supply Europe, but it is forwarded even to the "Eastern" or Atlantic States, often *via* that expensive route the Isthmus of Panama. In the State statistics for 1866, the amount of wheat* grown is set down at 14,000,000 bushels, and of barley nearly as much. The wine manufacture is fast becoming a leading branch of industry; over 3,000,000 gallons is now the annual produce of California, and the quantity will largely increase. The culture of the vine and the art of wine-making are, of course, in their infancy in a country itself so young; but some of the wines

---

* "In California one seeding and one cultivation suffice for two crops. The 'volunteer' crop of the second year is, perhaps, one-fifth less in quantity, but it is all profit."—'Overland Monthly,' San Francisco, August, 1868.

would compare favourably with French and German productions, although Californians *are* said to prefer sending
their wines to Boston and New York, and drinking foreign
wines themselves! This is, to an extent, true of San Francisco, but not of the people of the wine districts, who evidently
thrive on their own produce. Many kinds are made,—white,
red, and sparkling. The manufacture of grape brandy has
also been commenced on a large scale. Raisins, figs, prunes,
peaches, and apples are now dried in quantities. The climate
of California is such that the most tender varieties of European grapes, with the olive, orange, and almond, will ripen
in the open air. In Lower California, where there is almost
a tropical climate, the culture of coffee, cocoa, palms, and
bananas has been attempted successfully. In that part of
the country—as yet very thinly settled—the inhabitants are
said, but *not* on the best authority, to read the morning
papers (when they get them!) up to their necks in water—
where they are lucky enough to find any. Towels are an
unnecessary luxury, the heat of the sun causing immediate
evaporation. If you hang up a string of candles, in a few
hours the grease runs off them, and there is nothing left but
the wicks, and they are always, therefore, kept in ice till
required. Droughts are common, and whisky is said to be
cheaper than water, which, if true, may account for some
of the other statements!

The writer has from 1862-7, inclusive, repeatedly revisited
San Francisco, finding each time marked and rapid changes.
The once disorderly village of shanties and tents is now an
orderly city of 140,000 souls. Its best streets are almost
Parisian, its public buildings would be a credit to any city,
and its hotels are better kept and furnished than those of

New York, and that is saying much. A sea wall and docks, both long needed, are now in course of construction.

The State of California has steadily resisted the introduction of a "greenback" currency, or "shin plasters," as they are irreverently called, and those who attempt to pay their debts in this paper money at its nominal value, are advertised in all the papers of the country. There is still no money in circulation under a ten-cent piece, or "bit," as it is termed, while Californians can boast the handsomest gold coin in the world in their twenty-dollar piece. In the early days there was a still larger coin, one worth over 10*l.* sterling, a fifty-dollar piece, an octagonal "slug" of gold, not unlike a Japanese coin. They were made so carelessly that they frequently contained a dollar or two in gold above their supposed value. The Jews used to file and "sweat" them till they were not worth forty dollars; their coinage was in consequence discontinued.

The only city of the United States, outside of New York, which can compare with San Francisco in rapid increase of population, is Chicago in Illinois. San Francisco is as much the centre of American interests on the Pacific, as is New York of those on the Atlantic, and *her present population is as great as was that of the latter city in* 1820, two hundred years after her first settlement.

If it were possible to galvanize the Mexican ports of that coast into life, or if Victoria, Vancouver Island, had a good country round or near it, San Francisco might have a successful rival; as it is, she stands alone, and must be the commercial emporium of the coast. Again Fr'isco (as her citizens often lovingly call her) is the terminal point of that great enterprise the Pacific Railway, and by 1870, in all

probability, the Chinese, Japanese, and Oriental trade for the
States, and some of that for Europe, will pass through her.
A line of splendid steamers is even now running from San
Francisco to China and Japan.

The general prosperity of the people is very apparent.
Where else in the world do you find the labourer on the
docks, or the advertising " medium " walking with his boards
à la sandwich, jauntily smoking a ten-cent cigar?   Where
else do you find no beggars dogging you in every street, and
no crossing sweeper bothering you at every corner?   Men-
dicity is not *défendue,* it does not exist!   There was certainly
the "Emperor Norton," a kind of half-witted fellow, clothed
in regimentals, who issued pompous proclamations, and subsisted by levying black mail on those who were amused by
his fooleries, or on the " free lunches" of the bar-rooms.
There was certainly a huge Mexican female eternally smoking
cigarettos or munching fruit, the while she extended one
hand for alms ; but beggary of that painful kind, which is so
largely developed in every old country, is not known there.
Except in the sailors' quarters, in the lower part of the town,
no fallen women accost or molest the passing stranger ; there
are many of them, indeed, as elsewhere, but they are not
reduced to that depth of degradation.   Servant girls still get
their twenty-five dollars a month, and usually " engage " their
mistresses !   The labourer on a farm, or " ranch," as it is
invariably called, gets his thirty dollars, and is " found "
in board and lodging ; the skilled mechanic averages four
dollars a day.

Indeed, so scarce is female labour as yet, that I believe
the following anecdote—taken from a Californian newspaper
—may be regarded as true :—

T

"A well-to-do citizen of San Francisco, happening to be short of servant girls, was requested by his wife to call on a young lady who had expressed her willingness to engage, for a consideration, to spend a portion of her time in the residence of some highly respectable family, 'references exchanged,' &c. He called on the interesting female, and found her all his fancy painted her, and more, too; in fact, a masterpiece of the milliners', hair-dressers', jewellers', painters', plasterers', and chemists' art, and as airy as a redwood palace with cloth and papered walls, on Telegraph Hill. A few minutes' conversation satisfied him that he had opened the negotiation on a wrong basis, and in fact he was the party to be engaged, not the high-toned lady before him, who answered no questions at all, and questioned him with all the nonchalance of a practised horse-buyer, cheapening a three-legged nag at a Government sale. The interview closed as follows:—

"*Female.*—Where do you live?

"*Citizen.*—Well, out pretty near the Mission Dolores.*

"*Female.*—(With a doubtful shake of her head.) That is a

---

* This is the quarter round the old Mission San Francisco, erected in 1775-6 by the Spaniards, and which is repeatedly mentioned by all the old writers on the coast—Vancouver, Humboldt, Wilkes, Beechey, Forbes, &c. The old church still exists, and a quantity of Spanish MSS. and old books are to be found there. It is about two miles from the heart of San Francisco, but now forms an integral part of it. There are horse and steam "cars" running out to it, as to every other part of the city. Amusing stories are told of the Mission's early days, when the Indians would only keep working in the manufacture of adobes (sun-dried bricks) so long as the good Fathers kept singing to them. As late as 1849, large boilers were to be seen, in which oxen were sometimes boiled *whole* (I had almost said "in one joint!") for the Indians' consumption. See Hutching's 'Scenes, &c., in California.'

long way from Montgomery-street; almost too far, I am
afraid! How many children have you in the family?

" *Citizen.*—(Modestly.) We have four, madam.

" *Female.*—Four! That is a great deal too many.

" *Citizen.*—(Abashed and humbled, taking his hat in his
hand, nervously.) Well, madam, do you think you could get
along with two or three children?

" *Female.*—I suppose I *might*, but you say you have *four.*

" *Citizen.*—(Edging towards the door.) Yes, madam, I did
say *four*, but rather than give you offence and risk a failure
of the negotiation, I did not know but my wife might be prevailed on to *drown one or two of them!*

" With a look of insulted dignity the female rose and
waved her hand, as much as to say, 'You won't do! Get
from my sight!' and the citizen went out of her presence,
feeling, as he avows, at least a thousand per cent. meaner
and more contemptible, in his own opinion, than he had ever
felt or had cause to feel before. He says he is entirely satisfied with his experience in the line of hiring servant girls,
and don't want to try his hand at the business again."

Even if the above is not true in fact, it is in spirit. Let
those who expect to get domestics on the same easy terms as
at home, or to make them " keep their place " with deferen-
tial awe, stay where they are. So rare are female servants,
that a Chinaman or two forms a part of every large household
in city or country. Those who are lucky, get an Irish
" Biddy " or Kathleen, may-be, but it is very rare indeed to
find a *native* American in any menial employment whatever.

A tide of immigration is much needed and desired by Californians; the want of labour often seriously impedes the

progress of the country. The man who now goes there with
a little cash in hand may soon become a prosperous land-
owner himself. He will go to a country whose climate is that
of Italy, or the South of France, whose common productions
are the luxuries of other lands. The writer cannot name
edibles more abundant in their season in the San Francisco
market than salmon, venison, turtle, peaches, and grapes,—
things the very idea of which makes an epicure's mouth water.
The first is generally retailed at eight or ten cents a pound,
and the last are often sold five pounds for twenty-five cents
(about a shilling). But if these are not good enough, a
"royal" dish, the sturgeon, is to be had by any one who likes
that rather tough and indifferent diet.

The *carte* at a first-class San Francisco hotel contains,
in one harmonious whole, the delicacies of London, Paris,
New York, and—New Orleans. The verdant foreigner can
—till dyspepsia brings him back to sanity and plain living—
revel in waffles, buck-wheat and flannel cakes, fried and
boiled mush, hominy, corn bread, French and Spanish ome-
lettes, the national fish-ball, gumbo soup, terrapin stews,
clam and cod-fish chowders, potatoe salad, sweet potatoes,
oyster plants, green corn, elk meat, California quails, squash
pie, floating island, ice creams, and rose candy (candies and
sweetmeats often figure in the dessert of a dinner bill of
fare). The price of board and lodging at such houses is
two and a half to three dollars a day, (or by the month about
fifty-five to sixty dollars). This is one-third lower than the
New York charges. There are no extras (wines, &c., of course
excepted). *Servants are never charged,* nor—excepting for
special services—do they expect payment. Indeed, if you
offered a San Francisco waiter any remuneration (at the

European standard) he would probably punch your head, or leave you to wait on yourself. He would, however, readily "take a drink" with you.

Although San Francisco is full of bar-rooms, "saloons," and Dutch *lager bier* cellars (the German family are all called Dutchmen in San Francisco, and the same title is given usually to Norwegians, Swedes, and Danes,—I have even known a Switzer called a Dutchman!), there is little drunkenness to be observed. This is doubtless partly due to the prevailing American style of drinking—"small doses —and often"! There is one institution in the city—which is, I believe, peculiar to it—the "Home for the Inebriates." It is what its name implies—a temporary hospital for violent or incapable drunkards, or for those who are the victims of *delirium tremens*. We have, or had, an asylum for "homeless dogs," but we are not quite so lenient to our inebriates!

San Francisco has eight daily papers and a dozen weeklies.[*] One of these contains a new feature: "Divorces" are inserted in the column with "Births, Marriages," &c., and it reads, "Births, Marriages, Divorces, and Deaths"! In point of fact, the new heading is well supported! A Fenian paper, said to be printed in green ink, the writer was never able to discover.

The Chinese population is a great feature of this country,

---

[*] 'The Alta California,' 'The Bulletin,' and 'The Sacramento Union,' are papers of a very superior class, and are much a-head of the New York and Boston journals, in paper and type. A new magazine, 'The Overland Monthly,' very similar in appearance to 'The Atlantic Monthly,' has just (July 1868) reached England. It has commenced its existence with much spirit.

and is said to be 60,000 strong. "John Chinaman" you find everywhere; he is house-servant, cook, farm labourer, miner, even railway "navvy." * He does most of the laundry business, and it is a curious and rather unpleasant sight to witness him ironing out clothes, with a great open pan of hot charcoal, and sprinkling them by filling his mouth with water, and squirting it over them in a fine spray, through his clenched teeth. Their signs, Gee Wo, Hop Chang, or Cum Sing (actual names), are seen on every secondary street. And very strong-smelling is the special Chinese quarter, with its curious little shops, eating-houses, and laundries, where nine persons out of ten you meet are from the "Flowery Land," and wandering in which, you might imagine that you had lost yourself in Canton or Pekin.

These gentry have several "joss houses," and two theatres, where the performances are of an interminable nature, as they take the reign of an emperor, and play it through in detail night after night. Their gambling-houses are numerous, and their attractions are enhanced by (Chinese)

---

* Several thousands are now employed in building the Pacific Railroad. A late number of the San Francisco 'Bulletin' says :—" As a tunnel-cutter he was especially invaluable. During the progress of the great 'Summit' tunnel (through the Sierra Nevada Mountains) there was a strike in some of the Nevada mines, and a number of Cornishmen came up to work for the Company. But it was found that the Chinamen could do considerably more work and stand the fatigue and foul air of underground work much better. The Cornishmen tried it a while, but concluded to leave the work of boring through granite mountains to the more adaptable Celestial, and went away in disgust."

Three hundred are engaged at the " Mission " Wool Mills in San Fran-cisco, in the manufacture of cloths, flannels, and blankets from Californian wool.

wine, women, and opium. The police have some trouble with these establishments, from brawls not of a "celestial" nature. It is said that opium smoking is more general among them here than even in their own land; the facilities for obtaining it are probably greater, and, like many a better man, "John" is cut off from his own kindred, and is more dependent on his own resources to while away his leisure hours.

The larger part of the poor Chinese in California have been "imported" by some five or six companies composed of their wealthier countrymen, and it is a well-known fact that for a long time after their arrival they are in a species of bondage; paying off, in fact, their passage money, &c.

A tax of four dollars a head per month is imposed by the state on every Chinaman, and, though he forms an undoubtedly useful part of the population, it cannot be said that he has a very pleasant time in California. The "poor white man" looks on him as an interloper, who lowers the price of wages, and is consequently deserving of the worst forms of persecution; the "dead broke" or "busted" gambler in the mines, comes round with a bundle of papers and an inkhorn, collecting from his unsuspecting victim a "tax" on his own account, to enable him to start a montè, or faro bank, once more; and the Indian looks on him as his rightful prey, and murders him when the opportunity occurs. It is to be remarked that the Indians of the coast generally, as far as my experience goes, look on the negro also as a thoroughly inferior being to themselves. As a servant "John" is certainly better than the negro; he attends to his business, and is not so fussy. On the new China steamship line from San Francisco, Chinese waiters are employed exclusively.

In the mining districts "John Chinaman" is to be seen travelling through the country, carrying his traps on either end of a long pole, in the style depicted on the tea chests, familiar to us from earliest childhood. In this manner he "packs" much larger loads than the ordinary traveller. The writer well remembers a Chinaman he met, carrying at one end of his stick a bag of rice, a pick and shovel, a pair of extra pantaloons, a frying pan, and a billy-pot; whilst from the other depended a coop of fowls and chickens, of which "John" is devotedly fond. In this respect he is wiser than his betters; for while the ordinary "honest miner" is feeding on beans, bacon, and tea, he has eggs and chickens with his rice, and is very diligent in searching out and utilising wild onions, berries, and roots. In 1865, a number of Chinamen arrived at intervals, in several vessels, in Victoria, V. I., and a few hours after landing they invariably found their way into the woods, or on to the sea-beach, where they collected shell fish and many kinds of sea-weed, which they stewed and fried in various shapes.

But though "John" has no objection to live in California, and often has to die there, he will not consent to be buried away from the "Flowery Land," and every vessel for Hong Kong and Shanghai takes a cargo of defunct Chinamen; the wealthy ones put up in spirits, or embalmed.

Large and influential firms or companies of a better class of these people exist in the city, and they sometimes offer entertainments to "distinguished arrivals." In June, 1866, one was held in honour of the U.S. ministers to China and Japan, then waiting for a vessel to convey them to their destination, and was, in Californian phraseology, a "high toned and elegant" affair. The "carte" included sharks'

fins, birds' nest soup, reindeer sinews, geranium and violet
cakes, samshoo and rose wine, but was not deficient in the
good things of our *cuisine*, accompanied by an unlimited
supply of champagne. A toast to the minister to China,
concluded with a thoroughly Oriental sentiment,—" We wish
your Excellency ten thousand golden pleasures, and a happy
voyage to the Central Flowery Empire ! "

The wealthier Chinese merchants—many of them very
intelligent men—often wear European clothing, and their
pig-tails are then coiled up in neat *chignons* (I believe this
is the correct word ?) at the back of their heads. But the
tail is always there! and nothing would induce them to
part with it. When their hair is naturally short or scanty,
fine black silk, and sometimes real hair, is woven into it
to make up the deficiency. I have heard of something not
very dissimilar in vogue recently among our countrywomen,
but do not, of course, believe it !

CHAPTER XXV.

CALIFORNIA—*Continued.*

San Francisco society — Phraseology — Ladies of Fr'isco — Sunday in the
city — Free criticism on parsons — Site — Steep streets — San Francisco
calves — Earthquakes — House moving — Fire companies — "Wells
Fargo's Express" — The three-cent stamps — The men of the Pacific.

Society in the "Bay City," though still a little "mixed"—
to use a Californian phrase, is, taking it altogether, a much
heartier, jollier, sincerer thing than elsewhere. Californians
will have none of the airs of the high and mighty; they call
it "putting on frills," they say that sort of thing is "played
out," and recommend such to "vamoose the ranch," or get
from their sight. Ask them how they are, and the answer is
pat, "Oh, gay and festive," with probably the affirmative positive, "you bet," or may-be "you bet your boots." If a preacher,
actor, or writer, indulges in an exaggerated manner, they
say "he piles on the agony" too much, has a "spread eagle"
or "high-falutin" style about him. The derivation of the
last term is involved in mystery. Many of the common
expressions are taken from mining operations and experiences. "It panned out well" means that "it gave good
returns." "Show," or "colour," from the indications of gold
in gravel or sand, are words used in various shapes. "I have
not a show" means I have no chance. "We have not seen
the 'colour' of his money" means, he has not paid up a
farthing. "Prospect"—to search for gold—is used in many
ways; ask if a speculation promises well, they may answer,
"It prospects well, if we can only make the riffle," the last an

allusion to successfully getting over a " rapid " or " riffle " on a river. Or, if the thing has disappointed, it may be, " we got down to the ' bed rock,' and found it a ' bilk,' "—Californian for a humbug.

If one looks anxious, they say, " There's a heap of trouble on the old man's mind ; " and if one is got up elaborately in a "biled shirt " (i. e., white shirt), a "stove-pipe " (or as we say, "chimney-pot ") hat, and a suit of new broadcloth, one is apt to be asked, " You've rather spread yourself, haven't you ? " It is common for men to shave a good deal, and the city is full of barbers' shops, where you can get yourself shaved and your boots blacked at one and the same time. These establishments are often luxuriously fitted up, and beat anything of the kind to be seen in the " Eastern " States. Beards are termed " chin whiskers," and our " whiskers " are distinguished as " side whiskers." The terms for most things are on a more magnificent scale than with us. A bar-room is invariably a "saloon," an eating-house, a "restaurant" (pronounced in an Anglicised manner), and a shop is a " store." A good substantial repast is known as a " square " meal, all over this coast, and the same term is applied to many other things. A "square " drink is a " deep, deep draught," and a good " square fight " is an encounter or " muss " where the opponents were in earnest. Some of these terms are common to the " Western " States and outlying " territories," but cannot be regarded as full-blooded Americanisms. They attract just as much notice from " Eastern " men travelling in. California as they do from Europeans.

Listen to a quarrel in the streets : one calls the other a " regular dead beat !" at which he, in return, threatens to " put a head on him !" whereupon, the first sneeringly retorts "up a flume," the equivalent of a vulgar cockney's "over the left." If one or the other "weakens," or shows signs of "caving" in and leaving, he is said to "get up and dust." It is then the business of his opponent to "corral" him in a corner,—a term taken from the Spanish for catching and shutting up cattle in an enclosure. This last phrase is used in a variety of ways. A police officer "corrals" an offender, a greedy man at table "corrals" all the delicacies, and a broker "corrals" all the stock of a company, and controls the market, and so on.

But in justice to Californians, it must be stated that many of these phrases are—among the better classes—only known to be avoided. A stranger might be a long time in the country before he heard the whole of the above. A portion of them are, however, common enough.

A San Franciscan would doubtless detect something equally strange in the current "slang" of London, which we all know to be by no means confined to the lower classes, but which constantly crops out in the conversation of young men and even, alas! in that of the young ladies "of the period."

Although things have changed since the time when a miner would walk twenty miles to catch a glimpse of a female,—and when the steamboats advertised "*Four* lady passengers to-night!" as a sure bait to travellers,—they are still by no means at a discount, and in no place in the world does woman hold a higher place. Perhaps, in consequence, there is rather more heard and seen of her vanity, weakness, and extravagance. I have the best authority for stating that "Perhaps in no other American city would the ladies 'invoice' so high per head, when they go out to the opera, to party, or ball." But though there is a dash of

"fastness" on the surface, ladies, refined, educated, and vir-
tuous, are as abundant here as they are elsewhere, and the girls
born in California will bear the palm in a country famous for
its pretty girls, whilst their mothers, at a given age, are more
plump and blooming than those of the Atlantic States.

Here and there, it is true, you will find some prominent
citizen, who in early days "took unto himself" his washer-
woman, no better being then available; and I have native
authority for saying, that the men seem of a higher grade
than the women. Nevertheless, I am sure that a mixed
assembly of San Franciscans would compare favourably with
a similar one of New Yorkers, where the "shoddy" and
"petroleum aristocracies" have rather too much sway. In
the country districts, ladies who attend to their dairies and
gardens in the day, and in the evening are able to delight
you with the best and latest music, or tell you far more than
you know yourself of current literature, are by no means
uncommon.

In San Francisco Parisian fashions dominate, and any fine
afternoon a rich display of furs is to be seen *on* Montgomery
Street, (reader, it is always *on* not *in* a street in this country),
which might seem out of place in so warm a climate, but for
the fact that a cool wind blows into the city, with periodical
regularity, in the latter part of the day, more especially in
summer time. The winter season is by some preferred to
the summer, but the climate of San Francisco and its
immediate neighbourhood is not equal to that of California
generally. This is doubtless owing to the proximity of the
former to the ocean.

Sunday in this city has a decidedly foreign tinge, although
there is a large church-going public. When the writer was

first there, mock "bull-fights" and balloon ascensions usually
took place on the Sabbath; brass bands paraded the streets,
and it was a favourite day for excursions of every kind.
Some of this has been a little modified: indeed, if you took
the number of churches and chapels, Episcopal, Presbyterian,
Methodist, Congregational, Unitarian, and Roman Catholic,
San Francisco might be considered a very pious place indeed.
The Roman Catholics, considered as one sect, predominate:
the Jews are very strong; one of their synagogues is a prominent building in the city.

The demand in San Francisco is for liberal clergymen of
high culture, and it is indispensable that they shall have
good powers of oratory. Judging from what I have seen,
sect is of little consequence, and, in point of fact, you will
meet Roman Catholics at the houses of Methodists, and
vice versâ, and mingling as the best of friends. Before
leaving this subject, one point must be mentioned,—the
very free criticism the preacher gets, both in private circles
and from the press. In an American work, now lying before
me, the writer, alluding to a Rev. Dr. ——, says, he "is making his *début* as pastor of one of the Presbyterian societies, and
is drawing good houses"! The only objection that can fairly
be made to the preachers of California, and indeed of the whole
United States, is, that they are rather given to mixing politics
with their religion,—a very curious fact in a country where
Church has absolutely no connection with State.

The site of the "Golden City" was chosen rather for its
"water front" than for any excellence in itself. It is "built
on the sand," and this is ever before and also *in* your eyes;
it is one of the dustiest places on the globe, though otherwise a clean, bright-looking city. In the suburbs you may

see an enclosed, but unoccupied "lot," with the sand drifted
up to the top bars of the fence; and although the principal
streets are well covered in with stone, wood-blocks, and
asphalte, yet whenever they are taken up for repairs you
see the true foundation of the city. The main business
streets are level, but the side streets and suburbs run up
the hills, at angles often of thirty degrees, and it is even
troublesome to keep your footing on the wooden pave-
ments or "side walks." The houses seem, in places, to be
holding on with difficulty, as though a storm or earthquake
might shake them down in a general heap to the bottom.
Now-a-days, when the streets are being "graded," it frequently
happens that the older dwellings are left perched up in the
air on a rocky bluff fifty or a hundred feet above the road-
way, and their owners, who formerly walked from it direct
to their front doors, now have to climb a series of zigzag
steps to reach them.

This exercise has a beneficial effect on San Franciscan
legs, and no where are children's calves better developed!
As the ladies of "Fr'isco" do *not* put holland trousers on the
legs of their pianos and dining-room tables—as it is said
their more prudish sisters in the New England States are
in the habit of doing—this allusion may be permitted. San
Francisco would be an excellent place for a Pacific Alpine
Club to train in.

À propos of earthquakes, San Francisco has had many a
fright from feeble shocks, which have cracked walls and
brought down chimneys, but have hitherto done little
damage. But just as these latter sheets are going to press,
the telegraph informs us of the occurrence (on Oct. 21st) of
an earthquake in California, of a more serious nature. I

hope, and believe, that the damage stated to have been done to property in San Francisco, will prove to have been exaggerated, and that the uncertain allusions to loss of life, will turn out to have no foundation in fact. The recent terrible earthquakes in Peru, &c., will be fresh in the minds of every reader. The force of the subterranean disturbances, on the West coast of the American continent, appears to diminish as it proceeds northwards, though more or less alarming shocks are common, in point of fact, all over the Pacific, North and South. The writer has experienced such in California, Vancouver Island, and Russian America.* A theory was started recently in San Francisco, that these were simply the result of thunder-clouds rolling over the land! but few could be induced to see them in that light.†

---

* It is well known that shocks have been felt almost *simultaneously* in California, Oregon, British Columbia, and the Sandwich Islands. In 1865, when one of the worst earthquakes which have frightened San Francisco occurred—one of the two peaks of Mount Baker (a very fine volcanic mountain in Washington Territory, seen from most parts of the Gulf of Georgia, &c.) fell in partially. Smoke and vapour rise from this mountain, but there is, I believe, no record of lava or ashes issuing from it. Mr. E. T. Coleman of Victoria, V. I., a worthy pioneer of the Alpine Club of London, of which he is an original member, has twice essayed the ascent of Mount Baker, and although he has not yet reached its summit, I have no doubt he means to do it. The difficulties he encountered—dense forests, mountain torrents, and a lack of guides—are a fair sample of those which will beset all travellers in these half-developed countries. There will be almost as much trouble to reach the base of a mountain as its summit.

† A recent New York paper publishes the following telegram from California :—"On the 15th August (1868), a singular tidal phenomenon occurred off San Pedro, Southern California. A series of waves commenced flowing upon the coast, causing the tide to rise sixty-three or sixty-four feet above the ordinary high-water mark, which was followed by the falling of the tide an equal distance below the usual low-water mark. The rise and fall occurred regularly every half-hour for several hours, creating considerable alarm among the inhabitants along the coast in that vicinity."

All well-situated property in this city is held at a very high value, and the expense of housekeeping induces thousands of well-to-do people to live in the hotels, which are certainly equal to those of any country. But, notwithstanding this, the suburbs are full of cottages, villas, and mansions of a superior class, often surrounded by very handsome grounds. As the streets improve, the older board-and-shingle "frame buildings" are moved to the outskirts on rollers, and often on large, wide, low carts, with small wheels, drawn by fifteen or twenty horses. Sometimes the family continues to occupy it as usual, and you see the smoke issuing from the "stove pipe," or chimney, as it travels through the streets. The furniture and carpets remain "as they were," and are carried bodily with the house. A travelling hawker's caravan creates more notice here in England than this "house moving" does in San Francisco; it is a common occurrence in all Western and Pacific towns. A house is often deposited at the corner, or in the middle of a street, for the night.

The "fire-men" of San Francisco were long one of its most interesting and worthy features, and their brightly painted, brass and silver mounted, steam and other fire-engines and apparatus, rivalled the best that were to be seen in other American cities. The earlier buildings were all of wood, and even now in the suburbs are commonly of the same material. Fires of a terrible nature have devastated the city; it was, in its young days, three times almost destroyed.

It is obvious, that the "Fire Companies" were then, in-stitutions of no common value; they numbered, in their palmy days, three parts of the best citizens of the place—all volunteers. There were "crack" companies too, to which it was an honour to belong, whilst the "Chief Engineer" of the city was a very distinguished individual. But as San Francisco increased in size, these rather deteriorated in quality, and the "rowdy" element became rampant. In consequence, it was not uncommon for several rival fire companies to meet and fight at the corner of a street, or before the fire, sometimes using revolvers and knives, while the conflagration itself remained unchecked, and it became obvious that some other arrangement must be made. There is now a regularly organized, and *paid* Fire Department, which works in a satisfactory manner. It is an occurrence of every week, and frequently of every day, to hear the fire-bells tolling suddenly. The quarter of the town in which the fire exists is indicated by the number of the strokes.

One of the prominent "Institutions" of California, as of the whole coast, and in a lesser degree of the whole United States, is certainly the famous Wells Fargo's Express. An American writer before quoted,* says truly, "a billiard-saloon, a restaurant, and a Wells Fargo's office, are the first three elements of a Pacific Coast mining town." They forward goods everywhere, convey nearly all the "treasure" in gold or silver; do a general banking business, and are infinitely more trusted by the public with the transmission of mail matter than the Government Post Office. This great firm, or corporation, has first to buy the Government stamp, and then add their own to the envelope they sell you. In 1864, they purchased this way 2,500,000 of three-

---

* Bowles, 'Across the Continent.'

cent stamps,* and 125,000 of higher value. The quantity has now doubtless considerably increased. Their messengers, armed and wide awake, ride through the outlying unsettled, and more or less lawless, districts, and are met on every steamer of the coast.

From this rough sketch, it will be seen that the Pacific Coast is not behind the times, and that all the elements of life, energy, and civilization are represented. An early writer on California told us that "San Francisco exhibited an immense amount of vitality compressed into a small compass," and that "people lived more there in a week than they would in a year in most places." This is still true. It is a thoroughly "live" place. But it has still better features. Nowhere will you find a mass of more reliant, hopeful, kind-hearted, and generous men than on this coast: nearly all of whom have at some time "gone through the mill," and have come out strengthened by the process; and the writer, remembering the pleasant days spent among them, would conclude this chapter by saying, from the depth of his heart, and in their own language, "Long may they wave!"

---

* The three-cent postage-stamp of the United States is equal to the penny stamp of Great Britain. Affixed to a letter it will frank it from one extreme of the country to the other—from the Atlantic to the Pacific. We are justly proud of our cheap postage, but we have hardly attained that degree of cheapness—3000 miles for three cents! At the present time, too, that charge is hardly in advance of our own; three cents—paper —is little more than an English penny. But there is one terrible draw-back; excepting in the large Atlantic cities, letters are not delivered, but have to be called for. Every business man has his private pigeon-hole box at the Post Office, in which his letters are deposited.

CHAPTER XXVI.

CALIFORNIA AS A FIELD FOR EMIGRATION.

Early American opinions of the country — California steamers — The public lands — Extent — Price — Labour — Wages — The wine interests — Table of temperatures — Vineyards, &c. — Classes suitable for immigrants — Education — Schools — School ma'ams — Investments.

THAT California is a desirable country wherein to dwell, no one who has visited it will be disposed to doubt; yet for a long period, *even in America itself*, it was looked upon as of dubious value. A writer in one of the leading San Francisco newspapers, 'The Alta California,' speaking of his own countrymen last year, said, "The greatest number of those who returned East (*i. e.* to the Atlantic States), from 1849 to 1855, reported the State as, in the main, a barren desert, deluged with rain in winter, parched up with heat in summer and autumn, and wholly unfitted by nature for the uses of the farmer. At that early day, such opinions were common, and hardly to be wondered at, for the farming capabilities of the State had scarcely been tested. Our first peaches came into the market in 1854, and the man at that time, who would have ventured the prediction that this State might excel any State west of the Alleghanies in fruits, and any country on the continent in grapes, would have been rated a fool: for, four years later, we still imported the great bulk of flour, meal, bacon, butter, lard, beans, &c., from the

States * or from Chili.   Not that it would not have been profitable to produce these articles here, but because the vast
majority of the people did not believe in the capacity of the
country to produce them.   Mankind are slow to surrender
the prejudices and habits of early life; and if heaven itself
were offered to an Esquimaux, clad in the waving verdure
and flowery vestments which charmed the eye of Dante as he
gazed upon it from the banks of Lethe, he would probably
esteem it a wretched country without the regular complement
of darkness, icebergs, and walrus-fat.   The total absence of
rain from May to November, and the want of his regular
treat to thunder and lightning every two or three days, were
things altogether strange to the Western farmer, whose corn
and hemp, and vegetables, he thought could not possibly
mature without them.

"And so it came to pass that California had more de-

---

* The "States" and the "East" are terms which signify simply—when
used by Californians—the Atlantic States of America.   California is as
much a State as any other, but, as large parts of its population are from
New York and the New England States, they look to them as their old
home,—and proudly call them "The States."

There are a large number, also, of Western frontier men in the country,
whose lives have been spent like that of John Brown—in "marching on."
Born, say in Missouri, they commenced life by taking up land—clearing
and improving it for a year or two—and then selling it; they then moved
on to a fresher and wilder locality, repeating the process over and over
again, till they reached the "Farthest West" in California.   But civilization has no charms for them, and some of them having perhaps seen more
of it in a week in San Francisco than in their whole lives before—and
become much disgusted thereby—have started back on the *return journey*
across the continent!   But such men as these will make a howling wilder-
ness smile.   They are the true pioneers of civilization, though they fly
before it, as does the wild Indian before them.

tractors than eulogists for the first ten years after the discovery of gold. She was regarded as a very good gold-mine—nothing better;" and that view of the case did not assist in settling the country.

But now things are changed. When I left California last November (1867), there were three distinct lines of steamers for New York: the Mail and Opposition boats (viâ Panama) and the old Opposition (viâ Nicaragua). In addition, there was the regular stage-line across the continent, and every one was looking forward to the completion of the Pacific Railroad. Yet, with all these facilities for travel, the united population of the States of California, Oregon, and Nevada, with the Territory of Washington, does not yet number a million souls. That number—one-third of the population of London —is diffused over territories larger than those inhabited by the whole German family of sixty millions!

The expense* of reaching California is, of course, one great hindrance to a rapid increase of its population. The steam vessels on "both sides" of the Isthmus of Panama are of a very superior class, and usually charge accordingly. It has been proposed to employ a supplementary service of screw-steamers for emigrants and freight. Should this be done,

---

* This varies considerably. I have known the price of passage from San Francisco to New York range from 75 dollars (say 15l. 10s.) to 300 dollars (61l. 10s.) for first cabin accommodation. Owing to excessive competition, a steerage passage has been as low as 35 dollars (7l. 3s. 6d.), and at that rate was a loss to the Company. The transit across the Isthmus of Panama is always included in the charges. When the Pacific railroad is completed, the steamer fares will probably be much reduced. These boats have, on occasions, carried 2000 passengers, and very frequently 1000 or 1500.

and the Panama Railroad Company reduce its exorbitant fare—twenty-five dollars (£5), for a distance of forty-seven miles!—which they charge every passenger, of whatever class—California may get the labour she so much needs.

Last autumn, a number of Southerners, disgusted with politics, disgusted with negro supremacy in places where they themselves had reigned, wrote to the mayor of San Francisco, for information about the country; and, as the answers returned were printed in the Californian papers, I propose to clip from them a few items of general interest. The first query was this,—"Are the public lands entirely absorbed?" and the answer (returned by the Immigration Society, to whom it was referred) was as follows:—

" No. There are millions upon millions of acres yet in the keeping of the Federal Government officers, which can be had for one dollar an acre in gold. Only in the neighbourhood of the great thoroughfares, the navigable rivers, the fragments of railways yet constructed, the mining camps and the like, has ever the Government Surveyor yet erected his theodolite. There are plenty of good spots where small colonies of immigrants may squat and await for years the coming of the Federal Government Surveyor; and when he shall come, the dollar an acre demanded by the Government will have, long before, been realized out of the land.

" In the San Joaquin Valley, sixty miles back from Stockton (a town of about 5000 inhabitants and one night's journey by steamer from San Francisco), plenty of land can be got for one dollar in gold per acre, from the Government office in Stockton. This valley is about 100 miles long, by a width varying from ten to thirty miles, through which streams, navigable for flat boats, flow down to the Sacramento River.

The soil is deep and rich, and the bottoms near the water are exceedingly fertile, and able to support abundance of kine. This valley would absorb 100,000 settlers."

The Sacramento Valley also—especially in its upper portions near the source of the river—is a very promising field for the new comer, while—

" In the counties south of San Francisco—Monterey, for instance, two days' journey by stage from San Francisco—large tracts of the richest land, owned by easy-going people of Spanish descent, can be purchased or rented upon very advantageous terms: purchased for a dollar or two an acre, or rented on shares for one-fourth of the annual produce of the land. The chief and greatest cost is the expense of fencing.

" In many places the old Spanish settlers own tracts of thirty to fifty thousand acres, unfenced and undivided, over which numberless flocks of sheep and cattle roam, and breed, and die, without control or much care from the proprietors, who live in rude ease and almost secluded from the outside world. Their slumbers will soon be broken by the hum of busy immigrants, who will come crowding by sea and land into their fruitful territories. Farther south, towards Los Angeles, the best lands can be purchased from those old-fashioned settlers for a dollar an acre, or even less. There is very little timber to be cleared from any of these lands.

" To go upon those lands, several families should form themselves into villages, or companies, and go out together on the land and help each other. This coöperative system is sure to make the immigrants happy and prosperous."

The second prominent question related to the demand for labour, and the reply was so truthful, and at the same time so properly ·guarded from exaggeration, that 1 print it as it stands :—

" We are full of the great idea of inviting an extensive immigration from Europe, and from the Southern and Eastern States, to the Pacific slope, but we shudder at the thought of misleading any one. It is almost unnecessary to repeat that we have room and work for millions of people in our fields and mines, but the great trouble is to support people while they are finding the work suited to their strength, their habits, and their experience. The idea that fills the minds of many persons in making towards California is, that they shall go a gold-hunting in the mines, make lucky hits, and return at some distant day to their old homes in Europe or the Atlantic States to enjoy their good fortune. This idea has been the unseen rock that has wrecked many an immigrant to this golden land. None should come to the Californian *mines* but *miners*.*

" On the first discovery of gold in California, and for several years afterwards, every kind of labourer went to the mines, and many of them did very well; but of late years the Chinese have got in and have swarmed over the ' placer ' or stream mines, and, as they work in well-organised companies, and live upon little, they are able to scrape a living from the oft-washed sands in the older washing-grounds of the earlier miners. The principal mining now carried on in California is quartz mining, which is as like coal or iron mining as possible—penetrating the bowels of the earth

---

* A large number of Welsh and Cornish miners have—from the earliest days of Californian history—settled in the country, and are much esteemed as practical men.

several hundred feet—men working in gangs, in 'watches'
of eight hours each shift, so that the work never stops, night
or day.   For this kind of work miners get four dollars a day.
Their board and lodging in the neighbourhood of those quartz
mines comes high, about eight or ten dollars a week, as a
general rule ; two and a half days' wages is required to pay
for a miner's board and lodging for a week.   A great deal of
the work on the Pacific Railroad on our side of the Rocky
Mountains is performed by Chinamen, under white overseers.
They get about a dollar a day for their labour.   White men
could get such wages with board, but they won't work for it.
A dollar a day is the lowest notch which the strong man's
labour has touched in any part of California.   Common
labour, according to skill, ranges up to one and a half and
two dollars a day.   We are not now talking of skilled mechanical labour, such as carpenters, bricklayers, plasterers,
smiths, machinists, foundry-men, tailors, shoemakers, and the
like.   The labour of such men brings three to five dollars
a day in all the cities and in all the towns of the Pacific
Coast.   As to clerks and light porters,* and those who are
always waiting for an easy berth or something to 'turn up,'
there is little encouragement for them.   The cities are full
of them.   This kind of helpless people are the production of
an erroneous system of education, which has weaned the
boy from labour, and left the man a helpless, pitiable
mendicant.

    " You are, doubtless, impatient to learn, then, what sort of

----

* " Light porter " is a term often used in California, to designate one
who prefers an easy, half-lazy employment to more manly pursuits.   It is
not generally used in a very flattering sense.

people are likely to do well here, and we answer, any sort who are thoroughly determined to work—men and women, young and old.

" The lowest wages for labour amongst us is about twice the wages of New York, and four times the wages obtained in Great Britain, Ireland, or Germany. The price of wheaten flour is about one-half what it is in Liverpool or New York— eight dollars a barrel of 196 pounds just now. Tea, sugar, and coffee about the same as in England or New York. Clothing and house-rent about double the English rates, and about the same as in New York. All the foregoing rates are in gold.

" The total produce of our gold and silver mines may be set at fifty to sixty millions of dollars a year. Our farming and general agricultural products will very soon, if they do not now, foot up to fifty million dollars' worth a year. The value of the wheat and flour shipped from California since last harvest comes up to nine million dollars; and as fast as good ships come into the harbour they are engaged to take out wheat and flour, wool, hides, &c. The general demand for all sorts of mechanics in this city, and throughout the State, was never better. The wages, as we have said, range: for Chinamen, one dollar a day; common labourers, two dollars a day; skilled mechanics, three to four dollars a day; some of superior skill, five dollars a day; female servants, fifteen to twenty-five dollars a month, and board; farm labourers, thirty dollars a month, and board."*

---

* For precise and reliable information on the country, the reader is referred to Hittell's 'Resources of California,' and Cronise's 'Natural Wealth of California.' These works, the latter of which is a very recent

The wine interests, destined to become one of the most profitable pursuits, are at the present time beset by serious obstacles, from the high price of labour, materials, and especially of casks; but the climate, soil, and enterprise are there, and success is certain.

There are considerable variations between the mean temperatures of places in the country (and this, of course, affects the variety of grape most in vogue in each locality); a table of such temperatures is here given * (extracted from a recent number of 'The Alta California,' and including some Euro-

production, are both published in San Francisco, but can be obtained in London.

* TABLE OF TEMPERATURES.

DISTRICTS.	January.	February.	March.	April.	May.	June.	July.	August.	September.	October.	November.	December.	Average.
Dijon	33	36	48	51	60	66	70	72	62	53	43	35	52
Bordeaux	41	45	51	56	60	66	73	73	67	58	48	43	57
Marseilles	43	45	48	56	63	71	75	71	68	58	50	47	58
Madeira	60	60	62	63	64	67	70	72	71	67	64	60	65
Los Angeles..	52	55	58	..	..	73	75	75	75	69	59	60	..
San Diego	51	53	56	61	62	67	72	73	70	65	56	51	62
Monterey	52	50	51	53	56	57	58	59	59	58	54	50	55
San Francisco	49	51	52	55	55	56	57	57	58	57	54	51	54
Humboldt Bay	40	43	47	54	53	58	56	57	57	53	48	45	57
Fort Yuma	56	58	60	73	76	87	92	90	86	76	64	55	73
Fort Miller	47	53	56	62	68	83	90	83	76	67	55	48	66
Sacramento ..	45	48	51	59	67	71	73	73	66	64	52	45	59
Grass Valley..	27	37	38	44	49	52	63	58	53	53	43	36	46
Sonoma ..	45	47	51	53	62	71	66	66	67	66	58	46	58
Meadow Valley	34	32	41	..	61	66	71	68	57	52	44	32	..

(California. — bracketing Los Angeles through Meadow Valley)

pean districts for comparison). The figures represent the mean monthly heat in degrees of Fahrenheit (without fractions).

This table includes places which represent the furthest extremes of the State. The observations on Sonoma temperatures were taken by my friend Major Snyder, who has one of the most highly-cultivated vineyards in the country. There, and at the vineyard of a second friend, Mr. Craig, where I have passed many pleasant days, and at others in the same beautiful valley, I have had an opportunity of witnessing the culture of the grape under favourable circumstances. Mr. Craig, besides capital white and red wines, has succeeded in making some of the best grape brandy in the State; while Major Snyder's wines, some of them four and five years old, closely resembled high class Burgundy and Rhine wines.* It would astonish those who look upon California as not yet " of age "—which, in fact, she hardly is —to see the wine-presses of scientific construction, the wine-houses and cellars of Sonoma and Los Angeles. Most of the vineyards in Sonoma were in the valley, but the hill-sides will sooner or later be utilized; the vines of all varieties, and mainly European, were all dwarfed, staked, and kept carefully pruned.

Los Angeles (Pueblo de los Angeles), "the abode of the Angels," is also the abode of a large number of wine growers, who, if not angels, are at least jolly fellows! It is situated on the southern coast, and the county yields the largest returns

---

* Time has worked wonders. Wilkes, in 1841, " found the wines of the country miserable stuff, which would scarcely be taken for the juice of the grape."

of wine; Sonoma standing second, and Santa Clara County
third. It is much warmer, as our table shows, than Sonoma,
and the most delicate and tender grapes ripen there to perfection. The native American grapes (Delaware, Clinton,
Perkins, King, &c., all hardy varieties) are not much prized
in California, but in one or two counties the Catawba is
a great favourite. The Muscatelle, Isabella, and Mission
grapes are the commonest varieties grown in large quantities.
The grape vines when five years old yield plenteously. I
have before me a story of a vine of the Isabella variety,
which, in its *fourth* year, bore 1500 bunches, weighing
420 lbs. The "wonderful gooseberry" of periodical recur-
rence must evidently hide its diminished head, or burst with
rage ! *

Hops and tobacco are now raised in fair quantities, while
experiments have been made in the culture of cotton, and
the rearing of silkworms.

As I have before stated, immigrants are much desired
in California, and the question naturally arises which classes
of our population might most profitably venture there.
First and foremost stands the farmer. Farming in England
—though not quite so unprofitable as some grumblers would
have us believe—is, to the small tenant at least, no very

---

* Hittell tells us, in his 'Resources of California,' that in 1765,—
"Señora Dominguez, a native of Mexico, and a resident of Santa Barbara
County, rode from Monterey to her home, and, before starting, she picked
up a grape-cutting for a switch. When she had ridden twenty miles, she
saw that her switch was budding; she took care of it, and after getting
to her house at Montecito, planted it in the garden. The vine grew, and
now its trunk is 16 inches in diameter, and its branches are supported by
an arbour 114 feet long and 78 feet wide. Its annual yield of grapes is
three or four tons."

paying pursuit. Our small farmers, if possessed of a little
capital to start with, would soon rise to competence in
California. Next comes the man with a definite profession,
business, or trade; especially the skilled ˙ mechanic, who is
safe anywhere on the Pacific coasts, and specially so in
California, or Oregon; and, lastly, the labourer, and female
servant, who are perfectly sure of remunerative employment. Young men brought up in idleness, men of no definite
profession or business, petty clerks, counter-jumpers, and
the devotees of "genteel" callings, had better stay where
they are. California is no home for them, unless they mean
to mend their ways. The market even there is over-stocked
with such persons.

Although California was a loyal State during the late
civil war in America, there is much liberality of sentiment
there, and politics do not run as high as in the Atlantic
States. The Englishman * will find numbers of his countrymen, and there is no reason why he should not venture there.
If he goes, he will assuredly never reproach the writer for his
recommendation.

In the matter of education—one of so much importance to
the man who brings a family with him—California is by no

---

* With regard to the wine manufacture and the culture of the vine, it
is obvious that foreigners from the wine districts of the Continent—from
small proprietors to peasants—would each and all be specially welcomed,
and could very readily find remunerative employment in the vineyards of
California, and, sooner or later, become proprietors themselves. If they
go with a reasonable amount of capital, they can become such at once.
Already there are many intelligent Germans, Frenchmen, and Hungarians,
but the labour employed is mainly Chinese. Men capable of superintend-
ing vineyards are much desired.

means behind the rest of the country, and the United States may fairly boast of her school system.   In addition to any number of private schools and colleges, the public free-schools are of the most efficient kind, and in them the children of well-to-do citizens—as well as those of a lower grade—are frequently to be found, side by side.   The Lincoln school-house in San Francisco, which accommodates 1000 scholars, is a building which would attract notice anywhere, and 9000 children attend the public schools of that city.   They are instructed by a corps of 180 teachers, male and female, the larger part of whom hail from Boston, the centre—in the United States— of culture, refinement, and education.   To the other features of their school system is added that of furnishing a tolerably well paid employment to a large number of young women. The "school ma'ams"—as they are popularly known—are usually certificated, highly educated young ladies, who in the cities teach the younger children, but in the country sometimes take complete charge of a school, and often prove more successful than the rougher sex.   But it is hard work, as the jaded, fagged-out looks of some of these ladies prove; and I always rejoiced when I heard of the transformation of a "school ma'am" to wife,—not a very uncommon proceeding! In justice to California, it should be stated that these well-informed, sensible—occasionally a little "blue"—but often very attractive young ladies are at a premium.   I have no doubt that such would be equally so here in England if we had a similar system, and that the "girl of the period" —if she is indeed a fact—would be completely cut out.

With regard to the investment of capital in San Francisco, the central portions of the city are now extremely valuable. Still any new comer can readily acquire a "lot" in the

suburbs.   Many building and land associations—like those of
our own country—exist.   The usual price of an ordinary
plot of land for building purposes (in the outskirts of the
city) is from two to three hundred dollars (about £40 to
£60).*

The water frontage of San Francisco does not exceed nine
miles in length, and is, of course, very valuable, and likely to
become infinitely more so.   San Franciscans who believe
that their city will—as the best port of the coast, and the
virtual centre of commerce and manufactures—rival New
York, wish that the water front were larger.   Bad, however,.
as is the site in some respects, there is no better on the Bay,
and therefore the growth of the city must undoubtedly follow
its present course, and those who can afford to invest in
outside property, and wait ten or fifteen years, will most
assuredly reap a rich reward.   One of the finest sites in San
Francisco was purchased, in the early days, by a sailor who
left the coast for years, and who turned up one fine day, to
find himself—much to his own surprise—a wealthy man.
The sand-heap he is said to have bought in a drunken frolic,
and which next morning, he probably thought was a worthless bargain, is now in the very heart of the city, covered
with handsome buildings, enclosing a public " Plaza " with
shrubbery, &c.   The value of property in New York has
constantly doubled and re-doubled during the last thirty

---

* No respectable man will find any difficulty in getting a house put up
for him by the Societies above mentioned, to be paid for by monthly instalments, little exceeding the ordinary rent of a similar dwelling.   General
expenses are rather high in San Francisco, and the rents of ordinary
cottages or villas in the suburbs will average twice those of such buildings
in the outskirts of London.

years, and in spite of all unbelievers—and there are croakers
even in California—that of San Francisco will do the same.

The timid and doubting in such matters may advan-
tageously read the following New York anecdote, which I
recently clipped from an American paper :—

"A lot on Broadway, 25 by 100 (feet), and well up town, had
been sold for one hundred thousand dollars. Several prudent,
well-to-do citizens, were discussing the purchase, and, of course,
were certain that the price was greatly above the value, and
that the purchaser and his money had parted company for
ever. An elderly gentleman, sitting by, waited until all had
expressed their opinions, and then quietly said: "I have
known that lot ever since it was farming land. When first
sold as a lot it brought three hundred dollars. As the city
grew it changed hands many times, and brought two thousand,
ten thousand, thirty thousand, sixty thousand, and now one
hundred thousand dollars, and every time the buyer has been
called a fool!"

I trust that these pages will have proved that California,
and the Pacific coast generally, afford a wide and a fresh
field to the scientific man, the artist, and traveller, as well as
to the capitalist, the agriculturist, and the emigrant. When
London is within sixteen days, and New York within a week's
travel of San Francisco—as they will be on the completion
of the Pacific Railroad—we may reasonably hope to see the
coast become as well known as it certainly deserves to be.*

---

* Bayard Taylor states, in his recent work on 'Colorado,' that the
Pacific railroad track is being in some places extended at the rate of a mile
and a half a day. "Recently," says he, "*Two miles and seventeen-hundred
feet* were laid in a single day—the greatest feat of the kind in the history
of railroad building!"

APPENDIX.

———◆◇◆———

I.—THE PROPOSED OVERLAND ROUTE FROM THE ATLANTIC TO THE
PACIFIC, THROUGH BRITISH TERRITORY.

II.—THE W. U. TELEGRAPH SCHEME.

III.—NOTES ON SITKA.

IV.—PORT CLARENCE, NORTHERN ALASKA.

V.—INDIAN DIALECTS OF NORTHERN ALASKA.

VI.—NOTES ON THE GEOLOGY OF THE YUKON.

APPENDIX.

I.—THE PROPOSED OVERLAND ROUTE FROM THE ATLANTIC TO THE PACIFIC, THROUGH BRITISH TERRITORY.

MR. WADDINGTON's scheme for a railway and steamboat route from Canada to British Columbia, recently laid before the Royal Geographical Society, &c., has attracted some notice from the press. I do not, of course, propose to go into details; suffice it to say that by following the chain of the great Canadian lakes, the course of the Saskatchewan River for a distance of 1249 miles, and Fraser River, in British Columbia, for 260 or 280 miles—Mr. Waddington would take us 2400 miles, by water, out of the 3490 from Montreal to the head of Bute Inlet (British Columbia). By this route the fertile settlement of Red River, now detached and isolated, would be connected with civilization and the outer world.

The project has been branded as premature, and, judging by our standard at home, it is so. The construction of a railway here always presupposes a string of cities, towns or villages. In America it has been often otherwise: the railway has been the forerunner of population. Here the country makes the railway; there frequently the railway makes the country. The Illinois Central Railroad, and many others in the United States, furnish examples. The State through which the line passes concedes to the railway company large tracts of land at intervals on either side of the route, and the first dividends are paid out of the sale of that very land, itself much increased in value by the construction of the iron road. Land only worth a nominal price, which could be obtained previously for a dollar an acre, suddenly rises to ten or twenty dollars an acre, or much more. Eligible spots are selected for town-sites, and a population rapidly springs up along the line. Such roads are often roughly, too roughly, made: a single pair of rails is all that is deemed necessary: no expenses are incurred with regard to elaborate, or even commodious, stations and termini. But, as the district improves, the railway is sure, for its own interests, to follow suit.

Taking into consideration that the proposed line would connect Canada with British Columbia and the North Pacific—would pass through the prosperous and fast-improving Red River and Saskatchewan districts—such a project has points in its favour under any circumstances, and has more, in the first instance, to recommend it than many a similar line in the United States.

In the discussion which followed the reading of Mr. Waddington's paper at the Royal Geographical Society's meeting, Dr. Rae pointed out the shallowness of the Saskatchewan River. It would ill become me to criticise the statements of a traveller who has seen as much, or probably a great deal more, of northernmost America than any other man. Nevertheless, no one who is familiar with American river-steamers would lay much stress on this point. I have seen flat-bottomed, stern-wheel steamers built to draw no more than a foot or fifteen inches of water. On the Upper Missouri, on the Columbia and Fraser rivers, such steamers are common. I well remember, in British Columbia, passing through a " slough," as it was called, at which the passengers were asked to walk from one side of the boat to the other to assist it in wriggling through, and where a part of the crew and passengers got out into the water to help it on, much as we did with our rafts on the rivers of Vancouver Island. There are creeks in California where something similar happens, and where, if you are on the bank, a little way from the stream, the steamer appears to be travelling *on land*. (On this point, see an engraving and descriptive letterpress in Hutching's ' Scenes, &c., in California.')

In a paper read before the Royal Geographical Society, Nov. 25th, 1867, John Collinson, Esq., C.E., &c., mentioned, incidentally, steamers drawing, when laden, no more than ten inches of water.

With regard to rapids—often a worse obstacle than any other on the rivers of the northern continent of America—it may yet safely be stated, that nearly all or any of them are amenable to the influence of a little engineering skill. They owe their existence, of course, to either sunken rocks, accumulations of drift-wood, or sand-bars. A few hundred pounds of powder have often turned a brawling dangerous rapid into a comparatively quiet part of the stream. But here, again, the American-built steamers, of good power, often get over rapids which seem almost impassable. It is not many years ago that it was pronounced impossible to reach Fort Yale, Fraser River, on account of rapids (at Emory's Bar), and, in consequence, Fort Hope was, for a long time, the head of the navigation. This rapid is now passed many times a week, in both directions. A few rocks, &c., were removed at a low stage of the water, and flat-bottomed steamers of greater power were constructed for the route. In common with most visitors to British Columbia, I have passed over that part of Fraser River, have seen the steamer stick for half an hour together, wriggle from side to side of the stream, the while all her timbers quivered, and every available pound of steam was "got up." But art triumphed over nature—at the risk, perhaps, of blowing us all to destruction—and we "made the riffle." The excitement of the thing was worth half the money!

To Mr. Waddington belongs the credit of drawing attention to a comparatively easy route across the continent, and, although the Pacific railroad will be built and finished while this project is being discussed, there is no reason why we should suppose that one railway between the Atlantic and the Pacific would suffice for all that vast country. Most of us will, probably, live to hear of more than one such line in the United States; and Canada, backed by England, ought at once to be up and moving in the same direction.

II.—THE W. U. TELEGRAPH SCHEME.

(RUSSIAN EXTENSION.)

GREAT doubts were at times thrown on the practicability of this project, and it has for the present, at least, been completely superseded by the success of the Atlantic Cable. The work proposed was virtually the same—to unite the old and new worlds. The line, as proposed, was to extend the already constructed line in British Columbia, northwards through Russian America, across Bering Strait, and then proceed southwards through Eastern Siberia, till a junction should be made with the Russian lines already built to the Amoor. New York being in constant communication with San Francisco, and San Francisco with British Columbia, the connexions would have been complete.

I propose to notice some of the objections which have been at various times raised, but many of which entirely disappeared when our explorers had examined the country.

1st. "The difficulty of keeping up a line running through a more or less Arctic, thinly populated, and barren country."

Already, in the United States, some of the principal and paying lines run through country of doubtful value and thinly populated. The Russians, moreover, have a great line which enables them to communicate from St. Petersburgh to Irkutsk and the Amoor; and our proposed line hardly ran through wilder or more barren countries than those just mentioned. The W. U. line was to have followed, more or less closely, the courses of great rivers in many places : hence our explorations on the Fraser, on the Yukon, on the Anadyr. Such rivers furnish means of rapid transit in summer (by canoe), and almost equally rapid transit in winter (by sledging). Stations were to be erected at moderate intervals along the course of the line, and there was infinitely less to fear from Indian or other native depredations in Alaska and Eastern Siberia, than on telegraph routes which are already open in the United States. Furthermore, it has been found, that in lines passing through an alpine district, notably in those crossing the Sierra Nevada Range (California, Nevada, &c.), the poles, once firmly planted, remained in better order than those crossing countries enjoying a warmer climate.

2nd. With regard to the cable across Bering Strait, it was urged that icebergs would infallibly ground on it, and cut it up. The answer to this is direct: icebergs, properly so called, are never seen in Bering Sea or Strait. The prevailing currents set strongly into the Arctic Ocean—not from it. Floating ice, in deep packs, is, of course, abundant in the early summer; and for this reason, Colonel Bulkley, after a detailed examination, selected for the cable "landings," the deepest and most protected harbours he could discover. Port Clarence was selected for the American side. It has a good entrance, ten fathoms of water and a mud bottom. On the Asiatic side, Pentigu Gulf (or Aboleschef Bay), Seniavine Straits, was selected for similar advantages. St. Lawrence and Mechigme Bay were considered too exposed.

A part of the numerous soundings, taken by members of our expedition, in Bering Sea, have been already recorded on pages 87, 88. The moderate depth of the whole sea, and its soft bottom, seem points in favour of the proposed cable crossing.

A late Victoria (V. I.) newspaper states that the telegraph line already constructed from New Westminster to the town at the mouth of Quesnelle River (which was the first section of our overland telegraph), is to be extended to Cariboo. Those inaccessible mines, which seemed, a few years ago, as isolated from civilization as is Spitzbergen, will then be in direct communication with San Francisco, New York, and Europe.

The real obstacle in the way of our enterprise, especially in British Columbia and the larger part of Alaska, was the existence of densely timbered ground, where, in wintry storms, or by the processes of natural decay, the trees might be expected to fall on the telegraph line. To obviate this, it became necessary to clear a wide "track" on either side of the line—a work necessarily of some expense. But no part of the proposed line passed through a worse country, in that respect, than the first portion already constructed to the mouth of Quesnelle; and, as it has been since kept in good working order, the objection is not a fatal one.

It has been proposed to extend the same line to Sitka.

III.—NOTES ON SITKA.

LISIANSKI, Kotsebue, and Sir George Simpson are the only authorities on Sitka which we possess. Mr. Robert Brown, of Edinburgh, kindly informs me that the flora of Sitka was described by Bongard (in the 'Mémoires de l'Académie, &c., de St. Pétersbourg,' and also in a separate work), but the country generally has not been overdone by travellers.

Until last year (1867), Sitka was an inaccessible place, and there were no regular means of communication from any point. Now all this. is changed; steamers, touching at Vancouver Island, ply between San Francisco and Sitka, once or twice a month. In summer, this trip is likely to be a pleasant one; late in the autumn, it may sometimes be very much the reverse. The distance from San Francisco is (approximately) 1500 miles.

Sitka, itself built on an island, has no roads whatever from it, and the traveller must, therefore, thread the forests as we did on Vancouver Island, charter a canoe for trips in the immediate neighbourhood, or take his own yacht or other vessel. At irregular periods, there will, doubtless, be facilities for communication with the northern coast, the Aleutian Islands, &c. For these points, however, San Francisco, California, and Honolulu, in the Sandwich Islands, are the best starting-points. The whalers and traders almost invariably leave those ports for the north in the early spring.

IV.—PORT CLARENCE, NORTHERN ALASKA.

PORT CLARENCE and Grantley Harbour (an inner basin), were first explored and named by Captain Beechey in 1827. Point Spencer, the extremity of a long spit, which shuts it in, was determined by him to be in Lat. 65° 16' 40" N., Long. 166° 47' 50" W. It was frequently visited during the search for Sir John Franklin. H.M.S. 'Plover' (Captain Moore) wintered there in 1851-2, and H.M.S. 'Rattlesnake' (Commander Trollope) in 1853-4. See the numerous 'Blue Books' on Arctic Explorations, &c.

During the winter of 1866-7, and following summer, Captain Libby, of our Telegraph Service, with nearly forty men, stopped at this inaccessible place. At Grantley Harbour, a good station, and other houses (which have been left there), and portions of the telegraph line, were built by these men. It was, as before stated, the spot intended for the Bering Strait cable "landing" on the American side, and it has been already mentioned as the central point at which the natives of Kotsebue and Norton Sounds, and the neighbouring country, meet the Tchuktchis from the Siberian coast. Many whalers annually visit this harbour for trading purposes, and I expect to hear of a permanent white settlement being formed there. The experience of the earlier Arctic explorers, as of our telegraph men, shows that it is a good spot to winter in. Some of our men there, at one time very short of provisions, lived for months at an Indian village near Cape Prince of Wales. Supplies from the resources of the country were very uncertain. In 1866-7, the natives in the neighbourhood were almost starving, and were at one time reduced to boiling down their old boots and fragments of hide, in order to sustain life. " Yet," said a correspondent (a member of our expedition), writing from thence, "the party under Captain Libby, although without bread or flour for some weeks, escaped the scurvy entirely. The generally received opinion that scurvy is generated from want of flour, does not seem to be correct. At the station (Fort St. Michael's), where plenty of flour was received, and freely used, they were afflicted with this disease; while at Port Clarence, where they were almost entirely dependent upon the resources of the country for some weeks, living upon walrus and seal meat, without flour or bread, no symptom of scurvy made its appearance."

Very severe snow storms, called "poorgas," swept across the open and barren country, at times, during winter; but, nevertheless, our men persevered in what, eventually, proved a thankless task. They were often camped out at temperatures below the freezing of mercury. At the station, among other devices for passing the long winter evenings, our men concocted a MS. newspaper, which was entitled 'The Esquimaux.' This was afterwards printed in San Francisco, as a memento of the expedition.

V.—INDIAN DIALECTS OF NORTHERN ALASKA,

(LATE RUSSIAN AMERICA).

MALEMUTE VOCABULARY.

Words from the dialect of the Malemutes, Norton Sound, Northern
Alaska.—WHYMPER.

I - - - - - - Wounga.			Mouth - - - Kanuk.		
He - - - - Oona			Teeth - - - - Keeutik.		
We - - - - Wurgut.			Arm - - - - Tālik.		
You - - - - Itlepit.			Leg - - - - Neeyu.		
Man - - - - Inuet.			Hand - - - - Ashigītĕ.		
Woman - - - Achanuk.			Window - - - Egalook.		
Child - - - - Kakooshka.			House - - - Topek.		
Brother - - - Ungarunga.			Wood - - - - Kushuk.		
Sister - - - - Nooga.			Canoe, Ship - Omeuk-puk.		
Day - - - - Oblook (see also			Knife - - - - Chowik.		
Sleep).			Spoon - - - Athrotik.		
Night - - - Niptiga.			Cup - - - - Culoot.		
Morning - - - Oblaam.			Pot - - - - Klipseen.		
Noon - - - - Kolwāchtook.			Tree - - - - Napāktuk.		
Evening - - - Nakekiluskuk.			Gun - - - - Shupon.		
Month - - - (see Moon).			Powder - - - Agara.		
Sun - - - - Sickunyuk.			Caps (percus-		
Moon - - - - Tachkut.			sion) - - Cabiloo.		
Star - - - - Obloat.			Bullet - - - Cagarook.		
Land - - - - Noona.			Shot - - - - Cagariya.		
Water - - - Imuk.			Skin coat - - Atigee.		
Sea - - - - Tagaiuk.			Skin trousers - Nellikāk.		
Lake - - - - Nasuuk.			Skin boots - - Camook.		
River - - - - Coke.			Skin cap - - - Nasota.		
Snow - - - - Kanik.			Skin gloves or		
Ice - - - - Seko.			mitts - - Akatook.		
Rain - - - - Ebwinuktuk.			Hay - - - - Eweek, Penikiruk.		
Head - - - - Neakuk.			Rope - - - - Akloonuk.		
Face - - - - Keenyuk.			Chief - - - - Amaleek.		

Pipe - - - - Queenuk.
Tobacco - - - Tabac.
Needle - - - Mitkin.
Thread - - - Evaloot.
Bag - - - - Powuskuk.
Dance - - - Poolaruk.
Sleep - - - - Shineek (used to count time. So many " sleeps").
Bread - - - - Kakook.
Fish - - - - Ekathcthlook.
Bird - - - - Ekāshika.
(Reindeer) meat Nāga.
Sugar - - - - Kapsitaak.
Whisky - - - Tānuk.
Berries - - - Asheuk.
Grease - - - Ookarook.
Beaver - - - Palouktuk.
Sable (marten) Kavaitchuk.
Mink - - - - Tagiakpuk.
Bear - - - - Aoutkluit.
Squirrel - - - Chikirik.
Reindeer - - - Toontook.
Dog - - - - Camukter.
Musquito - - Keektagiuck.
Whale - - - Akiwik.
Seal - - - - Oogarook.
Walrus - - - Aiwik.
Wolf - - - - Amaouk.
Yes - - - - Waa.
No, Not - - Peechuk.
Big - - - - Ungidooruk.
Little - - - - Mikidooruk.
Few - - - - Ekeektuk.
Plenty - - - Amalacktook.
Good - - - - Nakuruk.
Bad - - - - Ashuruk.
Quick - - - Kelūmuk.
Slow - - - - Sikichuk.
Cold - - - - Allopar.
Hot - - - - Allopar peechuk (not cold).
Crooked - - - Chakoonaruk.
Straight - - - Nalooruk.

What - - - - Schuman.
Where - - - Nāmi.
Here - - - - Māni.
Now - - - - Puckmummi.
By-and-by - - Atachta.
Who - - - - Keena.
How much ? - - Capsenik.
Don't know - - Ki-yūme.
Come here - - Cakīnee.
Go away - - - Aunee.
Go on a journey Alachtuk.
Work - - - - Chawitka.
See - - - - Touktook.
Give - - - - Aichilunger.
Buy - - - - Etauchsik.
Sell - - - - Keepuchuk.
Laugh - - - Kachkuktuk.
Talk - - - - Ocaktuk.
Tell - - - - Kanucktuk.
Bring - - - - Taishkē.
Kill - - - - Takootka.
Shoot - - - - Shoopega.
Understand - - Tookshiruk.
Steal - - - - Tigaliktook.
How much for that ? - - Chimuk.
Thank you - - Koyana.

NUMERALS.

1 - - - Atousik.
2 - - - Ipar.
3 - - - Peeniuk.
4 - - - Seetimat.
5 - - - Talimanuk.
6 - - - Echukerit.
7 - - - Malounik shepnelik.
8 - - - Peenesheruk hsepnelik.
9 - - - Kolingneotilik.
10 - - - Kolit.
11 - - - 10 and 1 do, &c.
20 - - - Enuenuk.

CO-YUKON VOCABULARY.

—◆◇◆—

Words from the Co-yukon dialect, spoken (with slight variations) on the Yukon River for at least 500 miles of its lower and middle course. (Ingelete, a variety of same dialect.)—WHYMPER.

Good Spirit -	- Kanuckertoltoi.	Gun - - - -	- Eltudla.
Bad Spirit -	- Tcheklaker.	Caps (percus-	
I - - - - -	- Sĕ.	sion)- - -	- Onunkadadoi.
Thou - - - -	- Nĕ.	Powder - - -	- Kau koon.
He - - - -	- Ecossee.	Bullet - - -	- Kautla.
We - - - -	- Seyer.	Shot - - - -	- Koon
You - - - -	- She.	Knife - - -	- Kakikltaun.
They - - - -	- Nun.	Pipe - - - -	- Koniuk.
Man - - - -	- Tenalō.	Tobacco - - -	- Tabac. Tacona (fire).
Woman - - -	- Salturn.	Coat - - - -	- Taïak.
Child - - - -	- Tenaiyusa.	Trousers - -	- Kätchee.
Brother - - -	- Skitla.	Shoes - - - -	- Kakatauch.
Sister - - - -	- Städsa.	Cap - - - -	- Kakadalaion.
Head - - - -	- Se woiyer.	Kettle - - -	- Oclock.
Face - - - -	- Senun.	Axe - - - -	- Mukalklalla.
Forehead - -	- Sekäta.	Flour - - - -	- Klatsmitze.
Eye - - - -	- Se noga.	Fire - - - -	- Tacona. Klētcle.
Ear - - - -	- Se tsä.	Water - - -	- Too.
Nose - - - -	- Se nee.	Ice - - - -	- T'un.
Mouth - - -	- S'alotte.	Snow - - - -	- Nootaga.
Tongue - - -	- S'acloula.	Sun - - - -	- S'o.
Tooth - - - -	- S'uwyer.	Moon - - - -	- Taltolla.
Neck - - - -	- S'ukugl.	Star - - - -	- K'lune.
Arm - - - -	- Sekäner.	Day - - - -	- K'lut.
Hand - - - -	- Se lur.	Night - - - -	- K'liltahl.
Body - - - -	- S'kotit.	Morning - - -	- Kadamatona.
Leg - - - -	- Sowool.	Evening - - -	- Lalaatsun.
Foot - - - -	- Se ka.	Summer - - -	- Säner.
Bone - - - -	- K'lun.	Winter - - -	- Koidau.
Heart - - - -	- Se naiyitz.	Wind - - - -	- Atse.
Chief - - - -	- Kooka.	Rain - - - -	- Al'corn.
House - - -	- Konaugh.	River - - - -	- Suckener. (Small) Se-
Village - - -	- Zadlecle.		cargut.
Canoe - - -	- Metauī.	Mountain - -	- Klehl.
Paddle - - -	- Tauloi.	Island - - -	- Taash. New.
Bow - - - -	- Klintun.	Valley - - -	- Tekalculcul. Kona-
Arrow - - -	- K'au.		kon.

Stone. Rock	- L'orna.	Far - - - -	Neelot.
Tree - - -	- Chooma.	Who - - - -	Tewa.
Wood - - -	- K'aut.	Where - -	- Houghtee.
Swamp - -	- Munacut.	Yesterday	- Katona.
Birch-tree -	- Ki'e.	To-day - -	- Autakut.
Spruce - -	- Chumā.	To-morrow -	- Katooman.
Bowl - - -	- Kluck.	Yes - - -	- Ha.
Beads - - -	- Neltilla.	No, not - -	- Micullah.
Blanket - -	- T'suda.	Sleep - - -	- Littern.
Needle - -	- Klatakona.	Sit - - -	- Litto.
Bag - - -	- Melketla.	Give - - -	- Entar.
Berries - -	- Keeka.	Talk - - -	- Tini.
Fat - - -	- N'kau.	Shoot - - -	- Teltūdlā.
Reindeer - -	- Anoyer.	Work - - -	- Konitinē.
Reindeer tongue	Kakloula.	Now - - -	- Atakauch.
Moose - -	- Tanaiger.	By-and-by -	- Kl'at.
Rabbit - -	- Kaugh.	Quick - -	- Tow-wer.
Bear - - -	- Klāousa.	All - - -	- Etedsun.
Marten - -	- Carkayousa.	Hungry - -	- Kutlakat.
Mink - - -	- Tauchkousa.	Enough - -	- Koodar.
Beaver - -	- Carka.	Come here -	- Orni.
Dog - - -	- K'lick.	Go away - -	- Antouger.
Wolf - - -	- Yes.	How much?	- Tenaltai.
Grouse - -	- Telerbucker.	Thank you -	- Marci.
Duck - - -	- Nintaal.	How are you?	
Goose - -	- Titsena.	(salutation)	- Koyana.
Fish - - -	- Telamachkur.	Don't know -	- Testini.
Musquito- -	- Kl'ĕ.		
Big - - -	- Nekau.		
Small - -	- Nacoutza.	NUMERALS.	
Strong - -	- Kootclear.	1 - -	- Ketleket,
Old - - -	- Klokee.	2 - -	- Untĕ.
Young - -	- Ataltahai.	3 - -	- Taunkĕ.
Good - - -	- Nazoon.	4 - -	- Tinikĕ.
Bad - - -	- Satklaka.	5 - -	- Ketsnala.
Dead - - -	- Tult'lun.	6 - -	five one.
Alive - - -	- Toitlala.	7 - -	five two.
Cold - - -	- Azoo.	8 - -	five three.
Warm - -	- Azoo micullah (not cold)	9 - -	five four.
Many - - -	- Lorn.	10 - - -	- Nekoshnala.

* For some brief observations on these dialects, see the writer's Paper on the 'Natives of the Yukon River,' in the 'Transactions of the Ethnological Society of London' for 1868.

Y

KOTCH-A'-KUTCHIN VOCABULARY.

———•◇•———

Words from the language of the Kotch-a'-Kutchins—the Indians of Yukon River, at the mouth of the Porcupine River, in Northern Alaska.—KENNICOTT.

Good Spirit - -	Ti'h-hŭ-gun. (Lit., "My old friend;" supposed to inhabit the sun and moon, and to be powerless for good or evil.)
Bad Spirit - -	Chu't-sai^n. (This seems to be merely the spirit of death, and only for this reason bad. To it go all souls, good and bad.)
Man - - -	Tĭn'-jī.
Woman - - -	T'rĭn'-jōh.
Boy - - - -	T'tsī-āh.
Girl - - -	Nī-chĭt.
Infant - - -	Trī-ny'ĭn'.
Father - - -	Ti'h ; my father, tī'h-ē ; thy father, nē-tīh ; his or her father, vě-tīh.
Mother - - -	Hun (same as river ;) my mother, nä'-äh.
Husband - -	Kái-īh ; my husband, sē-kái-īh ; thy husband, nē-kái-īh ; her husband, vē-kái-īh.
Wife - - -	At.
Son (of father) -	Tĭn'-jī ; (lit. man.) My son, if spoken by the father, or as relating to him, sē'-tĭn-jī ; thy son, nē'-tĭn-jī ; his son, vē'-tĭn-jī.
Son (of mother) -	Zŭh ; my son, sī'-zŭh ; thy son, nī'-zŭh ; her son, vī'-zŭh.
Daughter (of father)	Chī ; my daughter, sē'-chī ; thy daughter, nī-chī ; his daughter, vē-chī.
Daughter (of mother)	Gē'-tsī ; my daughter, sī'-gē-tsī ; thy daughter, nī-gē-tsī ; his daughter, vī-gē-tsī.
Brother (elder) -	Dē ; my elder brother, sŭn'-dē ; thy elder brother, nŭn-dē ; his or her elder brother, vŭn-dē.
Brother (younger) -	Chāh ; "young," se'-chāh ; thy younger brother, nē-chāh ; his or her younger brother, vē-chāh.
Sister (elder) -	Chīh ; my elder sister, sē'-chīh ; thy elder sister, nē-chīh ; his or her elder sister, vē-chīh.
Sister (younger) -	Chĭdh ; my younger sister, sē'-chĭdh ; thy younger sister, nē-chĭdh ; his or her younger sister, vē-chdĭh.
An Indian - -	Tĭn-jī.

People - - -	Tĭn-jī.
Indian fashion, or in the manner of Indians - - -	Tin-jī-zūh.
White man - -	Man-o-tlĭt.
Head - - -	Tī'-chīh; my head, tī'-chịh; thy head, nī-chīh; his or her head, vī-chīh.
Hair - - -	E-gēh. (In speaking of a man's hair, " head hair," chī'h-gēh is always used ; my hair, sī'-chīh-gēh ; thy hair nī-chīh-gēh ; his or her hair, vī-chīh-gēh.
Face - - -	Chĭ'-nēh ; my face, sī'-nēh ; thy face, nī-nēh ; his, hers, or its face, vī-nēh.
Forehead - -	Tchun'-t'tsut; my forehead, sun'-t'tsut; thy forehead, nun-t'tsut ; his, her, or its forehead, vun-t'tsut.
Ear - - - -	Chĕ'-tzēh; my ear, sē'-tzēh ; thine ear, nĕ'-tzēh ; his, her, or its ear, vĕ-tzēh.
Eye - - - -	Chĭn'-dēh; my eye, sĭn'-dēh; thine eye, nĭn'-dēh ; his, her, or its eye, vĭn-dēh.
Nose - - -	Chĭn'-tsīh ; my nose, sĭn'-tsīh ; thy nose, nĭn-tsīh ; his, her, or its nose, vĭn-tsīh.
Mouth - - -	Chē-zhĭk ; my mouth, sē-zhĭk ; thy mouth, nē-zhĭk ; his, her, or its mouth, vē-zhĭk.
Tongue - - -	Chĭ'-chā; my tongue, sĕ-cha; thy tongue, nĕ-cha; his, her, or its tongue, vĕ-cha.
Tooth - - -	Chā'-gōh ; my tooth, sa'-gōh; thy tooth, na-gōh ; his, her, or its tooth, va-gōh.
Beard - - -	Chī-tē'-ai-gēh ; my beard, sī-tē'-ai-gēh ; thy beard, nī-tē-ai-gēh ; his, her, or its beard, vī-tē-ai-gēh ; (chin hair.)
Neck - - -	Chē'-kōh ; my neck, sē'-kōh ; thy neck, nē-kōh ; his, her, or its neck, vē-kōh.
Arm - - -	Chĕ'-kī-ĭn; my arm, sĕ-kī-ĭn ; thy arm, nĕ-kī-ĭn ; his, her, or its arm, vĕ-kī-ĭn.
Hand - - -	Chĭn-lī ; my hand, sĭn'-lī ; thy hand, nĭn-lī ; his, her, or its hand, vīn-lī.
Fingers - - -	Lā'-t'thuk; my fingers, sīn-lā'-t'thuk; thy fingers, nīn-lā'-t'thuk; his, her, or its fingers, vīn-lā'-t'thuk.
Nails - - -	Chĕ'-kaih ; my nails, sĕ'-kaih ; thy nails, nĕ-kaih ; his, her, or its nails, vĕ-kaih.
Body - - -	Chĕ'-zuk-taih ; my body, sĕ'-zuk-taih ; thy body, nĕ-zuk-taih ; his, her, or its body, vĕ-zuk-taih.
Belly - - -	Chĕ'-vut; my belly, sĕ'-vut; thy belly, nĕ-vut; his, her, or its belly, vĕ-vut.
Leg - - - -	Chĭ'-dhudh; my leg, sĕ'-dhudh ; thy leg, nĕ-dhudh; his, her, or its leg, vĕ-dhudh.

Foot	- - -	Chĕ'-kēh; my foot, sĕ'-kēh; thy foot, nĕ-kēh; his, her, or its foot, vĕ-kēh.
Toes	- - -	Chĕ'-kēh-chī'; my toes, sĕ'-kēh-chī'; thy toes, nĕ-kēh-chī; his, her, or its toes, vĕ-kēh-chī.
Bone	- - -	T'thun; my bone, sĕ-t'thun; thy bone, nē-t'thun; his, her, or its bone, vĕ-t'thun.
Heart	- - -	Chĭ'-t'trī; my heart, sĭ-t'trī; thy heart, nĭ-t'trī; his, her, or its heart, vĭ-t'trī.
Blood	- - -	Tăh; my blood, sĕ'-tăh; thy blood, nĕ-tăh; his, her,'or its blood, vĕ-tăh.
Chief	- - -	Kāh-kēh'.
Warrior	- - -	(No name.)
Friend	- - -	Sē'-chī-āh. (Lit., "My companion.")
House	- - -	Zēh. (Originally, an Indian lodge was probably Zēh).
Indian Lodge	- -	Nī-vī-āh'-zēh. (Nī-vī'-āh is "lodge cover.")
Village	- - -	Zēh-kēh. (Lit., "Many houses," or "many lodges.")
Kettle	- - -	Tī'-āh. (Nearly like father—a pot or cup is chūⁿ-tī-ah.)
Arrow	- - -	Kī'-ĕ.
Bow -	- - -	Uhl'-tīⁿ.
Axe -	- - -	Tā'-ĭⁿh.
Knife	- - -	Rsīh; my knife, sĭ'-rzīh; thy knife, nĭ'-rzīh; his or her knife, vĭ'-rzīh.
Canoe	- - -	T'-trīh.
Paddle	- - -	Tăh-ĭⁿh. (Very nearly the same as axe.)
Boat -	- - -	T'trīh-chō'h. (Lit., "Big canoe.")
Raft -	- - -	Hkāⁿ.
Indian Shoes	- -	Kēh-trĭh.
Bread	- - -	Klī'-uth-chū.
Flour	- - -	Klī'-uth.
Ashes	- - -	Klī'-uth.
Earth	- - -	Klī-uth. (Flour, ashes, and earth called precisely the same word.)
Pipe	- - -	Sē-tĭd-chĭ; my pipe, set'-se-tĭd'-chĭ. (Lit., "Tobacco stone."
Tobacco	- - -	Sē'-tĭd.
Sky -	- - -	Zi'-ē.
Horizon	- - -	Zī-ē-baⁿh.
Cloud	- - -	K'kōh.
Sun -	- - -	Drĭn-ūr'-zīh.
Moon	- - -	Tudh-ūr-zīh.
Star -	- - -	Suⁿ.
Day -	- - -	Drĭn.
Light	- - -	A-t'trí.

Night - - -	Hkāh.
Darkness - - -	Tudh.
Morning - - -	Vun. (Almost the same as " Lake.")
Evening - - -	Nā-chī-aiⁿ· (Lit., " Sun-set.")
Spring - - -	Taiⁿ·
Summer - - -	S'sïn.
Autumn - - -	Hkain'-sun.
Winter - - -	Hkaih.
Wind - - -	A'kh-traih.
Lightning - -	Nāh-tun'-kun. (Lit., "Thunder-fire.")
Thunder - - -	Nāh-tun'.
Rain - - - -	Tsïn.
Snow - - -	Zāh.
Hail - - - -	Chïn-lūh.
Fire - - - -	Kōⁿ·
Aurora Borealis -	Yā-kaiⁿ·
Water - - -	Chuⁿ·
Ice - - - -	T'tun. (A fragment of ice or floating ice is Thlú.)
Land, Earth - -	Nun.
Sea - - - -	Chōⁿ-chōh. (" Big water.")
River - - - -	Hun.
Lake - - - -	Vun.
Valley - - -	Kū-nā'-trī.
Mountain - - -	D'dhāh.
Island - - -	Njūh.
Stone, Rock - -	Chī.
Copper - - -	Thē'tsraⁿ·
Iron - - - -	Chī-tsīh.
Tree - - - -	Tĕ-chun'.
Wood - - -	Tĕ-chun' or Tsrōh.
Leaf - - - -	Chït-un.
Bark - - - -	Bä-trī. (The bark of the birch, however, is always K'kīh.)
Grass - - -	K'klōh.
Poplar - - -	T'tōh. (Populus tremuloides, T'tōh-zōh; P. balsamifera (?) T'tōh.)
Birch - - -	Hkā'-t'tōh; alder, kōh.
Willow - - -	Kaih-tluk'. (This is the common upland willow; another species on the low lands, and of which the Indians sometimes eat the soft, new wood, is kaihtzū'h— perhaps the true generic name for willow is kaih.)

Spruce - - -	T'tsī-vēh'.
Flesh, meat - -	S'sīh; salted meat, shō-vī-lĕt'.
Dog - . - - -	Hklaiⁿ; a small dog, thlug-a-tsul'; my dog, sī'-lĭk; thy dog, nī-lĭk; his or her dog, vī-lĭk.
Buffalo, fossil - -	Ah-kīh'; musk ox and domestic cattle, āh-kīh', (same.)
Bear (Black) - -	S'sōh; grizzly bear, s'sīh; white bear, sīh-tā'-kaih; red bear (cinnamon bear), s'sōh-tā-tsĭk'.
Wolf - - - -	Zōh.
Reindeer - - -	Vut-zaih'.
Moose - - -	Tĭn-jī-yuk'.
Beaver - - -	Tsē.
Fox - - - -	Nā-kudh', or nā-kuⁿdh; black fox, nā-kudh'-rzīⁿ.
Squirrel - - -	K'kluk'k. (Sciurus Hudsonicus.)
Marmot - - -	T'thâh. (Spermophilus Parryi.)
Rabbit - - -	Kēh.
Fly - - - -	Tīⁿ.
Musquito - -	Chīh.
Bird - - - -	Tzīh'-tsōh or nī'-un; a small bird, as a robin, black-bird, or smaller, tzīh'-tsōh; a large bird, as a duck, a grouse, or larger, nī'-un. In speaking, the distinc-tion is always made.
Egg - - - -	Chā'-h'gōh; duck's egg, tē-tsun'-hgōh; goose-egg, hkēh'-h'gōh.
Feather - - -	Tsuth.
Wing - - -	Chut-sun.
Duck - - -	Tē-tsun'.
Goose - - -	Hkēh.
Fish - - - -	T'thlūk or chī'-ē-lūk.
Salmon - - -	Thlūk. This is the large salmon—a smaller species is shīh.
Name - - -	Vōr-zīh.
Affection (I love him) - - -	Vat-ī'-nī-thun; I love you, nĕt-ī'-nī-thun.
White - - -	Tā'-kaih.
Black - - -	Tā'-rzīⁿ.
Red - - - -	Tā-tsĭk'.
Blue - - - -	No name, they call it " black."
Yellow - - -	Tā-tlōh'.
Green - - -	Tāh'-tlōh.
Great - - -	Nī'-tsīh or choh. Nī'-tsīh is applied to pronouns, and as we would use "is large"—as your dog is large,

				nī'-lĭk-nī'-tsīh. Chōh is applied to nouns; in other cases, as "*big-lake*," vun-chōh.
Small	-	-	-	Nĕt'-tsul or tsul. (*Is small*) nĕt'-sul, is applied like nŏt'-tsīh; tsul like chōh. A little, applied to quantity, kwīn'-tsul.
Strong	-	-	-	Nī-t'táih'.
Old	-	-	-	Saī^n-yī-dhĕlh-hkaī.
Young	-	-	-	Kē-chĭt-ē'-dha'.
Good	-	-	-	Nīr-zīh'. (Nearly the same as *your knife*, nĭ'-rzīh.)
Bad	-	-	-	Nī-zī^n'-kwāh.
Handsome	-	-	-	Mē-go-ná-thlīh.
Ugly	-	-	-	Trā-rud'ī-udh.
Alive	-	-	-	Kōn'-daih.
Dead	-	-	-	Ehl-chī^n. (Killed, trī-dhĕhl-kaī^n.)
Cold	-	-	-	Nī-k'kudh. (Cold water, chū^n-nī-k'kudh'.)
Warm	-	-	-	Nī-dhā'. (Hot water, chū^n-nī-dhā'.)
I	-	-	-	Sī. (Mine, sī-set'-sun.)
Thou	-	-	-	Nun.
He	-	-	-	Tā-tun.
We	-	-	-	Nākh'-hun.
Ye	-	-	-	Nākh'-hun. (Precisely the same as " we.")
They	-	-	-	Kā-tā'-t'tun. (Lit., " The others.")
This	-	-	-	Chī.
That	-	-	-	Tā'-hgut.
All	-	-	-	Tut-thuk'.
Many, much	-	-	-	Laī^n.
Who?	-	-	-	Chō'-tī-ĕn? (Whose? chó-tī-ĕn-vĕt'-sun?)
Where?	-	-	-	Kwē'-ē-chī?—Lit., " Where is it?"—where is my pipe? sĭt'-sē-tĭd'-chī kwē'-ē-chī?
Near	-	-	-	Nāh'-k'kōdh; far, nī-zhĭt'.
To-day	-	-	-	Chūk-dsrĭn'.
Yesterday	-	-	-	K'kāh'-taī^n.
To-morrow	-	-	-	Yīh'-kāh.
Yês	-	-	-	A-hā.
No	-	-	-	Nō-kwâ'.
Sit	-	-	-	Dhīn'-tih.
Stand	-	-	-	Nī'-nē-dhut.
Come	-	-	-	A'-nē.

NUMERALS.

1 - - Chīh'-thluk.	9 - - Mēn'-chudh-nē-kōh'-kwā.
2 - - Nē'-kaiⁿ·	10 - - Chī-thluk'-chō-tī-ĭn.
3 - - Tĭ'-ĭk.	11 - - Chī-thluk'-vī-dá-tuk.
4 - - Tāng.	12 - - Nē'-kaīⁿ-vī-dá-tuk.
5 - - Chīh'-tluk-ūn'-lī.	13 - - Tĭ'-ĭk-vī-dá-tuk.
6 - - Nīh'-kī-tĭ'-ĭk.	20 - - Nē-káīⁿ-chō-tī'-ĭn.
7 - - E'tse-dē'-tsē-nē-káiⁿ	30 - - Tī-ĭk-chō-tī'-ĭn.
8 - - Nīh'-kī-tāng'.	

VI.—NOTES ON THE GEOLOGY OF THE YUKON.

My companion on the Yukon, Mr. Dall, published a few notes on the geology of the region in 'Silliman's American Journal,' for January, 1868, some extracts from which are here given.

Speaking of the mountains known as the "Ramparts," &c., he says :—" They were entirely composed of azoic rocks, of which a silvery greenish rock of talcose *appearance*, but very hard, predominates. Quartz in seams, slates and quartzite rocks, are abundant, and a rock resembling granite—but with a superfluity of feldspar, and no mica—is rare. The slates generally have a north-westerly dip.

" True granite appears only once, near the termination of the Ramparts, and forms a ledge extending across the river, and making a rapid; not, however, a dangerous one. Fifty miles or less below the rapid the Ramparts terminate; the Tananá River (or River of Mountains) comes in; and from this point to the mouth, as a rule, the river is wide, with the right bank high and the left bank low, but occasionally with mountains in the distance, or a bluff on the river. From the end of the Ramparts to Co-yukuk River (250 miles) the right bank presents, in their order, conglomerate, quartzite, bluffs of yellow gravel, blue talcose slate conglomerate, hard blue slates and quartzose rocks, blue sandstones and a soft green rock (Plutonic), with light stellate spots in it. Granite is very rare, and mica also. I have found fine specimens of obsidian on the beach, and just above the Ramparts, pebbles of Niagara limestone, with its characteristic fossils. From the bend we find the following strata : blue sandstone (unfossiliferous), brown sandstone in beds at least 500 feet thick, containing vegetable remains in some layers, and, rarely, casts of mollusca,—all, as far as I have collected, *Lamellibranchs*. Thirty miles below the bend is a small con-

torted seam of coal between two thin layers of shale containing
very poor vegetable remains, and underlaid by the brown sandstone which overlies the blue sandstone, which, in its turn, I
think, covers the blue slates. The coal seam is very limited,
being on the extreme point of a bluff, and the greater part of it
has been denuded. The fossils are very poor, vegetable, and
resemble fuci. The coal is of good quality, bituminous, non-
caking, and leaves a gray ash. The seam is sixteen inches wide.

" The sandstones continue down the river some forty-five miles,
more generally with a N.W. dip, and always in gentle undula-
tion, sometimes continuous for miles, and often broken short off.
Below, the rocks for 300 miles are slates and eruptive rocks
of a pink colour, sometimes containing spathose minerals. The
formation changes at the Russian Mission from hard blue slate to
a volcanic rock, full of almond-shaped cavities, which are empty;
but certain parts of the rock are quite solid. It is black, and
contains minute crystals (of olivine ?). [It is roughly columnar
on Stuart's Island, Norton Sound, in five-sided columns on the
beach]. From this to the sea the banks are mostly low; but
when they approach the river they are invariably of blue, hard,
slaty sandstone, or sandy slate, the rock passing from one into
the other imperceptibly. This formation extends to St. Michael's,
nearly where the before-mentioned volcanic rock takes its place,
and continues up the shore of Norton Sound some thirty miles,
when it is replaced by the hard slates and sandstone, and I
have followed them up for thirty miles more to Unalachleet
River. Here you cross in winter to the Yukon, 200 miles of
portage.

" The entire country is sprinkled over with remains of pliocene
animals,—(?) *Elephas, Ovibos moschatus, &c.* Beds of marl exist
near Fort Yukon, consisting of shells (fresh-water) still found
living in the vicinity. The Kottó River, emptying into the
Yukon above Fort Yukon, is held in superstitious dread by the
Indians, on account of the immense number of fossil bones
existing there. The Inglutálic River, emptying into Norton
Sound, has a somewhat similar reputation.

" I have carefully examined the country over which I have passed for glacial indications, and have not found any effects attributable to such agencies.

" My own opinion, from what I have seen of the west coast, though yet unproved, is that the glacier field never extended in these regions to the westward of the Rocky Mountains, although small single glaciers have and still do exist between spurs of the mountains which approach the coast. No boulders, such as are common in New England, no scratches or other marks of ice-action, have been observed by any of our party, though carefully looked-for."

THE END.

LONDON : PRINTED BY W. CLOWES AND SONS, DUKE STREET, STAMFORD STREET,
AND CHARING CROSS.

Map of the

YUKON
or
KWICH-PAK RIVER.

The Mouths of the River are from the sketches of Mr E.E. Smith, of the
Western Union Telegraph Expedition.
The lower course is compiled from Lieut. Zagoskin, R.I.N. and other data.
The upper course to Fort Yukon laid down from the bearings, distances,
and notes of Mr F.Whymper.